# Three Worlds of Therapy

## An Existential-Phenomenological Study of the Therapies of Freud, Jung, and Rogers

ANTHONY BARTON
Duquesne University

 National Press Books

*To Professor Lloyd Easton,*
*a model of service to truth*
*and clear thought,*
*in gratitude for his teaching*

Library of Congress Catalog Card Number: 73-93339

International Standard Book Numbers: 0-87484-307-3 (paper)
                                     0-87484-308-1 (cloth)

Manufactured in the United States of America

National Press Books
285 Hamilton Avenue, Palo Alto, California 94301

This book was set in 11/13 Janson by Applied Typographic Systems
and was printed and bound by Kingsport Press.
The designer was Nancy Sears, and cover design was by Nan Golub.
Editors were C. Lansing Hays and Barbara S. Pronin.
Michelle Hogan supervised production.

# Contents

○——————————————○——————————————○

iii

# Acknowledgments

The text of this book is not a product of my work alone but is part of a common effort. To acknowledge this fact and to express gratitude to those who have helped to shape it is the purpose of this section. Most personal thanks must be given for the central contribution of Charles Maes, faculty member of both the Department of Psychology and the Institute of Man at Duquesne University, without whose teaching, discussion, and coparticipation in many courses, seminars, and practicums, this work could not have come to be.

Among my colleagues in the Department of Psychology, special thanks to Amedeo Giorgi, Edward Murray, Bill Fischer, Connie Fischer, Rolf von Eckartsberg, and David Smith, each of whom has contributed both spirit and content to the focus of this work. No less crucial is the contribution of the members of both the Institute of Man and the Department of Philosophy at Duquesne, who have indirectly shaped the thought expressed here. Adrian Van Kaam of the Institute of Man deserves special thanks, both for having brought me to Duquesne University and for providing the fundamental inspiration for a

ix

comprehensive existential-phenomenological psychology. Joseph Smith, Jan Van den Berg, Remy Kwant, William Luijpen, Joseph Kokelmans, Al Lingis, Hans Linschoten, Carl Graumann, and others have all contributed their thought through their lectures, writings, and discussions.

Among contemporary thinkers, Heidegger and Merleau-Ponty are most especially central to the present work. Without Heidegger's extraordinary insights into the centrality of language as the place where being illuminates itself, Merleau-Ponty's concrete, essential description of the place of the 'body-as-speaking', and Husserl's elaboration of phenomenological method, this work would lack center and sense. The author is greatly indebted as well to Sigmund Freud, Carl Jung, and Carl Rogers, whose work and thought have opened a field worthy of research.

To Thomas Tyrell, especially, and to many other students and research assistants who have given generously of their time, effort, and encouragement, my special thanks. I wish to express gratitude to the late Silas Pickering, a close friend, for polishing and correcting the manuscript, and to his wife, Ruth Pickering, who generously completed the preliminary editing so tragically cut short by her husband's death. Finally, my thanks to National Press Books, to Lans Hays and Michelle Hogan for their sensitive, intelligent help in dealing with me and my work, and most of all to Barbara Pronin whose thorough and rigorous final editing of the text was a delight to this most sensitive critic.

Hence, it must be seen that this work is *our* work. What is worthy of attention in it grows out of the thought, work, and goodwill of a multitude of others who live and have lived within a tradition of care for truth and for man.

# 1

# Introduction

○──────────────────○──────────────────○

## GENERAL SCOPE AND PURPOSE

This book attempts to answer the question what is psychotherapy by exploring the orientations and understandings that have been developed within a few of its schools. Conceived as an introduction to the subject, the text surveys several psychotherapies as they actually exist, are practiced, and are talked about by working theorist-therapists. These therapies are described and integrated on the basis of an existential-phenomenological viewpoint. The theories and methods of practice selected for examination are those of Freud, Jung, and Rogers, thinkers who have to some degree built on one another's insights, each correcting, expanding, and bringing further clarity to the field of psychotherapy. In order to articulate as clearly as possible the growing movement toward the understanding and practice of healing-speaking, it is crucial to use theorists who have built on one another's work. This insistence on a coherent, unifiable line of thinkers is partially a response to the state of affairs in contemporary psychotherapy-counseling.

1

Psychotherapy is an extraordinarily fragmented field at present. Strikingly divergent schools practice different approaches, espouse contradicting philosophies of life and of man, and employ a variety of techniques, and there is little agreement among them concerning either principles or practice. Depending on the attitudes of their adherents, they either engage in negative polemics against one another or maintain silence across the barriers of school and type of therapy. All of these therapies "work" in the sense that they are in some way satisfying to their adherents and are supported by some patients as well; but this does not mean that they work together to develop a coherent human science. If a coherent human science is to develop, the insights of each school must not be left to their sectarian adherents. A way must be found to absorb, comprehend, and use the rich resources of wisdom, knowledge, and understanding that now exist only fragmentarily. The existential-phenomenological perspective developed in this text is oriented toward a comprehension and integration of various schools of therapy.

## FOCUS ON THERAPY

This text focuses on therapy itself as a process to be comprehended and described. To this end, only those considerations absolutely essential to the development of a comprehension of psychotherapy are introduced. Hence, Freud's understanding of culture, Jung's understanding of history, and Rogers' understanding of education are not stressed.

As each theorist-therapist describes his views of what therapy is about, the reader is directed to apprehend what Freud, Jung, and Rogers have to say about the nature and scope of psychotherapy. Each will be asked to tell in his own way what the difficulty is that prevents the patient from being a nonpatient. Why is he seeking psychotherapy? In what way is he ill or disturbed? What was his condition before he came to the psychotherapist? As each psychotherapeutic orientation sees the patient differently, each gives a different answer to these questions.

Freud, Jung, and Rogers give answers that are both similar and yet strikingly different at the same time; understanding the implications of these similarities and differences is crucial to an understanding of psychotherapy itself. It will become clear in the course of this book that the differences are not merely "factual" but reflect powerful value-ideological factors inherent in the theories themselves. As paths of cure, help, and ways of understanding both the "bad" or "sick" life and the "good" or "healthy" life, these theories are richly expressive of value preferences and fundamental attitudes toward life and its meaning.

A set of related questions directed to each theorist-therapist deals with the pathway of therapy itself. How does the patient progress from disturbance or neurosis to a state of health? What is the actual therapeutic pathway? The text will lead to an understanding of what each theorist-therapist has to tell about the process of change and of psychotherapy.

In order to concretize the processes of Freudian, Jungian, and Rogerian therapy and to point up their differences and similarities, a single semifictional case will be taken through the three therapies. Further, through the analysis of concrete interactions, certain ideas present in each orientation take on fuller flesh when placed descriptively in a life context. Therapy involves concrete interactions between specific people with specific cultural-social and personal styles of living. Because Mary's case illuminates this particularity, it grounds the phenomenological analysis in the actual processes of therapy.

## Descriptive approach to each therapy

Throughout the text, an attempt has been made to remain true to the insights of the original thinkers involved. To facilitate comprehension, however, their understandings have been given in a descriptive language called English, using a minimum of technical language. Just by being cast in a common language, their understandings will be moved toward an implicit unity. In the process, however, an irreducible variation in language is uncovered which belongs to the therapy viewpoint itself. Each theory has its own particular modes of speech. The Freudian cannot speak like the Jungian, nor can either speak like the Rogerian. The speech itself carves out the areas of reality and of values which are the theory and which, as practiced, provoke the therapeutic transformation. Hence, the divergence in language, principles, and practice is discovered to be rooted in value-laden differences in approach to life itself. Each therapy is lived out as a certain vision of the good life, good values, a sense of what is proper to man.

Freud, Jung, and Rogers are outstanding thinkers who have revealed and articulated certain truths about man and psychotherapy. The existential evidence that each has a clear understanding of certain important realities is to be found in the fact that there are adherents to their viewpoints as well as patients who are genuinely helped by their therapies. Out of their individual angularities, each has been able to see some aspects of man with penetrating insight. The work of each must therefore be studied carefully in order to understand the nature of psychotherapy.

By considering each of the three theorists in turn, a way may be found to increase understanding in order to go beyond Freud, Jung, or Rogers and thereby to make use of other theorist-therapists as well. In this way, hopefully, a more adequate apprehension of psychotherapy, as well as a more comprehensive view of what each theorist-therapist is revealing, is attainable.

Freudian psychotherapy has been selected for study for both historical and substantive reasons. Freud initiated the field of "dynamic psychotherapy," and it is within this field that virtually all of contemporary psychotherapy is to be found. In addition to being a rich mine of insight into man, Freud proposed a systematic and fairly clear approach to therapy. Jung is included primarily because he wished to offer a comprehensive approach to therapy, a path toward the unification of various theories and approaches. Jung also had a profound appreciation and understanding of the power of symbolism in human life, as well as an understanding of the transformative possibilities of speech and human imagination. The third major figure of this work, Rogers' emphasis on the inner phenomenal world and on the empathic linkage of client and therapist not only represents a break with analytic tradition but also takes some first steps toward an existential-phenomenological understanding.

## Description and integration of differences

It is exceedingly difficult to elucidate an existential-phenomenological approach to these three therapies. Phenomenology is that discipline which seeks to arrive at descriptions, interpretations, and understandings linked to, and expressive of, fundamental structures of the life-world of meanings in an unbiased scientific fashion. The phenomenologist seeks to suspend those principles derived from science or philosophy which cloud an understanding of the fundamental structures of human reality. He seeks not only to suspend judgment but to allow the structures of reality to reveal themselves as they are. Because allowing reality to reveal itself is never without a purpose, a phenomenological project must seek to reveal its own approach and assumptions so that each reader may see them as clearly as possible.

For the purposes of this text, its approach to therapy can perhaps be best expressed by reflecting current psychotherapeutic practice, a reflection that reveals serious ambiguities in both practice and theory. Eavesdropping on a variety of therapies will expose the reader to the loud argumentative approach of "rational-emotional therapy" as practiced by Ellis, to the nearly impenetrable nondirectiveness and silence of the orthodox Freudian analyst, to the therapist of the Whittiker and Malone school who holds and rocks the patient, feeds him with a baby bottle, and so on. The differences between these schools are so sharp, their fundamental disagreements concerning attitudes, beliefs, approach, method, and technique so much at variance, that no integrative approach would seem to be possible at all.

However, it is the intention of this text to advance the work of integration necessary for the development of comprehensive psychotherapeutic theory. To do so, it is necessary to account for these differences, the sharpness of disagreement, and the animosity between the different schools. This proliferation of different approaches is itself a significant part of psychotherapeutic practice.

One approach to the confusion in the field is a simplistic, eclectic attitude which assumes that each psychotherapeutic group holds some portion of the truth and that the best attitude is one of open-mindedness to all claims and statements made by all therapies. But this sort of eclecticism can easily be unprincipled. In addition, it does not open a path through the cacophony of divergent voices. Without some principle of selection, the bizarre claims of the extremely one-sided therapist who jumps to the latest bandwagon conclusions are treated with the same seriousness and respect as the carefully thought-out conclusions of men of genuine scholarship, balance, and extensive experience. Perhaps psychotherapy today may be best approached by trying to understand why such extreme divergencies exist.

## LIFE-WORLD OF THE THERAPIST

On examining the childhood of a person who becomes interested in the problems of others—that is, the budding future psychotherapist— it is often seen that his relationship to others and to himself became problematic early in life. Freud, for example, had pondered the relationships in his family before he was five years old and has suggested that his discovery of the Oedipus complex was based on certain complications in his own early family life. In his childhood, Jung wondered about certain spiritual-psychic images, visions, and experiences which both disturbed and inspired him. Thus, life is often an early problem to the budding psychotherapist and is regarded as something to think about, to solve, to decode, to unravel, to find out more about. This early reflective attitude toward himself and others begins his history as a psychotherapist. Every psychological counselor, psychiatrist, or psychotherapist has his own somewhat involved story as to how he developed his professional interest, how he moved toward a psychological perspective in order to fulfill himself and to answer questions and problems that had become real to him.

Whatever else he wants from his work and specialization, he wants assistance in solving the problems that motivated him on this reflective path. Indeed, during his psychotherapeutic training when he is being schooled in a particular approach to therapy, he usually enters into personal psychotherapy as part of his learning experience. The total training that he undergoes, including the personal therapy, becomes powerfully influential on his view of himself and life. He finds that his own psychotherapy and career direction help to structure and give meaning to his existence. In his intimate contact with his own therapist he finds new ways to structure and give ground and sense to his own problematics. When he sees that this is helpful in securing a relatively less anxious life for himself, he is enormously encouraged to continue as a therapist within his particular orientation. At the same time, he also finds the approach being taught helpful in his work with patients.

He is encouraged by his growing social and professional contacts (often selectively limited to those who live their lives within a particular therapy orientation) to belong, to say the right words, to identify, and to become one with his mentors. He is encouraged by the fine experience of growing to be a member of the inner circle of those in the know. The insecure young therapist in training is uniquely susceptible to the kinds of learning that take place then. He learns to be horrified by the right kinds of things. He learns to move and live, to breathe, and to think within a unique subculture as his professors, supervisors, and trainers set the terms, teach the language, and mete out the social rewards and punishments.

There is considerable justification for this general approach. It is reasonable to learn one approach well before attempting any divergence. But the particular universes of discourse involved in the field of psychotherapy, the development of hothouse therapeutic communities which are more or less immune to outside influences, are unfortunate consequences of this way of training therapists. When this approach to training combines with the student therapist's inner reasons for moving toward psychotherapy, a rigidification of therapeutic theories occurs. The therapist now learns to live out a certain salvation code. It helped him, and it helps his patients by making him more secure, more expert, and more competent. His patients also find that this expert-oriented way-to-go is helpful. The challenges from outside the community are seen as ignorant or misguided, or they are tolerated as general proofs of the special gifts and intuitions belonging to "our gang."

After some years of training and experience, the practitioners of a particular therapy orientation have so well outlined and fundamentally packaged a world that they become virtually immovable by any other point of view. They now live out a particular world view as outlined by their specialist subculture, whether analytic, behavioristic, client-centered, rational-emotive, direct-analytical, Gestalt, or whatever.

## Advantages of traditional orientations

The problems of psychotherapeutic orientation and theory are partially unresolvable. It is absolutely essential that experts train experts; and in that particular, subtle, humane, and complex art which psychotherapy is, there is a need for specific orienting views. The therapist who does not know what he wishes to accomplish with his patient is unable to be a therapist. Nonetheless, the way in which the psychotherapeutic field has developed toward increasingly narrowed orientations and training does not seem a necessary condition.

The advantages of this kind of psychological background and training will be seen in greater detail as the processes of Freudian, Jungian, and client-centered therapy are unfolded from a phenomenological viewpoint. Obviously, the therapist's training gives him a sense of security. In order to be helpful he needs to have a more or less clear system of ideas and a way of proceeding. To exactly that degree to which he does know what is and is not helpful, he has a realistic sense of being an expert psychotherapist.

Also psychotherapy, through the therapist's orientation, becomes a somewhat orderly, logical, reasonable process. The orientation of the therapist gives (first for the therapist and later for the patient) principles of selection, ways of knowing what is important in the therapeutic interaction. Orientation in the kind of psychotherapy that now exists also makes it possible to read, understand, discuss, and share with a certain select group of colleagues one's professional life and understandings. It provides the real community for the therapist, either actually in the day-by-day sense or potentially, through books, publications, lectures, and so on. It will become clear further into the text how, in a much deeper sense, the universe of discourse which the therapist uses for his own structuring and sense making is of profound significance in the therapeutic process itself. Securing the therapist in his expertise, providing him with a community of experts with whom he can share his understandings and gain new understandings, are real benefits of traditional orientations.

## Disadvantages of traditional orientations

There are also some serious disadvantages to the schools of psychotherapy as they currently exist. First, the sense of security which the orientations now give to the therapist is partially misleading. Each orientation, when viewed from outside, represents an unnecessarily narrow specialization of understanding. Thus, while he is admittedly made secure and expert, the therapist is not able to be expert in all the things in which he should, or reasonably could, be expert. Orientations as they now exist give order and structure, but because they are not experientially-phenomenologically grounded, the order given is a subtly imposed one.

The structure grows out of neither the richest possible therapeutic situation nor the richest possible therapeutic understandings. The order is one which is already excessively pruned by the prejudgments of the therapist living within his narrowed orientation. The patient becomes "the patient about whom this therapist with his narrowed orientation is able to be expert." If the patient cannot become this, the therapy fails, a frequent practical problem in psychotherapy.

Further a narrow orientation makes it impossible to read, understand, discuss, and share professional experience with a large group of colleagues, which has the effect of narrowing down the community to a relatively small inner circle. Therapists often become unable to make use of the literary, philosophical, and meditative wisdom of the major traditions of the Western and Eastern worlds. Finally, because of the peculiar hothouse climate in which a band of dedicated insiders operate, therapists belonging to specific orientations tend often to overlook the most transparently obvious facts of life and of therapy. They often engage in fantastic linguistic and theoretical feats of legerdemain, which in many cases has the effect of obscuring reality for insider and outsider alike. Incantation, ritualistically conceived and lived, tends both to enrich and to obscure reality.

## AN EXISTENTIAL-PHENOMENOLOGICAL APPROACH

The phenomenological perspective which this text develops to some degree is based on the presupposition that reality can best be seen by allowing it to speak for itself. The unit of interaction and study will be the therapist and patient together in a dialectical situation. The behavior and beliefs of the therapist are as important to the study as are those of the patient. Our goal is to uncover the curious dialectic that emerges when a 'therapist-with-an-orientation' encounters a patient in need of help.

Certain fundamental existential understandings will be brought to bear as principles, the primary insight being that man is essentially not a solo phenomenon but a 'being-in-the-world-with-others.' This highly abstract statement is difficult to elucidate exhaustively. Emphasizing man's co-existential nature is a basic orienting attitude or intuition rather than a mere fact. For the purposes of this work, it means that our understanding of the therapeutic process will be dialectical. The patient must be understood as the 'patient-with-the-therapist.'

The patient cannot be understood outside the particular ways of interaction which are constituted by the patient with his therapist and vice versa. If this is true, it should not be surprising to find that the patient's problems, the very pathology which makes him a patient, are defined by the 'patient-with-his-therapist' and are not merely objective factors in his life situation. For the patient is not a 'patient-in-himself'; he is a patient only in his relationships. His immediate society makes him feel, or declares him in some way to be, crippled, inhibited, or experiencing some difficulty in meeting with life. Then his physician, psychologist, social worker, counselor, or educator, for whom he is a patient, makes him a patient.

No approach to psychotherapy which deals with the patient as 'he-is-in-himself' can possibly do an adequate job of encompassing the field of psychotherapy. Psychotherapeutic theory must be a descriptive theory of interaction between doctor and patient, therapist and client, and so on. It is therefore not acceptable to say that the patient's problem is basically an Oedipal problem or basically one of conditioned fear responses. The patient's problems are basically those which will be articulated in his relationship with his therapist. With some therapists, the basic problem to be articulated will be the conditioning and deconditioning of fear responses; with others, it will be the Oedipal problem. Which of these two viewpoints would best fit the particular patient is one whose solution we can hint at but which cannot be answered on the basis of simply which viewpoint—conditioning viewpoint or fundamental Freudian analytical viewpoint—is actually more correct.

An orientation to therapeutic theory must be a descriptive orientation to that dialectical situation in which therapy emerges between two people. For the purposes of this text, this is the concrete meaning of the fundamental existential insight that man is a 'being-with-others.' The patient's existence as patient and the therapist's existence as therapist are co-constituted between them. And this relationship in turn is constituted within the context of a larger cultural situation in which both patient and therapist are 'beings-in-the-world-with-others.' To describe this concretely, with fidelity to the Freudian, Jungian, and Rogerian therapies, is the task of this text.

## BIBLIOGRAPHY

Frank, Jerome D. *Persuasion and Healing: A Comparative Study of Psychotherapy*. Baltimore: Johns Hopkins Press, 1961.

A lucid account of healings and cures as they occur in society, in religious ceremonies, in doctor-patient relations, etc. The social surroundings supportive of help and the significance of expectation, hope, and faith are clearly described. Attention is also given to the development of ideological conviction, or conversion to a system of thought and interpretation.

Husserl, Edmund. *Ideas: General Introduction to Pure Phenomenology*. London: Collier Books, 1962.

A complex but thorough treatment of the rigorously detailed method involved in phenomenology as philosophic science, the method on which the present text is grounded.

Luijpen, William A. *Existential-Phenomenology*. rev. ed. Pittsburgh: Duquesne University Press, 1969.

A clear philosophical introduction to the fundamental movement and style of thought informing the present text.

Munroe, Ruth L. *Schools of Psychoanalytic Thought*. New York: Holt, Rinehart & Winston, 1955.

An excellent introduction to the psychoanalytic schools and the basic approach and premises of psychoanalytic thought, with special sharpness and completeness given to the theoretical and practical issues involved in Freudian thought.

Patterson, C. H. *Theories of Counseling and Psychotherapy*. New York: Harper & Row, 1966.

A clear, fair exposition of many schools of psychotherapy, showing the striking divergencies in philosophy, technique, theory, and viewpoint that characterize the field, and with commonsense conclusions concerning the basic qualities of good human relations as fundamental to therapy.

# 2

# Freud's view of the patient

## THE NEUROTIC PATIENT

According to Freud, psychoanalysis is based on the increasing attachment of the patient to the analyst and cannot be used with disorders in which such an attachment is not possible. Disorders in which the patient's interest, attention, and emotionality seem incapable of attaching themselves to the person of the physician or therapist are excluded from treatment. Freud considers the psychoanalytic patient to be neurotic, but a "good" neurotic who can make the necessary attachments.

By neurotic, Freud means that the patient finds himself split into two warring camps. Each neurotic symptom is seen as a compromise between these two camps or forces in the personality. The forces of repressed unconscious impulses seek expression, while opposing forces within the person seek to deny these impulses. Repression, as explained by Freud, is based on an incompatibility between the person's ideals and the impulses that are emerging. In some way the repressed impulses offend the person's aesthetic or moral sensibilities.

The following example should clarify this point. Imagine a young man in his early twenties, exceedingly polite and well-bred, who has developed as a standard in his life that he will never raise his voice in anger and will always exhibit proper decorum. Although his personality is characterized by exceedingly great socialization and lack of aggression, under certain conditions he develops anxiety attacks and is unable to catch his breath. On examining his case, it is discovered that he develops anxiety when his boss criticizes something he has done. Exploring this moment in detail, we find just beneath the surface of consciousness fragmentary murderous impulses toward the boss. As he approaches these impulses toward his boss in the psychoanalytic situation, the patient is not only anxious but also morally and aesthetically offended by them. He tells the analyst: "But that's horrible that I should have such feelings and thoughts. They seem so indecent, so gross, so out of keeping with who I want to be and who I think I am."

Freud teaches that this repression is based on the early childhood fear of retaliation and loss of love—fear that the person will not be loved, that he will in some way become less lovable, that he will be hated, that he will be directly attacked and destroyed by his parents. Stimulated by these basic threats, the patient not only suppresses his impulses but attempts to deny their existence altogether. He says, in effect, "I do not hate, I am not angry"—a very complicated process to communicate through the descriptive language of consciousness. Repression, as Freud described it, is a half-conscious half-unconscious process living itself out in a marginal area between consciousness and unconsciousness. Originally a person puts out of awareness that which offends him through fear. Soon he does not know that the repressed impulse exists. Like this young man, he experiences anxiety symptoms when aggressive impulses begin to emerge in him.

Freudian theory postulates that when aggression began to emerge in him as a child, he experienced sharply the threat of the loss of his parents' love and the fear of retaliation by one or both of his parents. These fears meant, for instance, that he may have gone through a period of temper tantrums and fantasized that his parents would retaliate by mutilating or destroying him, perhaps even by castrating him. Now the child, whose division line between consciousness and unconscious ness is not so clear, may actually experience a moment in which he says, "Well, I can't be angry like that any more. I mustn't think that thought any more." And the child puts it out of his mind, creating a repression structure, as it were, unconsciously. He no longer admits aggression into his ideas about himself, and he now lives out, in fact, the opposite. Reacting against the aggression, he becomes exceedingly meek, mild, polite, courteous, thoughtful, and so on.

At first this is more or less unconscious; later it is almost totally unconscious. But even in its adult form repression exists on the border between consciousness and unconsciousness. Glimmerings of hateful thoughts, hostile ideas, or aggressive impulses, pieces and fragments of angry talk, angry thoughts, angry feelings do occur to the patient in the course of his life. But he quickly glides over them, ignores them, and finds ways to defend himself against a clear recognition of his own aggressiveness, in this way maintaining his repression.

The neurotic person, then, in trying to make himself acceptable, lovable, or at least not altogether hateable, creates a division within himself. On one side of the split stand the forces of a trained taboo system, a system of predominantly negative injunctions that has been formed in the neurotic person, as in all persons, by the internalization of specific parental, as well as general, societal standards. The internalization of such forceful standards has to a great extent developed out of a fear of retaliation and loss of love. Being the part of the personality that forbids, it now demands that the repressed impulses stay repressed. The repressed impulses on the opposite side of the split self are constituted by sexuality especially but also by aggression, dependency, self-love, and so on. Freud admitted the theoretical possibility that any impulse could create a neurosis, but he learned in actual practice that the major active cause of a neurosis is always to be found in conflicts related to sexuality. Sexuality, however, is broadly conceived by Freud as the pleasure seeking of the body.

The split-self neurotic is thus caught between two demands within himself. One of these, the internalized value system, says, "Shape up, be virtuous, hide your shame," but the messages, while heeded, are barely audible to consciousness. The opposing side says, "I have strange hungers, needs, and wishes which must be expressed." This conflict goes on without any clear-conscious grasp; only fragments surface into clarity and are even then misunderstood and misinterpreted by consciousness.

## THE ACTIVE UNCONSCIOUS

Freud calls this absence of clear consciousness the "unconscious." The unconscious, repressed side of personality is not to be viewed as a mere unknown within Freudian thought. Unconscious processes are actually operative in the person's behavior, dreams, fantasies, hopes, and underlying motivations. To realize that the unconscious factors are active and more or less continuously in operation is crucial to a grasp of Freud's therapeutic understanding. Perhaps this can be clarified by elaborating the case of our polite young patient.

Suppose a young boy is repeatedly exposed to intense situations that arouse anxiety concerning castration—that is, he imagines or is told that he will be castrated if he is naughty. Also it seems to him from his own observation that females are males who have lost their penises. This brings home to him the terrible reality of the threat. If the child does develop such a castration anxiety—and Freud indicates that this is nearly universal in males—he will become exceedingly afraid to provoke such a punishment. In order to protect himself from the threat, he must control not only his external behavior but his thoughts and feelings as well. A thought or feeling can, after all, slip out. He could be "discovered" or "uncovered" as really having those nasty thoughts and feelings.

Freud tells us that each time this boy, and later this man, withholds aggression, he will actually be referring unconsciously to the active fantasy of the original castration anxiety. The child, as an inhibited adult, unconsciously but in fact experiences the whole fantasy drama of attack against the father and retaliation by castration. Thus, in the present situation with his employer, when the now inhibited adult fails to speak out, he unconsciously but concretely refers to the total fantasy and anxiety of the castration threat.

Freud is not merely saying that the original castration anxiety affects the boy by having ingrained an inhibited attitude. He is saying that every time the expression of aggression is inhibited, the whole unconscious fantasy of castration anxiety is actually evoked and activated. The original and underlying causes of the neurosis are, therefore, not merely something in the past that influence the person but something that continues to have an active though unconscious life in the remembering of the original fantasies and threats.

In his *Studies on Hysteria*, Freud says that the memory of the traumatic event is the direct cause of the hysteria. It is not a mere indirect cause; nor, he says, did the traumatic events merely shape the person in such a way that all other events are shaped differently. Rather, in the hysterical symptom itself there is a lively acting out of an unconscious fantasy. Some Victorian women, for example, displayed a symptom that is not often seen today. Having an almost totally repressed sexuality, these women would go into a convulsion during which their bodies would arch in their beds in an enormous semicircle, really "putting out," as it were, expressing themselves in an unconscious fantasy of sexual intercourse.

The repressed is exceptionally obvious in such classical hysteria, for the person "acts out" the unconscious fantasy. The hysterical woman, for instance, who had a bad relationship with her father and fantasized instead a seduction relationship often lives out her fantasized seductive relationship with her father with a current older man. It is not only that she had a bad relationship with her father and now has trouble handling men. Rather now, whenever she meets an older man she actively but unconsciously lives out the fantasized relationship with her father. The original underlying cause of the neurosis, therefore, is not merely something influential in the person's past. The activated memories or fantasies continue to have an actual, concrete unconscious life in the person. It is the continuation of the active, unconscious fantasy and its evocation by specific life circumstances that activate the neurosis and the symptoms.

In every respect, then, the unconscious psychic life is just as effective and actual as the conscious, except that the *un*conscious happens not to be conscious. Unconscious feeling, thinking, hoping, fantasizing, and willing are psychological processes lacking only one characteristic ordinarily associated with psychic life—consciousness.

One crucial difference between consciousness and unconsciousness, however, is that consciousness is more directly susceptible to planful and ordered action. I want something consciously, and I pursue it in a clear, conscious way, following pathways more or less well-ordered to the goal. But unconscious psychological processes cannot usually express themselves directly in rationally directed action. Thus, unconscious thinking, willing, wishing, and fantasizing usually express themselves indirectly in a variety of different symptoms, such as slips or errors in speech or action, in dreams, and in a number of aspects related to one's style of activity. It is, in fact, only insofar as these unconscious psychic processes actively interfere with a person's planful, rationally ordered, and deliberate life projects and provoke symptoms, inhibitions, or anxiety that the person is called actively neurotic.

## THE REPETITIVE UNCONSCIOUS

According to Freud, the usual insusceptibility of the unconscious to the rationally adaptive conscious psychological processes and activities results in the unconscious processes remaining relatively unchanged. At the most fundamental stratum of man's psychic life we find a relatively unchanging, repetitious core. Freud frequently refers to the unchanging character and timelessness of the unconscious, which is precisely the heart of the problem for therapeutic change. For if the unconscious *is* an unchanging striving for expression and, in the neurotic, is also a blocked striving which continues to be active and unconscious, then neurosis is a drama of fundamental repetition.

The neurotic person continues day by day to live out the unrelenting inner warfare between the split sides of his personality. The essential point is that the unconscious fundamentally does not change but is basically repetitive and follows the pleasure principle. In the neurotic, the unconscious seeks expression indirectly, by symptoms and other means that cripple him to a greater or lesser degree. But both sides of the basic neurotic drama are essentially infantile and refer to the past as it is relived again and again.

The person accepts the fantasized and real threats of the parents and continues to live out the inhibiting movement learned in child-

hood. Consequently, his moral, aesthetic, and social standards are infantile to the degree that they are neurotic. Such standards might have
been appropriate at a former time in some way, as when he was an infant with his parents, but infantile standards and taboos do not make
sense in the current situation. Nevertheless, they are lived out unconsciously, provoked by unconscious, repeating dynamisms.

The basic wishes are also fundamentally infantile. The neurotic is
unconsciously suffering from a perverse, immature impulsivity characteristic of young children who want things without respect to their
social desirability or acceptability. These wishes, first repressed or ban-
ished from consciousness because of real or imagined threats by the
parents, have had little chance to develop into any maturity. Therefore,
the polite, inhibited young man whose case we have been developing
thus far is not only unconsciously inhibited in a way appropriate within
his family to the behavior pattern of a "nice little child who doesn't
make trouble for his parents," but his impulses are also at the infantile
level and refer unconsciously but actually to the "enraged child who
would like to have his mother all to himself and murder his father."
Both impulse and inhibition have become fixated in unconsciousness on
infantile objects and fantasies.

The fundamentally fixed, unchanging nature of the unconscious,
which Freud referred to as "the true psychic reality," is thus established at the core of man's life. It is possible that this view of fixity will
turn out to be one of the basic weaknesses of Freudian theory as a therapeutic theory of change. The Freudian vision of man as fundamental
fixity may describe the unchanging nature of the core of the personality, but it leaves little room for a description of change.

## SUMMARY

The repression and splitting of the personality thus far described are,
as seen by Freud, the inevitable results of acculturation, civilization,
and socialization. The split occurs because the child must learn to repress the animal side of his personality and to shape it in socially approved ways. What makes a particular personality neurotic is only a
matter of degree or intensity. The neurotic person is the one whose

split into repressed and repressing forces provokes a conflict of sufficient intensity to produce severe disability. Freud indicates that inhibition is an integral part of the civilizing process, and he suggests that, for this reason civilized man can never fully enjoy sexuality.

The question of whether someone is neurotic depends, then, on the degree of rupture between the two sides of the split self and the intensity of the warring sides themselves. If the sensual or animal side is constitutionally very strong and the pressure to repress is also very strong, a clear-cut neurosis is almost certain to emerge. Still another important question is the degree to which a person can effectively redirect his animal instincts into culturally acceptable channels. If he is able to sublimate his aggression by, for instance, becoming a surgeon, dentist, or psychologist, this release of the unconscious need and its social transformation may obviate a neurosis.

## BIBLIOGRAPHY

Fenichel, O. *The Psychoanalytic Theory of Neurosis*. New York: W. W. Norton, 1945.

A thorough, comprehensive, scholarly treatise and veritable compendium of Freudian thought on the psychoanalytic theory of neurosis.

Freud, Sigmund. *Dora: An Analysis of a Case of Hysteria*. New York: Collier Books, 1963.

Freudian writing at its best—a lively, intuitive, speculative approach to an unsuccessful therapy case, with characteristic interpretations, understandings of neurosis, and speculative theorizing woven together into an intensely felt document.

_____. *A General Introduction to Psychoanalysis*. New York: Washington Square Press, 1952.

A comprehensive survey of psychoanalysis by its originating genius, with a good general picture of the Freudian view of neurosis in part 3, chapters 16 through 27.

_____. *New Introductory Lectures in Psychoanalysis*. New York: W. W. Norton, 1964.

Lectures 31 and 32 vigorously supplement, expand, and correct Freud's earlier formulations of personality and neurosis.

_____. *The Problem of Anxiety*. New York: W. W. Norton, 1936.

A somewhat technical exposition of Freud's later understanding of neurosis.

Freud, Sigmund, and Bruer, Joseph. *Studies on Hysteria*. New York: Avon Books, 1966.

A somewhat technical presentation of Freud's early cases, showing the skeleton of Freudian theory in concrete case-related terms. The emphasis on blocked effect, sexuality and aggression, and the theory of ⁀⁀⁀⁀⁀⁀  y clearly present.

ʰoanalytic Thought: An Exposi-
Integration. New York: Holt,

nmary of the Freudian theory of

# 3

# Classical
# Freudian therapy

○ ─────────────────────── ○ ─────────────────────── ○

## MAKING THE UNCONSCIOUS CONSCIOUS

The most fundamental purpose of Freudian psychotherapy is to make conscious that which is unconscious, to bring into the open that which has been shut off, to restore the faulty and amnesiac memory, to fill in the gaps of consciousness. "Where id was let ego be," said Freud, meaning that the powers of reasonable adaptability, of rational, logical, coherent, clear adaptive thought which belong to the personality, should move to first place in the guidance of behavior. The split in the personality between the warring conscious and unconscious should be healed through a widening of consciousness.

Freud had already understood by the time of his first therapeutic writing, *Studies on Hysteria*, that what is required in order to make the unconscious factors truly and effectively conscious is not a rational or intellectual awareness of the causes of the neurotic involvement but a concrete emotional apprehension of the experience. The basic    23 reason why the neurotic person cannot explain his behavior lucidly is because his resistive defensiveness has blotted out whole areas of personality. Gaps in consciousness, are indirect expressions of these blotted out or repressed areas and serve partially to disguise from the neurotic person his own real motivation.

In his first attempts at psychotherapeutic intervention, Freud hypnotized his patients, had them trace their symptoms backward in time to the precipitating events, and would then trace back to even earlier events that had in some way participated in the making of symptoms. These earlier events he understood to be the continuing primary active causes of the symptoms through being constantly relived in the patient's unconscious memory. When Freud abandoned hypnosis, he continued to use other directly suggestive techniques. When the patient's mind would go blank or some blockage of speaking would occur, the physician would place his hand on the patient's forehead, telling and even forcefully insisting that an image, thought, or idea would come to mind. The patient would then be asked, "What comes to mind?"

In his use of this "pressure technique," Freud saw clearly that the patient definitely resisted becoming conscious of his unconscious. Even with hypnosis, which appeared to bypass some resistances to remembering, Freud had noticed considerable resistance. The most well intentioned and intelligent patients showed remarkable lapses in following instructions: they suddenly went blank, criticized the analytic procedure, disregarded as unimportant an idea or image which they had had, and in a great variety of other ways opposed the specific instruction to say simply what came to mind. The resistance often concealed itself behind such excuses as "my mind is distracted today," or "the clock or piano in the next room is disturbing me." Once noted, however, resistance was seen to be the major problem in the success or failure of the analytic treatment. At once point Freud remarked that psychoanalytic treatment may be regarded in general as a reeducation in overcoming internal resistances. When a treatment is defined in terms of resistance, this becomes a central concept for understanding the treatment.

## THE PSYCHOANALYTIC PROCEDURE

Freud developed the psychoanalytic procedure proper when he gave up his "pressure technique." In general, the analyst invites his patient to lie down comfortably on a sofa while he sits behind and outside of his field of vision. The patient is asked "to let himself go" in what he says, to tell whatever comes into his head, even if he thinks it unimportant, irrelevant, or nonsensical. It is especially emphasized that no thought or idea be omitted because of its being embarrassing or distressing to the patient.

### Lying down

That the patient lies down provides a number of advantages. First, the patient is relaxed and more susceptible to saying whatever comes into his mind because the position itself invites a loosening of the rational structures of a hyperrational consciousness. Lying down also has the effect of making many of the usual social amenities seem irrelevant. It immediately undercuts many specific social conventionalities for the patient, for it is difficult to be pompous, to make skillful party chatter, or to lecture while lying on a couch. Many conventional social attitudes simply disappear when the patient lies on a couch.

Because lying down is a position for sleeping, it also encourages the emergence of the less conscious, more fantastic side of the personality. The patient is relaxed, afloat, and adrift, to a certain extent cut off from reality. He is literally not facing the world and is therefore not reality oriented in the everyday sense of the term.

Finally, the patient's lying down partially erases the distinction of high and low, the differentiation of the world into above and below. He allows both high and low to speak equally to him. Lying down, then, invites relaxation, a loosening of control, a diminishing of reality coping, and a certain unconventionality of social expectation. It is a very special thing to lie on an analyst's couch.

The analyst is also affected by the patient's lying down. That the patient lies down and the analyst does not is one of the most important aspects of the analyst-patient relation, because the analyst is then con-

firmed as being in a position of superiority and priority as regards the interpretation of reality. He is the one who has his feet on the ground and can see far. He may candidly admit that the patient is cleverer, more talented, gifted, and far-seeing than he. But in the analytic situation, when the patient is lying down, encouraged to relax and to say whatever comes into his mind, the analyst is given a certain priority with respect to judgment about what is real and important. The analyst is the "seer," and the patient "laid out before him" is the relatively passive producer of data to be understood and seen. The analyst is also affected by an empathic possibility for regression in himself. The fact that the patient lets down his controls helps the analyst to loosen his own control empathically—to be easy and free-floating with the patient because the patient is easy and free-floating with him.

## The analyst's invisibility

That the analyst is behind and out of sight of the patient further encourages the patient's loosening of reality ties and helps him to enter the special mood of the free association situation unmoored from the conventional signals of social reality. Indeed, he is virtually unmoored from *any* signals of social reality, not only conventional ones. He cannot tell which of his statements is arousing interest, astonishment, dismay, disagreement, joy, or disgust, because the subtle facial-gestural guidance system which carries approval or disapproval is no longer available to him. In ordinary social conversation, this complex guidance system enables us to change what we say immediately on the basis of another's reactions. In the analytic situation, however, this virtually disappears because the analyst disappears. The patient does not know what the analyst's reaction is and is thus thrown radically back upon himself. Very often he does not like this and tries, by craning his neck, to see the analyst.

Lacking clear cues as to the analyst's response, the patient must make sense from his own repertoire of experiences. He does this by means of fantasies which structure and clarify the analyst's role. Precisely because of the unmoored, uncanny, and progressively more fantastic structure of the analytic experience, these fantasies are often remarkably accurate reflections—indeed, amplifications—of specific past experiences of the patient. These past experiences, elaborated in fantasy—which is, after all, almost all the patient has in the analytic situation—are encouraged by the analyst's invisibility.

In other words, that the analyst is physically positioned behind the patient encourages transference, which is the reediting of old relationships with significant figures such as mother, father, and others. That the analyst is physically above the patient encourages amplification of these infantile fantasies. From the viewpoint of the reclining patient, this lends the analyst a certain fantastic omniscience, a certain superiority, which reestablishes the experience of childhood in relationship to significant adults as relatively omniscient beings.

The patient is forced to fantasize answers to the questions: "Who is there? What is going on with him? How does he feel toward me? Who is the analyst to me?" The analyst's intention is to arouse fantasy as much as possible and to become a screen for the play of the patient's fantasies. Freud frequently uses the idea of reediting in connection with the transference relationship, and he suggests that in some cases it is an almost exact reproduction while in other cases it has undergone considerable change.

The analyst is himself influenced by the patient's lying down, by his own sitting up, and by his own invisibility because he is not obliged to maintain a social facade or to exercise vigilant control over his facial expression, which would be necessary if the patient could see him. His invisibility means for him the possibility of having a receptive, relaxed awareness uncensored by social conventionalities. He is "seer" but not seen, which places great psychological emphasis on his power to see, comprehend, understand, and be free from the immediate pressure of the patient's imploring gaze.

The analyst also knows that, because of his invisibility, he will almost invariably find himself correct in attributing his patient's images and feelings toward him to the patient's past relationships. Inevitably the patient will judge him in terms of past significant figures. In one sense, the analyst makes himself neutral, but in another sense he makes himself a fantastic presence to the patient. By his silence, his invisibility, and the ambiguity of his nonjudgmental stance, he necessarily provokes a response grounded in the patient's past life. Within the ungrounded ambiguity of analysis, the patient must structure a meaningful figure. Having no ground in the situation for a realistic judgment, he is thus thrown back on himself and uses his own expectations and fantasies to make sense of the analyst. Within the analytic setting, this actually works. The transference interpretations are made to be true by the analyst and patient in dialogue.

The truth and reality of the transferential interpretation is enormously convincing within the analytical setting because the patient knows that the analyst is not really the fantastic ogre-father, threat, and so on. The analyst is, after all, the analyst, a professional helper of skill, learning, and sensitivity. "This is the way you saw your father, isn't it?" asks the analyst. In analysis, the patient understands this, and the analyst will always find that this is how the patient felt toward somebody in the past.

The analyst, then, creates a situation within which a whole horizon of analytic interpretations about the transference becomes true for both analyst and patient. By becoming a kind of powerful mirror or screen he takes away from the patient the full reality of perception and understanding even further. The patient increasingly finds himself in a fantastic life in which it is clear that he does not see the truth because his perception is clouded, distorted, emotionally tinged, and fantastic. Simply by pointing out how fantastic and emotionally clouded these perceptions are and how they must come from the past, the analyst establishes forcefully the fact of his priority in respect to the interpretation of reality.

There is an extraordinary power situation constituted here. The patient, in the free associative situation, is asked to relinquish his power to see accurately, to be rational. Increasingly he finds that he is unable to do what he wills to do, namely, to free associate. As he discovers ever more convincingly that he has all kinds of strange, fantastic ideas and feelings about the analyst, more and more he regards himself as infantile, stupid, irrational, unreasonable, and full of ungrounded passions. Meanwhile, the analyst establishes more solidly for himself his own realism, his own characteristically acute interpretation of reality, his own relatively resistance-free modes of commenting. The situation strongly affirms the analyst's priority as reality perceiver and speaker of the truth.

## Instruction to free associate

*Influence on the patient.* The instruction to free associate probably constitutes the most basic agreement between analyst and patient. It tells the patient explicitly that he is to open up in an honest, unconventional, and somewhat uncontrolled way at the verbal level. At the same time, this instruction contains the implicit promise that the analyst will neither apply the usual standards of social relations to his patient's statements nor use conventional standards in listening to his patient.

It implies further that the patient's whole psychological life is of interest, not only some details of it, and that anything that comes up is worthy of analytic attention. The analyst asks directly that the patient adopt a new, less immediately functional, less technical attitude toward himself. He is not to see himself as a problem or as someone with an illness to be cured but as a whole psychological being, whose total thought, feeling, sensation, and imagery is worthy of attention, reflection, and analysis.

The patient who comes to the analyst expecting to have a symptom treated is taking a technical, problem-solving attitude—"I have this phobia that I want you to get rid of for me." He is immediately thrust into a situation in which that technical, illness-curing, problem-solving attitude is disconfirmed by the instruction to free associate: "Anything that comes to your mind, anything whatsoever, whether it seems irrelevant, nonsensical, embarrassing, distressing, or what have you, is worthy of attention, so please mention it."

In the course of analysis, the instruction to free associate becomes the rule of rules for the patient for a variety of reasons. First, by inviting him to give up his rational control, the instruction to free associate causes the patient to become a source of analytic data. His utterances are now items in need of interpretation. How this structures the analytical situation will be seen in more detail later. Secondly, that the patient is chronically unable to free associate after he has agreed to do so becomes for him the central, most convincing proof of his irrationality, compulsivity, defensiveness, and resistance. This inability and the variety of ways in which the patient fails to spin his web of words freely are proof of his own blockage.

Through the free association process the patient is to let statements, as it were, pour out of him. He is not to stew over and deliberate about what he is going to say. He thus leaves questions of control and the priority of interpretation to the analyst, because he formally gives up his own selective, screening, interpretative function.

In return for this relinquishing of control, the analyst becomes the one who will maintain control and some realistic vision of what is allowed. "I ask you not to maintain your realistic vision of what is allowed but simply to let go and speak whatever comes to your mind, without regard to relevance, rationality, or reasonableness. Those are all words which suggest that you would have the interpretive power to understand what you say, and you are specifically asked to relinquish them. I as analyst must in some way fill in for you here."

*Influence on the analyst.* The fact of the patient's free associating is a fundamental difference between patient and analyst. The patient's task is to reveal himself to the analyst by speaking out without self-censorship. The analyst's task is to understand, interpret, and tune in on the patient's conscious and unconscious worlds. Thus, the basic attitudinal set within the relationship, already established when the patient lies down and the analyst sits up, is radically reinforced. The analyst will be in the most fundamental way "the" powerful person who has the priority of vision and understanding in the analytic situation. The setting itself is designed to increase his vision and understanding and thus guarantees a fundamental priority to the analyst. The patient then becomes a source of data for him.

The patient talks and the analyst listens and understands. The patient is invited to be more or less passive to the surgery of the analyst's interpretive intervention. In this way, the analyst is made to give priority to his own function as "seer," connector, instructor, interpreter. It is understandable that once the analyst has asked the patient to relinquish his own rational, orderly, ordinary social self-control, it must be provided for somewhere in the analytic situation. The analyst replaces the patient's control and vision with his own control and vision. While this can never be absolute, it is clearly the direction of the orthodox analytic situation.

## The analyst's evenly hovering attention

The analyst strives to maintain toward his patient an evenly hovering attention. He is not to focus selectively on this or that theoretical point, to select evidence for an interpretation that he has in mind, or to engage in any other activities that narrow the focus of his observation. This ideal attitude on the part of the analyst is the exact counterpart of the patient's instructions to free associate. Analyst and patient alike are to allow their attention to flow evenly and to hover, to allow all images or ideas into consciousness without preconceptions as to propriety, sense, logic, morality, aesthetic or even theoretical considerations. The analyst cannot, of course, divorce himself totally from such considerations any more than the patient can freely associate. Freud asks both the analyst and the patient to do what they cannot fully do.

*Effect on the patient.* In any event, the analyst's attention is implicitly promised to the patient at the outset. By telling the patient to say whatever comes to mind, an implicit promise is communicated that all these things will be granted attention. To some degree, in a good analysis, this evenly hovering quality of attentiveness is realized. The analyst's silence and, over a long period of time, his wide-ranging interpretive remarks show the patient that he is listening in a way that is free from the normal expectations of social life and that he is willing to allow his consciousness to entertain a great variety of possibilities.

Because the analyst does not impose, the patient is expected to be free from the suggestive possibilities of other, more activistic therapies, with the result that he is radically thrown back upon himself. Even the therapist's interests and theoretical predilections are supposed to be left obscured, providing yet another reinforcement for the patient's repetition of past experiences as he continues to maintain the analyst as a kind of screen. In a sense, the analyst is everyone and no one. This nonintervention is concretely learned in the analyst's training, even to the point that he is taught to disappoint expectations that have built up in his patients.

Everything in the analytic session is seen as belonging to the patient. The analyst, by his own quality of attention, is to give back to the patient what the patient gives to him. The analyst is deliberately a kind of mirror, helping the patient to clarify and understand himself. The analyst also provides the patient with a consistent security as the patient finds himself in this carefully nurtured atmosphere of objectivity. The analyst does not rush in with a wild idea of his own or with some experience he has had. He is an unemotional, level-headed, imperturbable observer who gives the patient back to himself realistically, firmly, and without bias. It becomes part of the analyst's growing rational authority if he does this well. His rationality, reasonableness, and openness become virtually palpable to the patient.

*Effect on the analyst.* By giving himself the task of maintaining an evenly hovering attention, the analyst can discern to what extent he lacks the necessary objectivity to carry on the analytic task. He is quickly able to uncover the beginnings of distortion, emotional involvement, and tendencies to collusion in himself. He can note when he has departed from this ideal attitude and has gone into one or another fantasy of the patient's world, or he can find himself beginning to theorize. In all such instances, the analyst is warned that he is straying from the strict, ideal attitude of objective impartiality—that is, that he is confronting resistance in himself now, resistance to being the analyst.

By striving consistently to maintain an impartial, evenly hovering attention, the analyst's coolness and distance are further reinforced. He does not become overly involved in one or another aspect of the case but maintains an overview attitude, a readiness to see or hear whatever is forthcoming in the patient's free associative ramblings. In this way his capacity to remain the understander, the comprehender, the grasper of connections, and integrator of data is maintained and fostered. In this way he fosters his own capacity to be the optimal producer of analytic understandings and interpretations.

## THE ACT OF INTERPRETATION

For the analyst, the whole point of the analysis is summarized in the experiences fostered by, surrounding, and leading into the act of interpretation. His 'tuned-in-ness', the evenly hovering attention, the cool surgical distance, the instruction to the patient to free associate, the respective social, psychological, and physical positions of patient and analyst—all of the relatively elaborate structure detailed above comes together at the moment of interpretation.

By interpretation is meant any statement by the analyst which points to a way of understanding the actual motivations that inspire the patient's activities. Interpretations can vary enormously in their extensiveness. In a preliminary interpretation the analyst may do nothing more than connect one behavior with another ("I notice that you smile when you say that"), but he has an idea that for this patient the smiling and the saying somehow connect in a special way. The analyst surmises that if this is pursued it will probably be seen to have roots deep in the patient's past and touch a pattern of reaction which somehow has a substantial place in the patient's neurotic life. In that respect, "I notice that you smile when you say that" is already within a larger horizon of interpretation and may even lead to the reconstruction of a major piece of past history.

The interpretation could also be more elaborately constructed. Noticing the patient's smile, the analyst might say: "You know, it's very interesting that whenever you say something that is a little bit nasty to anyone you smile. After you've been a little bit aggressive, you become *very* agreeable and nice, and I notice it here. I wonder if when you were with your father you discovered that the only way to keep him from attacking you was to become more sociable, amiable, in this kind of smiling, passive way. You have not told me this directly, but it surely must have been so." This rather elaborate interpretation connects a whole pattern of activity in the patient's life—a certain kind of smiling

passivity—to both a behavior in the analytic situation and to a relationship in his past life as well. Thus, current events in the session can be
connected with events outside the situation, with events during recent
years, and even with early childhood in one differentiated interpretative
construction.

The ideal interpretation is one which the patient is so close to grasping that it comes to him as a sudden shock of recognition; it makes real,
rational, and affective sense at the same moment. The patient can see
that it connects whole realms of experience and feeling which he had
hitherto regarded as more or less separate and distinct. The interpretation not only makes sense but rings true to the patient's experience.

*Effect on the patient.*   For the patient, the interpretative act and its
incipient beginnings in such little connecting remarks point also to the
root meaning of the analysis. To the degree that it rings true, makes
sense, and vivifies, it is in the interpretation that the patient discovers
the fundamental point of the analysis. He begins to understand himself
analytically and to anticipate being able to control the behaviors that
fall under the interpretation. In a moment he sees: "Yes, I really do get
this nice, smiling, benign attitude when I am a little annoyed. It really
has been that way all of my life, and I really did learn it first from my
father." Seeing sense and daylight, he hopes now to be able to control
this behavior and to have himself back in his own hands.

## THE PROBLEM OF RESISTANCE

### Making the reflective act concretely real

The wish of both patient and analyst that the interpretation will have
immediate and extensive power is usually disappointed in a short time.
It does, indeed, have some power but not as extensive a power as either
patient or analyst would hope. Why does the interpretation not usually
result in a transformation? Why can the therapist not see the patient
for a few weeks, uncover his major dynamics, explain him to himself,
and have this be therapeutically effective? The answer lies again in the
problem of resistance, a recurring theme in Freud's therapeutic
writings.

The early analyst had hoped for a quick change, especially through the intervention of an intellectual comprehension and grasp. It became rapidly evident, however, that such an intelligent comprehension, and perhaps an accurate general understanding as well, could exist but still leave the patient's ongoing activities relatively untouched. Indeed, the patient could write a book analyzing his own case in detail and still remain as disturbed as before.

It gradually became evident that the task of interpretation was to open up a horizon of *possible* but not yet *actual* connections. However interesting it may be for a patient to understand that he is inclined to be passively agreeable as a defense, this understanding indicates only in the vaguest, most abstract way what he does, how he does it, and why. He has not yet seen in an extended actual situation how completely automatic his smiling acquiescence is. He has not yet experienced in concrete detail his fearfulness of his own aggression or his terror before someone else's anger. He has not yet felt how utterly impotent he makes himself or how totally dependent he becomes on the approval of the other.

For these connections to become effectively conscious involves their becoming concretely embodied in the actual moment-by-moment description of events lived by the patient every day. For the term "passive acquiescent tendency" to be meaningful, he has to become aware of, for example, his tendency to swallow often when someone else is assertive, his failure to object when someone pushes ahead of him in line, his hesitation to ask a waiter or clerk for attention, his tendency to wait for others to start a conversation, his tendency to become anxious and sweaty instead of angry, and so on. He must see and interpret all of this as "fear of aggression," "castration anxiety," or whatever. This must occur repeatedly and be seen and understood by him repeatedly.

For the interpretation to be fully effective, it must be so well learned and concretized that the behaviors which it covers or subsumes are virtually always accompanied by the interpretive understanding. In this way, the repetitive pattern of neurotic fixity is frozen, stopped in a self-conscious, explicitly knowing reflection. It is characteristic of human life that the automatically functioning patterns of skills and habits with which the person constantly lives without reflection are disrupted by the act of reflection. For this reason such skills as typing or walking become awkward and uncoordinated when reflected upon directly. The interpretation of a neurotic behavior, then, breaks the automatic unfolding of the pattern when it directly accompanies that behavior as a reflective act.

Interpretation becomes effective as an accompanying conscious commentary that interrupts the smoothly flowing sequence of repetitive patterns of behavior. It is the structured bending back upon the activity in reflection which disrupts and freezes otherwise automatically unfolding behaviors. Thus, interpretation is one of the primary ways by which the structured neurotic patterns are destructured.

The interpretation depends for its effectiveness on its ability to provoke in the patient that concrete sense of self-awareness that disrupts ongoing patterns of automatic functioning. If this is to occur, the patient must not only find the interpretations convincing but be willing and able to utilize them concretely in his ongoing life. He must reach the point where he cannot say "I'm sorry" without thinking at the same moment that he is probably being "passively acquiescent" again. This is called the "working-through process."

Only actual, concrete, affectively lived interpreted connections have the power to make a real difference in the patient's life and to help him live in an analytically rational way. No longer does the person being badgered by his boss automatically accede to the smiling agreeability that has been part of his pattern. As he approaches his first temptation to smile and acquiesce again, he catches himself, and, slightly annoyed, resists the temptation. He discovers in the moment that he asserts himself a small fragment of what he needs to know radically, which is that when he is a bit assertive or aggressive, the world does not end. This he must learn to live and believe.

As the interpretations become more and more concretely engraved on the patient's consciousness, a transformation process gradually occurs. The repetitive patterns, now illuminated by analytic insight, no longer compose the dominating theme. The voice of analytic reason gradually gains strength in the patient's life. The old patterns are blocked by the reflective, self-conscious bending back of consciousness and thereby make room for new learnings.

## Resistance in the classic analytic sense

A second aspect of resistance is resistance as conceived in the classical analytic sense. The analyst's fundamental task is to help the patient to see his resistances and to break them down, because the resistances which the patient manifests in psychotherapy are the same that prevent him from being free from neurosis.

The neurosis itself, according to the Freudian analytic scheme, is rooted in the person's unwillingness to face the reality of his impulses. This resistance manifests itself in psychotherapy in the patient's almost constant inability to free associate or to let the different aspects of his psychic life touch correctively against one another. For example, the patient wants to lie on the analytic couch and claim that he has no strong dependent feelings. Despite the fact that his own arms cradle him as a mother cradles her child, he wants to say that this gesture is meaningless and that he puts his thumb in his mouth at a certain tense moment in the therapy does not refer to his infantile, security-seeking dependent self. He does not wish to suffer this embarrassment; and in not wishing to admit or confront the darker, impulsive, less constructive aspects of his existence, the patient has developed his neurosis. In the therapy situation itself, he continues to live out the neurosis, resisting the fantasy humiliation and fantasy retaliation from the therapist.

The moment of classic analytic resistance, then, is complex. First, the patient's consciousness does not wish to admit a certain factor of his motivation or life. His aesthetic standards, his standards of propriety and moral valuation reject with horror the idea concretely realized that homosexuality or strong feelings of dependency exist in him. He would feel guilty and attack himself if he allowed himself to have these feelings. The moral standards that he absorbed from his parents—to be a good, strong boy and not a crybaby—these standards, as he begins to have a sense of weepy dependency, begin to assert themselves in him, not clearly but unconsciously, in a certain tightening up. The patient now begins to experience a certain blocking in the analytic situation.

To make these observations more concrete, imagine a patient free associating. And as he is free associating he is lying on the couch speaking of an incident that happened that day with his boss. What he is speaking of is that one of the salesmen, in relation to the boss, is ludicrous to the rest of the staff because he seems to overadmire the boss, hanging around him like a puppy. Suddenly there is a blockage. The stream of association stops. The patient draws a blank. His body tenses, he becomes slightly rigid.

What has happened? According to the analytic schema, the patient is probably now approaching his own feelings of dependency, of admiration for the analyst. He, too, feels a sense of what a wonderful man this analyst is. Like the salesman, he, too, is feeling dependent, proud of belonging to the analyst. But he cannot allow himself these feelings forbidden by his own standards—standards which he learned originally from his parents and which now live themselves out in him. "As a child I learned not to let my dependent side be seen as I would only be ridiculed as a crybaby. Now, in the analytic situation, I feel again this weepy, needy desire to be comforted, and I feel also the terrible danger that I will be ridiculed. This is my half-conscious half-unconscious resistance to letting myself get in touch with all my feelings, which I have been invited to do in the analysis."

The whole analytic situation encourages the repetition of such infantile patterns of response and feeling. It does this in large measure by reducing the patient's freedom to act as an adult or by increasing his freedom to act as a child. Analysis is more or less an explicit invitation to repeat early patterns, to return to modes of experience belonging to childhood, and in response the patient often resists.

The resistance has a twofold structure. On the one hand, it is the withholding of a certain content, attitude, feeling, or remembering. On the other hand, it is a withholding from the analyst, who is now transformed into that feared person for whom the patient originally withheld this content earlier in his life. This is of great practical importance to the analyst's work because it provides him with a more elaborately specified horizon of accurate understandings of the patient.

Every time the patient blocks, the analyst knows: (1) that the patient is withholding something, and (2) that the withholding is in part a response to a change in his perception of the analyst. That is, the analyst is being experienced as if he were someone else, and this is making it impossible for the patient to avoid withholding. In other words, the resistance is occurring because otherwise the analyst would behave as the parents, brother, or sister had behaved toward the patient, or as he fantasized they would have behaved toward him. This is the unbearable, feared thing which caused the repressive, resistive structure in the first place. As he begins to approach a particular taboo experience, he is still afraid that he will be horrible and rejectable. Every resistance has this element of transference from childhood in it, at least implicitly.

The patient has learned from his parents "don't do that, don't feel that, don't think that." This learning has resulted in an inner structure of taboos partly unconscious and partly conscious, which is strongly activated whenever a taboo is directly or indirectly touched upon. The forbidding parents inside the patient continue strongly to influence the shaping of his resistances. This personality structure forbids impulses from the lower regions. The moment of resistance is, however, not completely an internal event. It is also a moment in which the analyst, as transference figure, undergoes a change ranging from slight to great. To the analyst are attributed the standards originally learned from the parents. The analyst is now seen as like the father and mother.

As the patient lies in the unstructured and ambiguous atmosphere of the analytic session, he begins to feel that it is the analyst who would disapprove. He may only have the fragmentary thought, "I wonder whether the analyst feels that I am cooperating or not as a patient." In some way, the moment of disapproval, the moment of threat of retaliation which originally instituted the repression into the unconscious of the impulses which just now are beginning to come up in the free associations of the patient—this threat is now experienced as coming from the analyst. The patient does not recognize that it is his own standards which block him and his parents who taught him the standards that he now carries within him.

Rather the patient experiences dimly, or sometimes with vivid clarity, something like, "If you saw me as a whiny dependent person, you would despise me. I'm not going to be that here." So in the moment of resistance the patient experiences a very complex process in which his own inner resistance is lived out in the situation between himself and the analyst. The resistance to speaking becomes a resistance to being demeaned in the analyst's presence, to being attacked by the analyst, as well as to allowing the unconscious impulses to manifest themselves in consciousness.

This form of resistance, as classically conceived, is the major cause of difficulty in the analytic treatment. The patient has to be taught repeatedly that the analyst will not retaliate against him; that the analyst is trustworthy, will not hate him, will maintain equanimity toward feelings and thoughts that had horrified the patient's parents, and will accept all relevations, however primitive, unformed, chaotic, perverse, disgusting, or horrifying.

Again and again the patient imagines that the analyst is secretly harboring a grudge or a disgust, secretly patronizing him or finding him revolting, because that is what he feared if his parents had ever known what was inside him. That is, indeed, what the patient unconsciously thinks of himself, and that is what he gradually has to work through in the analysis. He has to discover that the analyst continues to provide cool, reassuring, interpretive support without disapproval, hatred, recrimination, or attack.

## Resistance to being a patient

When the patient consents to the instructions of orthodox analysis, he consents in very general terms and makes a very general contract which he only vaguely understands. He consents to try to free associate but is unable to do so. He is not able to relinquish his aesthetic, moral, or rational standards, partly for the reasons indicated by the theory of orthodox analysis, which suggests that resistance is a living out of the neurotic repression.

By agreeing to free associate, the patient agrees to become a source of data for the analytic interpretation. That is, he agrees to strive to do away with his own schemes of interpretation and to allow his psyche, so to speak, to do the work of producing data. When he agrees to this, however, he does not yet grasp the radical degree to which he will abdicate to the analyst a virtual priority of vision and truth. In his free association, for instance, the patient tells the analyst about a freshman in school who is terribly funny, awkward, and nervous in her newness in the school situation. He mentions that when no one is observing her, the freshman does not shake and is not nervous. Some moments later the analyst asks, "Do you feel looked upon and judged by me?" The patient had merely intended the anecdote as an entertaining way of starting the session. But he suddenly realizes that the analyst was listening with the special intention of viewing what he was saying as a source of data about feelings, complexes, difficulties, state of transference, and so on.

The patient's realization that the analyst treats his utterances as data begins at this moment, and the patient may not like it. Recognizing some conflict in intentions, he may object: "You make too much of what I am saying. I only meant to talk about this interesting, amusing freshman girl. You assume that I was referring indirectly to myself." The analyst's reply may be silence, at which an extraordinary realization may dawn on the patient: "Why, he does not even consider whether my objection is valid. The objection itself is merely another source of information about me." In such moments the patient discovers that having one's statements taken as data in need of psychological interpretation involves a peculiarly, perhaps unpleasantly felt reduction of himself.

He discovers that he has given up something that is taken for granted in ordinary discourse—the primitive fact that his behavior makes sense to him within a preinterpreted schema which always has radical priority within the everyday social world. He discovers further that he cannot relinquish the priority of his own understanding in any real sense. His own understanding of himself as an intentional-being who makes sense to himself is his only point of departure. From this place, it may be possible for him to learn to make sense as the analyst does; but he will be able to do this only to the degree that he lives in a coherent sense-making world just as the analyst does.

The patient may think, at moments when he objects to the analyst's making too much of his statements: "Why does my analyst presume that he is right when he makes an objection to what I say, interpreting it as resistance, for instance? But when I make objection to what he says, I am breaking the pact and showing even more resistance."

The analyst has only to point out that the patient has agreed to free associate, relinquish control, and open himself up in order to understand more about himself; by engaging in rational arguments or objections he disobeys these instructions and can therefore properly be interpreted as resisting. Indeed, the resistance is not only to sharing a certain content with the analyst or to the analyst himself conceived as a threatening figure from the past. It is also a resistance to giving the priority of interpretation to another, to entering a radical self-and-other deception.

The analyst, then, places the patient in a paradoxical situation. On the one hand, the patient is asked to relinquish control of his utterances and to suspend the rational sense-making operations which structure his life. On the other hand, he is asked to make himself docile, even with resistance, to the rational sense-making activities of the analyst.

It is therefore permissible for the patient to disobey the instruction to free associate only if the analytic truth or analytic process is thereby fostered. He is allowed to be rational and logical only in the service of fostering analytic truth. If he is rational or logical in the service of any other truth, this is interpreted as resistance. And resistance it is, but a resistance to being reduced to a source of data in need of analytic interpretation. It is a resistance to being reduced to an object.

To relinquish the right to speak his own truth, apart from the truth spoken by the other, is temporarily at least to give up his sense of being a person. To become nothing but a source of analytic data in need of interpretation; a poor, incomplete, amorphous, confused, determined, helpless, source of data; an object buffeted by the winds and tides of life within, unable to steer his own course—to become all this is something which many resist. It may well be that in so resisting, the patient is not always mistaken. He may sometimes speak from a more comprehensive vision of reality and a better grasp of the truth of human life than the analyst himself. By refusing this reduction, he may be trying radically to maintain his integrity.

The analytic instruction to let go of all controls in speaking is *not really meant fully*, however. Analysts have themselves recognized that genuinely randomized free association as practiced by some patients is "defense." The patient must keep his head enough to be relevant to the analytic project, to obtain some understanding from analytic interpretations, and to produce appropriate memories, images, and ideas. Even not finding in therapy the experienced transformations of the analyst into threat, hated father, etc., totally convincing means to maintain some grasp of reality. It means maintaining a background of realism, objectivity, and the capacity to keep a centered meaning and sense in the ordinary everyday sense. If the patient believed *completely* that the analyst were actually bent on destroying him, the analysis itself would be destroyed. The patient's rationality and capacity to continue to make sense from his own center is actually counted on by both analyst and patient as the ground for making analysis possible.

## THE TRANSFERENCE EXPERIENCE

The transference, or carry-over experience, refers to whenever the patient acts or feels as if his analyst were like some significant figure or figures in his past life. Transference is an everyday phenomenon, for we often act as if someone is like someone else previously known. In analysis, however, it is a crucial element because the whole success of the analysis depends upon the handling and *understanding* of the transference. The core of the resistance to allowing taboo impulses to enter consciousness is lived out by the patient in the transference. Just as the threat of loss of love and hateful attack by the parents led to the original repression, so now in the neurotic patient's adult life the threat of loss of love and hateful attack from the analyst is the ground for maintaining the repression in therapy.

The patient's moment-by-moment, hour-by-hour expectation that his analyst will lose respect for him, attack, hate, dislike, reject, lose interest in, or insist on absolute compliance from him, smother him with commands, or make him feel guilty, is the transference. The major resistance to bringing the unconscious into consciousness is to be found in these transferred expectations from childhood. Here, according to Freud, is the battleground on which the analysis will be successful or not.

Lying on the couch, the patient begins to experience the analyst as one or another single or composite figure out of his past. He is encouraged to do this by the analyst's invisibility, silence, and adult position, which is distinguished from his own babbling, visible, self-exposing, childlike position. In relation to the analyst, the patient is the infant or child, and he brings to life again precisely those fantasies upon which the original repressions were built, vividly recreating just those parents, just that disapproval, which led originally to his unwillingness to let himself know and experience some parts of his life.

As it is brought to life again, this transference ground is *the* ground on which the fundamental analytic movement must be made. The patient does not merely remember his past but recreates it in the open space into which the analyst invites him. Always in the background of the analysis is the analyst's promise to assist in unraveling this complicated web, to be a reliable guide who has traveled down these paths before and knows the way. With this trust in the background, the patient is able to amplify and relive those buried aspects of his life. Usually, though, the first movements involve a transference and resistance to the process of remembering. Instead of remembering, his natural tendency is to relive and repeat. Instead of remembering his tendency to fight every authority, he fights the authority of the analyst.

The analyst must show the patient repeatedly that this is a transference until the patient is unable to resist the authority without remembering that this is just like his fight against his father. After awhile, repeating the rebellion becomes increasingly difficult. The behavior itself, of becoming impotently angry in the face of authority, is now accompanied by a reflective awareness in the form of an analytic interpretation.

This reflective interpretation makes the behavior pattern itself a kind of "object." The patient looks upon the behavior analytically, so that its spontaneous, automatic unfolding is frozen by the very act of looking. In that moment the patient repeats the objectification of himself which he first experienced when he angrily accused the analyst of being authoritarian; when the analyst noted in his cool and objective voice that the patient seemed suddenly to be very angry about that and he wondered why. The patient's anger is shut off and transformed by the new task of self-observation which the analyst has suggested. The self-conscious, reflective looking upon the flow of experience as data to be interpreted and understood is already a transformation of that original experience.

The structure of the analytic situation makes it relatively easy to show the patient to himself; for it is clear that the patient repeats and relives the past, and that this is so can be made quite convincing to him. In the transferential interpretation of this carry-over, the analyst returns again and again by implication to the realistically sensed ground which the patient must maintain: "I, the analyst, am an understanding, patient, skilled, and professional person. When you see me as different from that, what you are experiencing is a carry-over from your past." In this way the patient, unless he is to reject the whole process, necessarily comes to experience his own preset categories and prejudices, his own interpretations of other people, his own transference categories, or carry-overs from his past life.

He comes to realize concretely the power that these shadows have over his life and thus comes to understand and to grasp them. Through this understanding of the transference, the patient comes to grasp the living sources in his life of the anxieties, inhibitions, and symptoms which brought him to therapy in the first place. A very important psychological shift begins to occur at the moment when he really begins to grasp the transferential nature of his interaction with the analyst. Instead of being swept over by the fear of retaliation and loss of love, he stands in some way above these. The neurotic begins less to live the repressive impulses that would seek to express themselves but to come to grips with the basis for his condition.

To describe how this moment of apprehension comes to its usefulness, it must be understood that in the analytic situation the patient experiences sharply and rather consciously powerful fears of rejection, of domination, and of being overwhelmed. The analyst becomes "the one who will catch me in his net, who will spy on me and accuse me of my guilt." He becomes for the patient that horrid mother who never quite existed perhaps but who was constituted through the child's paralyzing fear and the guilt. These basic fears, as they are directed toward the analyst, are redirected to the patient by the analyst's interpretation. They are seen to be the patient's own inner psychic realities transferred onto the person of the analyst. When the patient experiences convincingly that this is true, it is an enormously reassuring relief. He suddenly discovers that this terrible fear that grips him belongs not here but to the past; that the fear and dread do not belong to the reality of the analyst; that, in fact, it is inappropriate ever to have thought so. By means of alert and skilled interpretation, the patient's expectations of chastisement, punishment, or guilty accusation are met by the directly contradicting reality of the analyst's accurate understanding and interpretation.

In principle, once this happens, the active transference is shattered. It may have to be repeated again and again; but when the first movement of incipient fear begins again to manifest itself, the patient now has some secure ground for seeing more accurately what the real situation is in his analysis and, *in principle*, in the rest of his life as well.

## CHARACTERISTIC CONTENT OF THE ANALYTIC INTERPRETATION

Analytic interpretations and constructs and the initial remarks leading to them almost always point predominantly toward the patient's past and to his internal life. In order to make conscious what is unconscious, to destroy amnesias, and to liberate strangulated affect, the analyst seeks to reconstruct the patient's past in a lively way. He repeatedly communicates to the patient that certain specific past events and relationships continue to exercise a far-reaching inward power over his life. This can sometimes involve elaborate reconstructions, especially with patients who have severe amnesias for certain significant events in their lives.

A female patient, for instance, may tell the analyst, "My father is an alcoholic, and my mother used to leave the house and take the children to our aunt's." It appears that there is some blockage of memory here involving something that was going on between the parents—the patient cannot remember exactly what. A very nice and proper lady who does not curse, the patient, a first child, had been "premature" by two-and-a-half months. Over a period of listening to her free associations, the analyst begins to construct a probable story: "When he was very drunk, your father used violent and abusive language toward your mother. Your parents married because your mother was pregnant, and so your father would say things like, 'You were not such a God damned holy virgin when I married you. When we got married, you were knocked up.' "

If the analyst has grasped the situation correctly, he will be correct in essence if not precisely in detail. The point is that his most fundamental interpretive work is always aimed toward the past, directed by the patient's past difficulties and their continuing power in his life. Infancy and early childhood especially are seen as the primary conditioning factors for understanding the patient's behavior. Implicitly and explicitly, the analyst guides the patient's free association toward those early dependent relationships. As already described, this emphasis on the past also occurs through the analyst's interpretation of the transference. About the past, the analyst asks further, for example, "When did you first notice it? When did it start?" calling explicit attention repeatedly to mother, father, sister, brother, and early childhood.

Although the past is emphasized, the interpretation is also directed toward the whole network of the patient's life. The analyst not only says, "You feel timid because you were made timid by the fear of your father's retaliation," but adds, "Your timidity manifests itself here in the transference, in your work as a student, in your professional life—indeed, in the clothes you wear and the friends you have." The patient's behavior is thus interpreted on a twofold basis: (1) here is the nucleus, which is unconscious and from the past, and (2) here is where we find the influence of this nucleus in your everyday life, in your relationships with others, and in the analysis itself.

The present, then, is interpreted in terms of the past, as repetition. In the Freudian analytic framework, this is conceived as psychically identical reenactments of original unconscious fantasies and wishes which repeat themselves over and over again with only minor situational changes, variations, and adaptive nuances. Hence, the behaviors of the patient are reduced in the analytic interpretation to the repetitive patterns, melodies, and strategies which are still the same, not figuratively but literally. In Freudian therapy, the unconscious is viewed as an active agent—as the "fundamental psychic reality." The patient is taught to believe that these repetitions, fantasies, or wishes live in him and use him as an instrument for their repetitive gratification patterns, an idea which involves a radical specialized transformation in perspective for both analyst and patient.

## Influence on the analyst

The analyst's interpretive intention formalizes explicitly his standpoint as objective observer and articulator of data—the data being 'the-patient-in-his-total-behavior-as-a-living-of-his-past' during the analytic session. From this formal standpoint, the patient's statements and behaviors are seen to have a fundamentally unreal structure. The patient does not and cannot really mean what he says or intend what he apparently intends. His ordinary everyday consciousness is a deceived or misled consciousness which does not know what it is about. The real meanings of his behaviors are inaccessible to the patient, revealing themselves only to the analytically attuned eye and ear.

These are meanings, however, which move away from the immediate here and now of the patient and are therefore not given in the patient's utterances. Rather they are inferred through the constructions of the observer-analyst, who penetrates the veils of the merely given to the hidden unconscious reality that lies beyond the patient's conscious sight.

This formal standpoint greatly emphasizes the analyst's capacity as comprehending theoretical intellect and schematizer of reality. Schematizing the patient removes the analyst from immediate observation of the here and now and reinforces his cool, surgical distance. He replaces the immediately given with the theoretically constructed. The analyst stresses finding the truth, reaching an understanding, comprehending, constructing, and reconstructing, making coherent lines of interconnections between the different aspects of the data which the patient speaks to him. He lends himself formally, by contract, so to speak, as agent-intellect, as the person who can make intelligibility live.

The analyst's attitude is therefore largely determined by his characteristic style of interpretation. The basic mode of analytic interpretation not only gives a specific content to the analysis but also determines that for him, finally, everything in the analytic situation is seen in the light of 'fostering-the-optimal-truth-within-the-analytic-framework.' At the same time, this defines as negative everything that impedes the analytic interpretive task. If the patient's feelings interfere, this is called resistance. If the therapist's feelings interfere, this is incompetence or countertransference.

To illustrate, let us consider the case of a fatherly analyst with a young college fellow. The young man is very disturbed because he has expressed his love for a young woman of his acquaintance and has been rebuffed. The patient may want reassurance from the analyst, or self-justification, or merely sympathy. The analyst in turn may feel sorry for him, remembering himself how it feels to be turned down. But if the analyst responds expressively in terms of his own feelings or in terms of spontaneous reaction to the felt-need expectations of his patient, this will be evaluated negatively from the analytic perspective. The analyst will be seen as contaminating with countertransference his meeting with the patient. Rather, his task in this situation is to illuminate either the transference reality of the patient who turns helplessly to "daddy" when rebuffed by the world, or the repetitive unconscious reality which led to his making a bungling choice of love object.

This example reveals another important aspect of the formal task of interpretation, which is that the analyst lives out with his patient a bifurcated, or twinned, consciousness. The first consciousness is the formally contracted analytic consciousness whose task is to shed light on behavior as repetition from the past.

At the same time, the analyst lives out an everyday consciousness of himself and others which dedicates itself, mostly without formal awareness, to the task of living together with others. It is this consciousness which leads the analyst to a noticeable softening of tone and slight increase in warmth when he experiences the other as wounded, rebuffed, and unhappy. It may lead him not to interpret something as repetition because he senses that this would be insulting, and also because at the everyday level he sees that what the person is referring to can stand on its own feet, with its own given meanings, without the benefit of analytic interpretation.

This form of consciousness takes clear precedence when the patient's father, mother, wife, child, or close friend dies or is severely ill. The analyst, like everyone else, expresses sorrow out of an ordinary social concern. The liking between analyst and patient, the feeling of mutual concern between them, the overlooking of bungled interpretations and awkward silences—in short, the thousand little events that make and sustain their relationship are to be found in the everyday consciousness rather than in the specialized analytic consciousness. In truth, analytic consciousness is grounded on and arises from the everyday world. For instance, everyone knows in an ordinary way that persons misunderstand one another by assuming correspondences with other times and other persons. Analytic consciousness only focuses on and radicalizes this everyday truth to a high degree.

The analyst not only twins his consciousness, which is unavoidable in any form of reflective consciousness, but he declares the formal analytic consciousness to be the one true consciousness dealing with the fundamental reality of his situation with his patient. For the analyst, this means that truth lives itself out in the analysis only in the form of analytic truth. Since the whole structure of the analytic situation emphasizes that the 'past-living-its-life-again-now' is *the* truth, it is understandable that both analyst and patient may succumb to the self-deception of declaring it to be the primary truth. In this way the accent of reality is given to the formal analytic consciousness as being the only true consciousness. The moment-by-moment everyday consciousness is relegated to a subjective or epiphenomenal status. In short, the ordinary relationship, including concern, friendship, and cooperation, without which there could be no analysis, is thereby overlooked. The tender regard which the analyst actually has for the patient, which makes it possible for the patient to overcome his expectation that all men will reject him as weak, is overlooked or only mentioned in passing as relatively unimportant.

The analyst's special consciousness, his formal allegiance to analytic schemes of interpretation, therefore does not foster that optimal awareness of some of the most important factors in the analytic process. His

actual sincerity, honesty, warmth, care, and down-to-earth reasonableness are crucial determinants of his helpfulness, but none of these
things can be properly described within the accented reality of the
psychoanalytic scheme.

## Influence on the patient

By agreeing to reduce himself to data to be understood, the patient
agrees to relinquish rational or normal sense making in favor of becoming a 'psyche-to-be-analyzed.' He begins to realize the import of
this agreement only when he is faced with the characteristic content of
the analytic interpretation again and again. The patient, from his own
center of everyday meanings, often experiences himself as merely
being cooperative, or amiable, providing additional helpful information,
or engaging in other normal everyday tasks with his analyst. The
analyst insistently refers these behaviors to unconscious motives belonging to the past and treats the commonsense motivations which the
patient experiences as real as being actually a deceptive covering-over
of the fundamental unconscious reality.

The following hypothetical situation illustrates. Let us suppose that
the analyst has just made an interpretive remark, and the patient replies,
"Let me mention something I neglected to say before that might clarify
that." The analyst notes that the patient is giving a kind of apology.
"Did he unconsciously mislead me into a mistaken interpretation? Is
he trying to obscure and qualify the interpretation out of existence?
What unconscious motivations are inspiring this apparent helpfulness?
He certainly isn't just spontaneously associating." The analyst might
remain silent, the patient continuing after a pause: "Well, I didn't
mean that I neglected to say it, rather that it just hadn't come up before
and I thought it might help you to see—"—(pause)—"I'm having a hell
of a time trying to talk about something I just thought of. I guess I
just don't want to bring it up."

Reflecting on this example sharpens an awareness of the dialectic
between the analyst and his patient. It is noteworthy that the patient
does not trust what he himself says and also that he is self-aware and
partly blocked by that awareness. He first speaks in an everyday mode:
"Let me mention something that might clarify." He is then met by a

vigilant, reflective self-consciousness which suspiciously asks what he meant, questions the reality of his everyday motives, accuses him of "neglect" in not having mentioned the thing before, causes him to justify himself and then self-consciously to become aware of justifying himself. Finally, he beomes aware of the most *real* motive, which is of wanting to hide the truth, and then interprets his whole activity retrospectively as "avoiding saying what was on my mind out of fear."

It is clear in all of this that the patient distrusts his own sense making in his everyday awareness of himself as a self-understood being. This self-distrust is a learned counterpart to the analyst's distrust of the patient's statements and everyday meanings. Now both patient and analyst have a twinned consciousness. There is, on the one hand, the patient's everyday consciousness of self and world and, on the other hand, a new analytic consciousness which is incorporated into whatever reflective self-consciousness the patient brings into therapy. It is this budding analytic consciousness which the patient gradually learns to trust at the same time that he is learning to distrust his normal everyday consciousness.

With the gradual refinement of the analytic mode of interpretation, the patient begins increasingly to see that his thoughts and feelings are to be understood as repetition from childhood rather than as valid response to reality. This growing realization is a paradoxical one, already foreshadowed in his *rational* assent to the *unreasoning* action of free association. He increasingly fosters in himself an awareness of his own irrationality shaped by the past and driven by dark forces from within. He thus undermines his own ground of reason and sense making while presuming that he can and does make sense through the development of his budding analytic consciousness. He presupposes the power to see, comprehend, and validly understand by showing to himself, through the analytic perspective, that he does not see, comprehend, or validly understand.

The trust-distrust dialectic is simultaneous. With every analytic understanding, he is helped concretely to trust the sense and meaning that he sees only insofar as it agrees with and reflects the analytic interpretation. At the same time, since the analytic understanding is distrustful of the given, he learns to distrust the ordinary everyday sense of things and people as fundamentally unreliable and merely symptomatic of deeper underlying realities. This paradoxical development of self-distrust in order to develop self-trust is very much in accord with the paradoxical qualities inherent in the whole analytic situation. The patient makes himself young in order to grow up, makes himself unreal in order to become real, makes himself uncanny in order to be canny, and reduces himself to unreason in order to grow reasonable.

## THE OUTCOME OF SUCCESSFUL ANALYSIS

When analysis works, the patient is freed of his enslavement to the repetitious pattern of his neurotic life. Both within and outside the analytic sessions, he sharply experiences a variety of emotions and situations, which he transforms through immediate analytic interpretation and reconstruction. When, for instance, he is inclined to be neurotically agreeable, he learns to say, "Here is mom telling me to be nice again." The transformation of the experience within the analytic consciousness changes its structure and meaning in such a way as to make it less binding and enslaving. The inclination to be nice, for example, is no longer seen as a valid expression of normal sociability but rather as neurotic repetition. Seeing a behavior in this way tends to freeze it reflectively, to stop it in its tracks, as well as to take away its validation or justification.

Thus, the patient learns to live increasingly in the truth as he has learned it from the analyst and less in that implicit neurotic view of reality learned first from his parents and later socially reinforced. He trades his old parents with their inadequate structures of understanding and evaluation for a new parent, the analyst, who has taught him ways of living, thinking, valuation, construction, and interpretation that free him from his old neurotic binds. In other words, he trades a neurotically inadequate repressive conception and experience of reality for a new analytic interpretation of reality. He is cured when he is able to be his own analyst.

But there is also considerable learning in a successful analysis that is not clearly wedded to the analytic perspective. The problematics of the therapeutic dialogue are always lived out between a specific analyst and a specific patient, each of whom brings to the therapeutic situation certain individual traits, qualities, and aspects that are not adequately encompassed in psychoanalytic theory. The patient will have learned much, for example, from some implicit attitudes of the analyst. The hearty warmth of one analyst may open for the patient a whole world of open-handed, warm spontaneity that he had lacked before. The cool, pleasant, wry toleration of human weaknesses and strengths characteristic of another analyst may initiate a patient into a more relaxed attitude toward himself and others.

From the specific virtues of his individual analyst, the patient learns not only concrete embodiments of the analytic vision but certain socialized human qualities that make for a better life as well. To understand the working of psychotherapy more adequately, therefore, it is necessary to give closer attention to some actual therapeutic events and to inquire further into their nature. This will be undertaken at length and in detail in the following chapter, in which Freudian therapy is concretized in the case of Mary.

## BIBLIOGRAPHY

Boss, Medard. *Psychoanalysis and Dasein Analysis*. New York: Basic Books, 1963.

An excellent comprehensive attempt to existentialize analytic practice in the light of Heidegger's vision of man. Boss' description of the fundamental meanings of analytic praxis serves as a background to the more concretely detailed description of Freudian therapy in the present text.

Freud, Sigmund. *Analysis of a Phobia in a Five-Year-Old Boy*. Standard Edition, vol. 10. Edited by J. Strachy. London: Hogarth Press, 1955.

Analytic interpretation and treatment brought together with vivid clarity in a lucid case presentation.

_____. *Dora: An Analysis of a Case of Hysteria*. New York: Collier Books, 1963.

Concrete dialectics of the therapy process brought sharply to focus in the drama between Freud and Dora.

_____. *Therapy and Technique*. New York: Collier Books, 1963.

A collection of most of Freud's articles on psychoanalysis as a therapeutic approach, containing the basic rules of conducting psychoanalysis in four essays of recommendations for physicians, some notes on the interpretation of dreams in analysis, and other essays.

Freud, Sigmund, and Bruer, Joseph. *Studies on Hysteria*. New York: Avon Books, 1966.

The therapeutic approaches of remembering, interpreting, bringing the past to conscious life, and transference are described as the fundamentals of psychotherapy in section 4, "The Psychotherapy of Hysteria."

Munroe, Ruth L. *Schools of Psychoanalytic Thought*. New York: Holt, Rinehart, and Winston, 1955.

The second part of chapter 7 offers a clear descriptive account of psychoanalysis as a treatment method from within the psychoanalytic view.

Schutz, Alfred. *Collected Papers. The Problem of Social Reality*, vol. 1. The Hague: Martinus Nijhoff, 1962.

A collection of profound phenomenological essays on social reality, grounding the specialized fragmentary worlds in the ordinary social order, and emphasizing the priority of self-understanding and self-interpretation—a background for the present text's understanding of the relationship of "specialized analytic interpretations" to "the analyst and patient getting along together."

# 4

# The case of Mary

## INTRODUCTION TO MARY

Mary is thirty-two years old—a plump woman, younger looking than her age, and rather unfeminine, the latter emphasized by the bland, tasteless, sexless, sacklike clothing she wears. Slightly intimidated by the newness of the situation she has entered, there is nevertheless immediately perceptible about her a kind of directness and clarity of movement and manner which suggest a person who is accustomed to being decisive and clear rather than vague and indistinct.

She is just reaching out to shake hands when the analyst directs her to the chair rather than to the couch. As she sits down, she sighs and begins immediately to give her history, understanding as a physician herself that a history will be necessary. She describes her father as a good and simple man who was rather overwhelmed by the mother. Her mother she describes as exceedingly anxious, hypochondriacally concerned with herself and her daughter. "If I'd let my mother have her way," she says, "I'd never have left the house. She kept telling me not to overtire myself, not to get too cold or too hot, to be in all ways careful—in short, not to live too much." An only child, the patient spent all of her younger years in a small town in the Midwest. She is a Protestant who, raised by nonreligious parents, considers herself to be more religious than they. At one point she had attended ministerial school with an interest in pursuing a career in religious education. She has come to psychoanalysis seeking answers to certain dissatisfactions, although she does not consider herself to be either very disturbed or very neurotic.

Nonetheless, certain recurring problems plague and puzzle her, the most disturbing of which is that no one ever treats her as a woman. She is always treated as a person of ability, competence, and stamina, as a strong, adequate person, but always as a kind of "pal" or "buddy." By some people she is treated as a mother figure but never as a female peer, and this disturbs her very much. She also explains that she has recurrent periods of overeating followed by periods of dieting and that she is approximately fifty pounds overweight. She is not especially nervous, however, nor does she suffer from deep fatigue. She sleeps well, does not dream—at least she does not remember dreaming—and her symptoms are on the whole few and minor. She is not severely neurotic.

Further details of the family history clarify the picture she has already given of her family structure. The mother was, and remains, a severely disturbed woman who had been hospitalized a number of times for a psychotic condition, the hospitalizations beginning when Mary was in late high school. It is further discovered that Mary slept with her mother in the same bed from the age of about two until she was about sixteen. Following her birth, the father had slept in a separate room. After several preliminary interviews the analyst and patient agree to begin a trial analysis, which means that for three weeks, Mary will come five days a week for an hour each day. At the end of the three-week period they will evaluate whether this is a fruitful therapeutic approach for her.

## The analytic view
The analyst has decided at this point to consider the patient neurotic rather than psychotic, even though her early family life was such as to suggest profound disturbances at deeper levels of her personality.

When the conscious defensive structure of a competent, adequate, professional woman is pursued through the analysis, the analyst will expect to find levels of profound pathology. He already expects that the repressed or unconscious side of her personality will exhibit certain specific dynamic problems.

The analyst expects to find strong repressed dependency feelings, manifested especially in Mary's eating behavior. The tendency to gain and lose weight as she does indicates an important area of severe conflict relating to her early dependent relationship with her mother. Further, she says that people in general treat her as adequate, competent, self-sufficient, and independent, which means that she must give them good grounds to do so. These traits are directly antithetical to strong dependent leanings, strivings, and behavior. Thus, within the model of psychoanalysis, at the unconscious level, much of her character is built against being dependent and weak, and it is only in her eating (and perhaps in other areas not yet known) that there is some symptomatic manifestation of an early hungering, needful self.

The analyst also expects to find both homosexual and heterosexual strivings repressed and maintained in unconsciousness. The homosexual striving would exist at the deepest level, of course—"of course," because the homosexual tendencies would be the most taboo and therefore the most repressed. Already she says that no one ever treats her as a feminine woman, a peer woman, or in any respect as a sexual being. In her daily behavior, she reacts against her own femininity.

That the defense against homosexuality is a very important part of her character is surmised on the basis of two lines of evidence. First, she slept in the same bed with her mother, which would necessarily create powerful sexual tensions in a young child, especially if the parents were separated from each other as they were in her life. Secondly, we find a symptomatic expression of a certain masculinity, a striving to be unfeminine as well as positively masculine, in some details of her clothing and appearance.

The total style by which she defends herself against dependency and sexuality, both homosexuality and heterosexuality, are blended in the way she has developed the character of a competent, intellectual professional woman. She enters analysis suspecting that this is not the whole story about herself and with the beginnings of a desire to allow herself to become more than this competent professional woman. Beneath the layer of competency the analyst expects to find, for instance, that in her fantasies she will become extremely passive and dependent, and, if encouraged in that direction, would produce, almost literally, oral fantasies of sucking and being taken care of—whether literally or not would depend to a great degree on the analyst. Before any of these unconsciously active fantasies, hopes, or aspirations were uncovered, however, layers of defenses would emerge, especially intellectualization and high moral and aesthetic standards which will produce much resistance in the psychoanalytic process. Images of abandonment will emerge: "I am all alone; there is no one; I am desolate in a desolate world, and no one cares for me." The analyst will be seen as "a cold and heartless bastard" when he fails to meet her dependency needs. Quite late in the analysis Mary would eventually begin to produce homoerotic fantasies of some sort. She will almost certainly act out what she claims other people do to her (that is, what she does to others as a way of preventing the emergence of strong dependency needs). She will say to the analyst, in effect: "You and I are equal in this situation; we are both physicians, brothers under the skin," not noticing that her analyst is a man and that she is not his brother.

The above hypotheses are extremely sketchy and are given only to elaborate further the notion of consciousness and unconsciousness as fundamental negative polarity in the neurotic personality. The notion of the unconscious, as a Freudian understands it, is such that when he talks about homosexuality components, he would expect literally that there would be fantasies—fantasies that will emerge into consciousness, literally, from their unconscious origins. Homosexuality is not a trait or habit learned in early childhood. A person's unconscious is seen to be activated literally and actually full, as it were, of these kinds of components—dependency, infantile oral fantasies,—but not seen clearly because in the unconscious things are unclear and murky. But they are really there nevertheless, and they will emerge in the analysis.

## INTRODUCTION TO DR. R.

Dr. R., the analyst, is a forty-two-year-old man who dresses conservatively, is somewhat overweight, likes his work very much, finds people interesting, and enjoys the sense of mastery and intimacy that accompanies getting to know people well professionally. He is definitely a thinker. From early childhood he has read a lot, primarily in science and philosophy. He will admit that he has never been much of a socializer, preferring serious discussions to parties, and was never very good in sports or political competition.

In spite of all his training and knowledge, including an M.D., two years of personal analysis, training at an analytic institute, and about fourteen years' experience as a doctor and therapist, he is shy and tends to be awkward and self-conscious in groups, as well as in directly expressing his feelings to another person. He feels most comfortable and natural when pursuing a line of thought or in intellectual discussions. Although he secretly admires them, people who are extremely emotional or spontaneously and easily expressive make him uncomfortable. By temperament he is optimistic, congenial, and inclined to think the best of people rather than the worst.

## A happy beginning

During their first few meetings, before the beginning of formal analysis, Dr. R. and Mary find that they get along well. Dr. R. asks the kinds of questions that Mary finds sensible and relevant. He seems direct and straight with her, not playing at being mysterious, which is one thing she had feared from an analyst. She notes with amusement that he, too, is overweight. In some ways he reminds her of some easygoing professors she had especially liked in school. He is attentive and serious and exhibits a lively interest that not only encourages her to speak and sparks her own interest in understanding herself but at moments arouses in her a mixture of enjoyment and tingling fear. She is herself rather intellectual and is pleased that her analyst-to-be seems intelligent and intellectually oriented. She already looks at him as someone who will know her better than anyone in the world, and that is a frightening thought to her. She also feels, though she would not yet dare put this into words, that he likes her.

For his part, Dr. R. is relieved and happy to be speaking with a patient who seems so amenable to his analytic understanding. She has taken up with alacrity the hints contained in his questions, already seeing that her feelings toward her mother might have something to do with her unwillingness to be feminine. He finds her direct, honest, and open with him, qualities he has always admired and often found lacking in women. There is about her a strength of character, a steadiness of purpose, and a commitment to values and goals similar to his own that he finds very likable. She is not given to self-pity or despair, nor is she a raving emotional hysteric. While recognizing that part of his task will be to loosen the very controls that he now admires, Dr. R. always feels more comfortable, and has found himself to be therapeutically more effective, with people who suffer from such inhibition of emotional expression.

From the standpoint of an *everyday* understanding, this is a happy beginning to a psychotherapy. Patient and therapist find each other natural, comfortable, and agreeable to be with, like each other, are compatible in style, and in agreement concerning fundamental life values. Because of this natural, social ground of liking between them, both are livelier, warmer, more interested, and more cooperative. The very tremor of fear that Mary experiences at his lively interest in her, which from an analytic viewpoint is a clear transference reaction based on early childhood, is also grounded in his reaction to her as "someone I want to know."

## A less happy beginning

Let us suppose, on the other hand, that Mary had gone to an analyst who was fond of, and comfortable with, highly expressive emotional people and uncomfortable with cerebral female types. If this were the case, he would find Mary dry, a dull intellectualizer, too tough, unyielding, and cold. He would find her competitive and striving to keep the therapy in her own hands. In short, he would probably dislike her personally and experience her as someone he would ordinarily avoid outside of his professional commitment. With that sort of personal feeling, he might ask her fewer questions and those cooler and drier in tone. Instead of asking sympathetically, "Do you suppose your mother's overemotionality has perhaps made you suspicious of emotions?" he might ask clinically, "Do you think that people don't respond to you warmly because you are cold and unemotional unlike your mother?"

In response to this kind of reception, Mary might well be more tightly controlled, less lively, and allow less emotion to show, experiencing the therapy hours as threatening, freezing, and difficult. She would be more blocked, less fluid and easy going and would experience the analyst as one who "stares" and makes her feel "like a laboratory specimen." Encountering a basically nonconfirming attitude from her analyst, she would actually look, and therefore be, more rigid, more "sick," more overcontrolled, more compulsive, less emotionally free, and less likable.

This co-constituting of the degree of pathology of the patient is inevitable in therapy, because the patient is sick, blocked, or neurotic with his therapist, not in a vacuum. It is important to observe that this applies not merely to the therapist's judgment of pathology but also directly affects the patient's behaviors, making him become more or less sick or disturbed. Thus, getting along well together and liking each other is crucial to the therapeutic process. It is a life-world background that colors every interaction between patient and therapist, and it is against this background especially that the patient's degree of pathology is defined and demarcated.

## A question of fact

To pursue the importance of patient-therapist interaction, how would Dr. R. and his opposite answer the question, How did Mary get along with her father? To ask this within an analytic perspective is to observe the transference reaction in therapy. Dr. R., who likes Mary, would be inclined to postulate that there must have been some basic good core of relatedness to the father which now makes possible her relatively good relating within analysis. The analyst who does not like or get along well with Mary will indicate that the father-daughter relationship must have been very destructive, offering as proof the incredible rigidity, fearfulness, and overcontrol in the analytic sessions. He would say that no one who had felt acceptance and liking from the father would be that tied up in knots in analysis. It is a natural temptation to ask which of these viewpoints of the father-daughter relationship is the more true, but to ask this is to miss the crucial insight—namely, that in the process of psychotherapy, either of these viewpoints may be *made true* between analyst and patient. Which viewpoint is made true depends on the dialectical unfolding of their relationship.

The patient's concrete past, which will be made to live between analyst and patient, is also co-constituted between them, not only by analytic theory but by the exigencies of the particular relationship itself. Thus, Dr. R. will see Mary's relationship with her father as a support—limited, to be sure, but real nonetheless—that sustained her. Out of this bias, Mary will be encouraged to seek and find not only the weaknesses and difficulties of her relationship with her father but also the good that there was between them. She may even eventually identify her father as the one without whom she would have gone completely crazy.

For the therapist who finds Mary stuffy and cold, the father will be seen as totally rejecting, indifferent, unsupportive, and neurosis inducing. Mary's attempts to find something good in her father will be seen as a defense against facing her real hatred. Her difficulty in relating to men will be seen as belonging in a special way to her relationship with her father. The cool, slightly negative flavor of the relationship between this analyst and Mary will foster hatred of the analyst as well as more resistance, all of which will constitute proof of the extreme difficulties that existed between Mary and her father. In this context, Mary's picture of her father will therefore undergo a transformation in the direction of antagonism, blame, and hatred.

## ANALYSIS WITH DR. R.

*The first month.* Because Dr. R. has decided to undertake an essentially orthodox analysis with Mary, they meet five times a week for forty-five-minute sessions. He instructs her in free association and sits behind and out of her visual field as she lies on the couch. In her first month or so she finds it very difficult not to look frequently at her analyst and cranes her neck again and again to see him. Also during the first several weeks, her posture lying down is rather wooden. She seems unable to relax and does not free associate by even the most generous definition of that term, being completely unable to speak everything.

A conscientious, hard-working patient, she often mentions something that she neglected to mention when it first occurred to her. It becomes increasingly evident both to her and to Dr. R. that she hangs on tenaciously to being a doctor, a competent professional woman, in the analytic situation. The analyst mentions this a few times, and she experiences it sharply, in tensed muscles, craning neck, intellectual forays into analytic interpretation, and a chronic inability to allow herself to flow easily. She tells highly connected stories about her life, often emphasizing this or that point with expressive gestures appropriate to normal social conversation.

As expected, she has read a bit of psychoanalytic literature in order to "cooperate better and with more understanding," as she puts it. Her analyst gently reminds her that such intellectual analytic work tends to defeat the task of letting go and relaxing vigilance in the analytic sessions. With the best will in the world, she finds it exceedingly difficult to let go of her controls in the sessions.

Thematically, during the first month, she has been developing the original complaint that men do not treat her as a woman. After several days of complaining in an organized manner about this, she begins to talk about how unfair it is that men seem to respond so positively to women who are brainless nincompoops. One day she delivers a forty-minute diatribe against the weakness and stupidity of women who, in blind, cowlike submersion of themselves, try to please men. During the following session, she is somewhat muted, a bit apologetic about this outburst. The analyst remarks with gentle irony that it is curious to be apologetic about her first actual relaxed letting go and points out that these emotions are usually prevented from entering consciousness by her overcontrol. Noting his approval of her self-expression, she pursues the theme of those "stupid, disgusting women" with renewed vigor. At the end of several more interviews devoted to this theme, the analyst observes that although she desires to interest men herself, she finds what women do to interest men disgusting.

In response, Mary spends three full interviews directly and indirectly justifying her disgust, proving that being womanly in the sense that she despises really *is* horrible. The analyst calls her attention to this defending behavior several times—first, as an indication of a very sensitive point, and second, as pointing to her need to be justified before him. It becomes quite clear now how much she fights the idea of being in any way submissive or dependent on anyone; the analyst stresses her fear of this and any feelings that might be connected with it.

## THE EVERYDAY USES OF INTERPRETATION

On several occasions during Mary's first month in analysis, the analyst's interpretations have meant much more to both of them than merely an accurate reconstruction of the motivations of her behavior. The analyst's interpretive remarks have served a variety of purposes in fostering the therapeutic dialogue. Dr. R. remarked to Mary, for example, that her apologizing for being too emotional on that first occasion fitted well with her general overcontrol. She and he both understood perfectly well that he was expressing approval and encouragement of her emotional expressivity. He interpreted her psychoanalytic reading as reflecting an attempt to maintain a defensive control of herself, and in this he was expressing gentle disapproval of her excess intellectuality, encouraging her to give it up in favor of a loosened expressivity. By interpreting her as needing self-justification before him, he was also reassuring Mary that she did not always have to be right with him.

In addition, there is a basic reassurance integral to the very act of interpretation. By giving an interpretation, the analyst asserts a fundamental "psycho-*logic*", sense-making understandability and humanity to the patient's behaviors. Even the most hostile and unpleasant use of interpretation restores the patient's behavior to the level of the generally human. In an everyday sense, through the interpretive act the analyst also presents himself as one who understands and is not dismayed.

The interpretive act carries an enormous communicative weight, since it is in a radical sense the only formally allowed and approved intervention of the analyst with his patient. The thrust of the analyst's total style is carried communicatively within the framework of a series of interpretive interventions. Thus, his tolerant, warm, open geniality or his sharp, acerbic, negating wit will be lived out in the context of his analytic interpretations. The analyst's pessimistic, depressive view of human possibilities or his optimistic seeing of the best in others will express itself in his mode and manner of handling the acts of inter-pretation.

Again it is necessary to concretize this in order to grasp the central-ity of the everyday uses of interpretation to the analytic process. Dr. R.'s interpretation of Mary's analytic reading as defense could be taken as a starting point. The manner in which he communicated this to Mary manifested to her a gentle toleration of her foibles, a continued approval of her, a steady, patient encouragement of a gradual loosening in her communications, and a basic trust that with such slight help and support she could overcome her rigidities. By a less gently congenial analyst, the same interpretation could communicate to Mary a basic disapproval, the impossibility of ever winning approval, a continual nagging and picking apart of all her behaviors for criticism, an impa-tient prodding to change, and a basic distrust of her ability to overcome her rigidities. This can be seen in the difference between remarking gently, "It is very difficult for you to give up intellectual control," compared with the accusation, "You have to hang on to control and pretend to be a man."

The whole mood and manner of analyst-patient interaction are set differently by these two remarks. The milder approach leads much more readily to a cooperative working together to resolve the difficulty; the accusatory mode leads much more readily to a power struggle be-tween analyst and patient. Again, this indicates concretely the ways in which patient and analyst 'make-each-other-be'. The accused patient shows herself to *be* more competitive, more power hungry, less agree-able and yielding, and therefore invites attack, strong interpretation, and forceful intervention. The more affirmed patient shows herself to *be* more cooperative, less power hungry, more agreeable, more yield-ing, and therefore invites softer interpretations and weaker interven-tions. Thus, the everyday structures of getting along with each other have a fundamental priority in the unfolding of the analytic process and are, in fact, basic to the relationship between analyst and patient. It is this actual everyday relationship between them which is the ground on which the analytic interpretations and interventions live themselves.

*The second and third months.* As Dr. R. and Mary enter the second month of analysis and Mary recapitulates her hatred of weak, weepy women, the therapist remarks upon her extraordinary vehemence and suggests that perhaps Mary had found her mother weak in this way. This leads the patient, who is now strongly emotional about this, to a bitter description of the constant battle that she had had to wage against her mother in order not to be crippled or paralyzed. Her mother was constantly telling her: "You poor, weak thing, you must take care of yourself and keep your health. You must be careful not to strain or overexert yourself."

Mary had had constantly to fight this in order to avoid becoming a psychic invalid or to be taken over. Nothing was private to her mother, who pried into everything, including Mary's bowel movements. If she were not having them often enough, the enemas would begin. Her mother would wash her all over her body, and Mary always felt there was something sick, queer, and overinterested in the way her mother did this. By the time she was five years old, she had rebelled actively against these intrusions by locking her mother out of the bathroom and insisting that she be left alone. They continued to sleep together in the same bed, however, which the patient knows to be a fact but can remember nothing about.

Going over this same ground often, Mary begins to remember a variety of incidents which flesh out the basic story, and each time she returns more strongly and in somewhat more detail to feeling her mother's intrusiveness. With each repetition she understands a little more concretely how she had been forced to hold herself in, to control herself, in order to defend herself from her mother's enveloping eroticism.

As she enters the third month of analysis, after approximately fifty interviews, Mary begins to wonder why she is unable to remember anything about being in bed with her mother. The analyst decides that this is a very important amnesia, noting that her free associations have tended to circle around the theme of what it means to be a woman, how disgusting women are, and, more recently, her relationship with her mother, whom she found to be queer and slightly disgusting. He suggests to Mary that she is blocking out something important having to do with being in bed with her mother, suggesting interpretively that her mother must have been awful to cause such a rebellion. In response to this evocation of the past, Mary says: "I feel very funny in here now. It's strange, because I used to enjoy coming before, but now there is something I don't like in here. I was really starting to relax on the couch, but now as soon as I lie down I feel a tightness in my stomach. I feel a little suffocated, like I can't breathe."

The analyst responds, "I think that you are afraid of what we are reminding you of from your past relationship with your mother. Just tell me whatever comes to mind and we will see more." He is encouraging and reassuring her, realizing that by evoking the past he has made her uncomfortable. He wants her to relax, and he speaks more soothingly than is customary in the analytic ideal of cool, surgical distance. He is certain that while lying on the couch the patient is feeling a literal repetition of what it was like to lie in bed with her mother. She is literally making herself tight and stiff in order to avoid the experience of intimate bodily contact with her mother. When he had first seen Mary, he had noticed that she held herself away from physical contact. He had not then understood it, but he now begins to see it more clearly as she lies there, really quite paralyzed, asking, "Can't you help me out of this terrible feeling?"

## THE PATIENT'S INVOLVEMENT IN ANALYSIS

By the time a patient has entered his fourth month of analysis, he has already spend about sixty hours in session with his analyst. He has been going five days a week and committing a sizable proportion of his income, even going into debt, in order to stay in analysis. In following the directions to free associate, however imperfectly, he has revealed more to the analyst, both in fact and in textured personal nuance, than he has ever revealed to anyone before. He has discovered with extraordinary concreteness the considerable degree to which he is unfree, blocked, and tied to the past. He has experienced the relief of confessing shameful things without retribution, of discovering and expressing faults without being blamed, and of relaxing verbal constraints without punishment. At the same time he has been learning to view feelings, current happenings, relationships with others, and the various exigencies of his life in the light of the analytic vision of the past repeating itself in the present.

Throughout this process, he has been experiencing the careful, disciplined attentiveness of an understanding analyst who has made penetrating guesses about things in the past, has shown himself able to comprehend the patient's feelings and thoughts, and has been tolerant of the patient's difficulties. More than ever before, the patient has been exposed to a continual, relatively steady care provided by the analyst. The quality of this attentive care may be a gentle background of warm liking and acceptance within which an accurate analytic vision is fostered, or it may be a cooler, less involved, more cerebral care which searches out suspiciously the underlying motivations that inspire the patient. In either case, the patient is exposed to a degree of attentive care probably hitherto unparalleled in his life.

As the analysis continues, there develops between analyst and patient a common history out of the common sharing of space and time, a history which incorporates into itself the totality of the patient's history. The patient has chosen to bring his past into the light of analysis, thereby to interpret and understand his life story. He is encouraged in this by the analyst, who points him in many directions but most explicitly, through the retrospective glance of the analytic interpretation, again and again to his own past. The person's history as *his story* is being recapitulated and reinterpreted within the analysis itself. The very sense and thrust of his total life is receiving a fundamental evaluation and restructuring in the analysis.

Hence, the patient finds himself increasingly involved deeper in the process of being in analysis. He has shared more, exposed himself more, been more carefully attended to, more intelligently understood, and brought more of the meaning context of his life into being between himself and his analyst than he has ever done with anyone before. He has done this in the hope that his life will become better and that he will understand himself better.

This deepening involvement in analysis means that he increasingly treats the daily events of his life as data to be understood. To understand and interpret becomes a second life that he lives within and alongside his everyday life. He lives more fully what his analyst says to him than he lives his job. Where he is, what he feels, what he thinks, and what is happening to him are more and more answerable in terms of what is happening within analysis. More succinctly, the patient *is* now *in* analysis.

*The fourth month.* At the beginning of the fourth month there have been about seventy-five interviews, and Mary is becoming annoyed at the contrast between her increasingly emotional involvement and the analyst's maintenance of cool rationality. She is not feeling cordially cooperative with him now and begins frequently to criticize him, directly and indirectly, consciously and unconsciously. She speaks in complimentary ways about a psychiatrist she has met socially who uses a highly interventionistic, activistic approach to therapy. She mentions reading about different schools of therapy and that she likes some of the more manipulative, active ones. She experiences the analyst as "just sitting there like a God damned bump on a log." Her resentment against him, her disappointment that he does not just continue to make her feel good, the evident fact that he feels that things are satisfactory when she feels terrible—all of these combine to increase her annoyance. Toward the end of the third month, the analyst had noticed that she was annoyed with him, his detachment and coolness. However, as the patient is herself oriented toward cool rationality and had previously found it a congenial quality in him, he looks upon the anger as unearned and as a repetition of previous relationships.

Until recently in the analysis, the father has been conspicuous by his absence. Now it appears that Mary had experienced real disappointment in her father, and she is reliving just that disappointment that she experienced when she realized that her father would not involve himself enough to protect her from her intrusive mother. Again she feels miserably beset as the man in her life (this time the analyst but the first time the father) sits by as an onlooker and does not move to protect or spare her. She had thought when she was a child, as she does again now, that somehow her daddy was strong enough to relieve and protect her; but he had chosen not to, or so it seemed. Now the analyst chooses to refrain from intervening, even though he softens his voice and is slightly warmer in response to her suffering. From Mary's viewpoint, he is commenting coolly on her suffering, and he still *does* nothing.

The analyst notes not only that she is reliving a disappointment and anger that belong to her father but also that the demanding, helpless, nagging behavior which she directs toward him now seems to resemble the behavior of her mother toward her father. The patient understands this, and yet she would still like the analyst to involve himself more. He does seem somehow cooler and more distant. They do not move in harmony now with a lively flowing of interested speaking on her side and mild, gently evocative interpretations on his. Rather, his interpretations now break into her flow of feeling and thought, and she experiences this as intrusive, negative, indifferent, and lacking in appreciation of her burden.

## THE STRUCTURE AND ENFORCEMENT OF ANALYTIC DISTANCE

It has been seen that the particular way in which Dr. R. and Mary handle distance and intellectuality originally fostered a rapport, liking, and even warmth between them. This was based, however, on the fundamental harmony of their attitudes. As soon as the patient is somewhat less sympathetic to analytic distance, cooperativeness is undermined. At this point, the analyst moves either gently or pointedly toward becoming an explicit enforcement agent, intervening strongly in the noncooperativeness and interpreting it. Because noncooperativeness does not accord with the fundamental agreement of analysis and also threatens the relationship, the analyst must powerfully reintroduce the agreement and find ways to undermine the tendency to resist.

In an everyday sense, the analyst and patient now become adversaries. The analyst affirms that he is doing what he should do and that the patient is introducing negative static from the past. The patient is at least half-heartedly affirming that the analyst is not doing enough of the right or the needed things and that this is why the analysis is not

going well. If the analysis is to survive this phase of "negative transference," the patient must submit to the analyst's interpretation and
move toward giving up the noncooperativeness, which may not be
easy for him. The analyst's attitude also undergoes a transformation
through this process, especially in cases where the noncooperativeness
and negativism become very strong.

The analyst becomes cooler and more distant—this is the heart of the
structural change which strong interfering transference produces—in
exactly that degree to which the patient's positive or negative feelings
toward him become intensely interfering in the analytic project. The
patient says, for example, "I just like to spend time with you, it doesn't
matter what we say"; or, "I feel like I don't want to have anything
to do with a pompous ass like you." In both cases the analyst, with
increased sharpness, distance, and accuracy, indicates strongly that
what the person is doing is *data* which they together must understand
and interpret. Because the patient no longer fully agrees to this, the
analyst now becomes the enforcer.

The analyst becomes structurally insistent until the patient moves
more fully to cooperative participation in the analytic project. This
insistent, strong pushing of the other to remain faithful to the analytic
project is already more cool and distant. The shared space between the
analyst and patient within which they move toward and with each other
is diminished to the degree to which the patient radically objects to the
agreed quality of that space.

At this point the analyst frequently reminds the patient of the promises made at the beginning of analysis and forcefully encourages him to
remain faithful to those promises, however difficult this may be. Often
the analyst becomes annoyed and exasperated with his patient's stubborn refusal to cooperate. The fundamental response of distancing or
anger as a reaction to the other's unwillingness to participate remains
basic to the shared life of analyst and patient. The analyst cannot feel
as close or move as warmly toward the patient who will not move
cooperatively within the space provided by analysis. The patient no
longer permits the analyst to be fully analyst-for-the-patient, and this
leaves the analyst in a peculiar position. The good analyst remains calm
and patient, but he feels better, can move more freely, and be warmer

when he and the patient return to a more harmonious 'being-together-cooperatively-in-analysis'.

*The fifth month.*   At the beginning of the fifth month Mary is fairly well over the phase of noncooperation and resistance. She is more relaxed on the couch, not as stiffly wooden as at first, and moves in a natural way. She appreciates that in spite of her negativism and unpleasantness, which she now sees as a reliving of both her own and her mother's complaints against her father, the analyst has continued steadfastly and kindly to help her see herself clearly. Even though she now feels grateful and warmly affirmative toward him, she still feels somehow uneasy about him. It occurs to her that she may have nagged and beat at him verbally to keep him at a distance, in this way repeating her mother's behavior toward her father. Dr. R. is very pleased by this insight, which had not been that clear to him until she had said it. This reopens for Mary the whole question of being afraid of, and yet interested in, moving toward men.

She sees that she has lived through with a series of men the same thing that she lived through with her father and the analyst. First she would build them up as wonderful, stimulating, and great; later she would be disappointed in them and finally quite angry with them. She had experienced this with some teachers, several ministers, and some male friends as well. The one thing to which she cannot yet assent is that she felt the same emotions toward her father. Intellectually she gives assent to this proposition, but whenever she admits it she invariably follows with praise for her father. The analyst notes this and remarks on her reversion to defensive praise, but he does not push it. He understands that by tactfully not pursuing her remaining negative feelings toward her father, he leaves in her a reservoir of negative feelings toward men and toward himself. He clearly foresees the possibility that there will be a resurgence of these strong negative feelings, but he chooses not to pursue them as long as the analytic work is going satisfactorily.

Outside the analysis Mary has been growing more comfortable with men, though she has noted with alarm that men on the street sometimes notice women in a very sexual way. She is beginning to flirt shyly and tentatively with some men in her life. She also changes her hair style and is thinking about developing a more interesting wardrobe. Until just a few years before, her mother had always helped her select clothes, and it was she who had encouraged the relatively colorless, sacklike garments. Thus, Mary takes the first tentative steps toward establishing herself as a woman. She continually seeks her analyst's assurance that what she is doing is to his liking. He preserves the appearance of analytic neutrality but indicates clearly through the modalities of interpretation his preference for colorful feminine clothes. With genuine enjoyment he remarks on her buying a red dress in spite of her inhibitions: "Your mother didn't win out that time, eh?"

Mary is, in fact, feeling so much better at this point that she wonders whether she really needs more analysis. During some interviews she speaks of superficial things, focusing primarily on her social life. The fact that she has always done rather well at everything she has undertaken has caused her to feel basically secure about her abilities. She is grateful to have escaped problems of inferiority and is happy to be sure of her competence. She weaves this theme into a great number of incidents, almost through her whole history, before she begins to doubt its truthfulness.

In response to the analyst's remark, "At least you could always be competent, even against your mother," she feels slightly depressed. She now underscores the limitations of her competence, stressing that it is only in very special situations that she feels competent. It is only when oriented toward work, tasks, or intellectual problem solving that she experiences herself as competent. In ordinary social conversations she falls silent. She remembers that she used to feel superior to such conversations, feeling that "only idiots engage in chitchat." This has been her way of justifying her social incompetence, but now she sees that she really lacks social grace. She does not really know what to do or how to act except within her rather mannish, competent professional or quasi-professional style.

All of this is rather depressing to Mary, and her associations now return to her childhood home life. She thematizes the fact that her parents had no friends or social life. Except for her parents, no one was ever there; she didn't even bring her school chums home. Every time she describes her home life now, she experiences a depressing sense of deprivation. She wishes keenly that she had had brothers and sisters.

It seems that being an only child in such a house has left her feeling empty and unsure, unable to be comfortable with people. She feels at times that she has no body. The analyst remarks, "You must have been so afraid to have a body that you had to do away with it," and, "You must have felt that your mother wanted your body—to do something—to possess you?"

Shortly after this Mary begins to have troubled sleep and to remember for the first time moods and fragments of dreams. All she can recall is a feeling of violence, fear, and frenzied activity and some details of people being cut apart, torn into fragments of flesh. "Your mother's violence?—yours?—your father's?" the analyst asks. Again Mary returns to the theme of her mother's intrusive, possessive, probing taking over. "Where is your father?" is repeated several times.

The theme of abandonment emerges again more sharply, and once again it is first experienced in relation to the analyst, who appears cool, distant, and detached. This time the reaction is not anger but depression, loneliness, and unhappiness. Mary continues now at a slower pace, experiencing that no one cares deeply for her. Dr. R., the person who knows her best, is after all a professional. She has friends, but they count on her, she cannot count on them; she is the one who always saves them from depression and unhappiness. There is no one in the world who is *for* her.

The analyst interprets her experience of abandonment as a reliving of her past experience within her family; specifically, that the feeling of abandonment is in response to her father and is generalized to include all men. She is living out the life of someone for whom there is never anyone who can be counted on. This is the pattern. There was mother, from whom she had to steer clear and keep her distance. There was father, who was not there to help her against her mother. You can count on no one in the world except yourself—Mary's basic motto since she was five years old.

Hence, she really feels depression and deprivation. The analyst is experienced again as distant and uncanny. She is told, and tells herself, that much of her being strong and competent was a defense against just this sharp sense of abandonment that she now is experiencing. To avoid the despair of loneliness, she had made herself strong, competent, somewhat masculine, logical, and intellectual. First she could not afford to be needy with her mother because she experienced her mother as devouring. Then she had to hold the great reservoir of need at bay in her adult life because it would come out (as it had in her mother) in an infantile, nagging, petulant, demanding way. That kind of hungering subservience was disgusting to her and would surely elicit absolute rejection from any decent person.

*The sixth month.*   Mary has now had about 110 sessions in analysis and is remembering her dreams fairly well. She begins the month with an uncanny dream about being in a complex prison structure, deep down in some dungeons, in a cell with another woman inmate who is lying naked on a cot. The other inmate has a sickeningly sweet look on her face. Mary picks up the woman, places her hand on the genital area, and asks, "There, is that what you want?" Mary's associations to this dream are a flood of memories of her mother, who used to have just that kind of smile on her face when they went to bed together. She can remember the filmy pink nightclothes her mother wore and the visible sagging breasts. "I used to lie in bed there, waiting for her to come to bed, feeling like I wished I could make myself into a block of wood." The analyst remarks, "You nearly succeeded."

   Little interpretation by the analyst is needed here because Mary can see clearly how she had defended herself against her mother's sweet, maternal, homosexual seductiveness. The patient is several times on the verge of asking the analyst whether she is really homosexual and whether she can ever hope to escape that. Almost by accident, in speaking to her of the defense against homosexuality, he says, "Once you can see and feel clearly that it was against homosexuality that the original defense was designed, then you can drop it." Without deliberate intention, he communicates to her that she can be a normal woman.

   Such *communication by implication* is a central part of the structure of psychoanalysis, as it is of every human relationship. The analyst and patient come to see that Mary's mother was unquestionably in a prepsychotic borderline state. The arrangement of the home, the estrangement between husband and wife, the increasingly bizarre behavior of the mother—all point to the severity of the mother's disturbance. In developing her defense of competent stiffness, Mary had been defending herself against a hurtful and destructive influence. Mary begins to feel somewhat better about herself as these revelations emerge. Her behavior and reactions were normal and understandable considering the stress she had been under, and this is a real relief to her.

At the end of the sixth month the patient has succeeded in losing about thirty-five pounds. She has completely restyled her hair, has bought an attractive new wardrobe, has gone on some dates, and is growing seriously interested in a man who works in the same hospital as she does.

## CONSTITUTING A NEW WORLD FOR LIVING

It is clear that new worlds of reaction, response, and feeling have already been opened for Mary. Through his approving, careful, patient encouragement, the analyst has opened up for her a variety of new experiences that have an *affirmable* sense. She has come sharply to experience the structure of her life as a normal, sensible response to difficulties. She has been allowed, even encouraged, to experience a whole range of culturally forbidden and individually shameful negative experiences within a context of basic acceptance.

The context of acceptance and expectation normalizes and makes interpretable horizons of experiences which had previously been excluded from Mary's life. Hatred, lust, homosexual yearnings, clinging dependency are all experienced in a context which allows them to be, actualized verbally. To express these underlying feelings is seen as admirable and brave, as deepening one's honesty, overcoming taboos, and heroically facing the dragons of the netherworld. Thus, the doubled consciousness of psychoanalysis is seen to rest on a vision of the analytic consciousness as heroically defending the real underlying truth rather than the everyday truth of the cultural and familial world that has constructed these taboos and thereby caused the neuroses.

With the analyst's encouragement, Mary experiences how much she was tempted to succumb to her mother's soft seductiveness. Fleetingly, because quickly brushed aside, she has often been tempted to succumb in adult life to a loving sexual intimacy with her women friends. That she admits this within analysis both she and her analyst regard as a proof of her fidelity to the analytic venture. To face the shameful truth—shameful to an everyday consciousness conditioned by bourgeois culture—that she has homosexual inclinations is surely an achievement.

But she must see that facing it in order to live it, as many practicing homosexuals do, is not the achievement implied here. The achievement is to face it verbally in analysis, to expose it to the analyst and to oneself. By examining it within the framework of analytic truth, it becomes an honest self-revelation which sacrifices comfort or facade for heroic self-evaluation. If, instead of facing it, a patient should simply succumb to homosexual practices, the analyst would speak of a weak ego or of poor analytic techniques. In some such way he would indicate that giving in to impulses simply because they exist is not the appropriate practice of analytic virtue.

A world of human virtue is thus constituted in analysis and a world of vice as well. Virtue includes all those things that foster analytic honesty about motivations ordinarily not held in esteem. Vice includes the things that hinder analytic openness. The analyst reproaches the patient for resistance, and the patient's appropriate virtuous response is eventually to admit the resistance and give an account of it as based on defensive motivations. To speak truthfully becomes identical with speaking about culturally nonesteemed motivations which reside in the infantile unconscious and belong to one's self. Strength becomes the capacity to face these motivations without panic, excess shame, or guilt.

Thus, in the first several months of analysis Mary might refer indirectly, unclearly, in a veiled manner to the possibility of something not altogether fully adult about her sexual feelings. Later she speaks of her homosexual impulses directly, as making sense in the light of her mother's sweet eroticism, as having been indirectly expressed in her relationships with women friends. It is notable that those homosexual impulses and/or the admission of them would be grounds in the everyday social world for loss of esteem.

In analysis, however, their admission and the concrete exploration in fantasy, thought, and image are schematized as forays into the darkness, or explorations of underlying unconscious motivations. As such, they become a part of progressive self-enlightenment and are therefore transformed into experiences which even make one more acceptable than before. For now the depths, the mysteries, the shameful truths have been courageously faced; the anxiety of exposure has been overcome, and the real underlying realities have been touched and known.

One then moves into that world of meaning which belongs only to those who have paid the price of exposure, suffering, fear, and anxiety and who have dared to see what is really there in the unconscious. Thus, what would, on the face of it, seem to lead to a loss of self-esteem and a denigration of self becomes in the constituted world of analysis a ground for self-enhancement. Analysis and its constituted world then become a possible new world for living. If the patient's degree of involvement in the process of analysis is understood, this new world of affirmable life can be seen as becoming the fundamental reality for the patient, as becoming therefore *the* world in which the patient lives.

*The seventh month.* As Mary goes into the seventh month of analysis she has had 126 interviews. She is feeling livelier and happier and she looks better, not only because her weight is considerably down and she is dressing more attractively but also because her eyes are lively, she smiles more readily, even her skin looks more alive. She has also lost to a great degree that overserious, somewhat ponderous emphasis on being and appearing competent and independent.

She meets a man, they begin to date and become fairly involved in rapid order, spending time together every evening, playing tennis or picnicking on the weekends. The patient speaks of nothing else. Although everything is going well between them, she becomes very concerned about how to behave, how to be with him, whether he will continue to like her, and so on. The analyst interprets this concern both as fear of entering womanhood—a repetition of the expectation of rejection by the father—and a reliving of the mother's constant reminders that she was unable to be or do anything. "You expect that this man will desert you as your father did and leave you in your loneliness and isolation."

Throughout this period she is feeling very buoyant, delighted by her new discovery of herself as a woman. Her free associations become more happily slapdash, and she is more often humorous in her sessions. For the first time she becomes rather freewheeling in a pleasantly crazy way. The analyst tactfully does not interpret this newfound freedom as resistance, though he notes aloud that on several occasions she uses it to steer away from discussing conflict areas involving her boyfriend. But she begins to feel somewhat more anxious as her relationship with Bill grows more involved and notes herself that she is "doing something funny with him."

*The eighth month.* Bill stops seeing her at the beginning of the eighth month. Previous to the break, Mary had been excessively demanding, nagging him when he was late, fussing when he did not call. Immediately she goes into depression and relives her abandonment experience. "Just as I expected, it didn't work out. It never will work out," she says over and over in a depressive monotone. In response to this mood and mode, the analyst becomes more frequently and more strongly interpretive. His basic line of interpretation is, "You made it happen. You drove him away by nagging and pushing at him." At the everyday level he wants her to understand that she is not doomed to rejection by every man. He wants to encourage and reassure her that she can have a good relationship with a man. But Mary seems to reject all this. She says again that it will never work out, and she also becomes annoyed with the analyst. "You always say that it's my fault; you always blame me. But even if I didn't do all that nagging and whining, no man would really want me."

The analyst interprets her giving up, even her depression, as a protection against getting too involved with men. In this way she keeps her independence; she keeps her penis, her masculinity, and does not have to share or give herself to a man; in this way she never quite faces her fear of men. She avoids finally even the feared rejection by causing it to happen before she is too involved and too vulnerable.

The analyst plays this polyphonic harmony of interpretation in response to the patient's statements, consistently making a connected and logical story of her relationship with Bill in particular and with men generally. In response to this, the patient dreams a vague dream that she can hardly remember. "Somehow it seemed like we were together in this room—maybe I was sitting up or—I don't know—it's all very vague and fuzzy—but you weren't in your usual place. There was something like a penis attached to you, but the way the thing was acting —it was funny how it just kept flipping up and down like it must have been on a hinge. It just kept flipping up and down very fast."

The dream is interpreted as a confirmation of her basic ambivalence toward having a man be a man. The back and forth ambivalence is expressed in the up and down of the "something like a penis." Mary experiences the analyst's penetrating understanding of her as a kind of sexual assault, especially as he has spoken assertively to her rather recently. She wants him to be powerfully masculine and for her to be receptive, just as she wanted the relationship with Bill to continue and get better. At the same time she is terribly afraid of "being a woman," of allowing the man to be assertive, intrusive, and penetrating. Her style of life, until it began to be influenced by the analysis, is understandable as a way of fending off the possibility of closeness with men. This fundamental fear-desire, the wanting and fearing of men, was expressed in her relationship with her father, with a series of teachers, with Bill, and now with her analyst. The analyst insists on this fundamental ambivalence in the subtle, quiet way that is characteristic of him personally.

He takes for granted in an everyday sense that he and Mary get along well, that he has already been helpful, that in spite of all her resistance, and fussing, and fuming against what he says she takes it seriously. Because he is basically secure and comfortable with her, he can simply repeat gently whenever it becomes appropriate the fact of her ambivalence as it manifests itself in different ways. Frequently he also points out that she resists this general interpretation more powerfully than she has ever resisted anything and that this means something. In the structure of the analytic situation, as it is individually humanized and lived by Dr. R., who likes her, the quiet voice of reason is taken up by Mary.

She first says, "Well, you are probably right, *but* . . . ," and later, "I can see and feel the ambivalence, *but* . . . ." Finally, she actively explores the roots of the ambivalence in her life, seeing clearly and affirming that she both wants and is afraid, both likes and hates men. She sees this as grounded in her past, expressing both her disappointment with her father and the nagging expectation of disappointment characteristic of her mother. She now concretizes this in detail, showing how she got rid of her boyfriend by acting sick, tired, depressed, unhappy, anxious, and nagging. She shows that these things would tend to occur at moments when she might otherwise be growing more intimate with him. She sees that she lived out with Bill the style of involvement that characterized her mother, first always being too sick, scared, or not in the mood, later accusing and blaming *him* for being cool and distant.

## ANALYSIS BECOMES THE PATIENT'S STORY

Human beings live in time, which means that they project themselves from now into the future and that the *now* is at every moment moving into the past. In many subtle, unreflective ways this living in time is always a story, a history, however diffuse and unclear it may be. For man not only lives but also lives a story, and this story or fundamental theme undergoes a transformation through analysis, when it is successful.

Mary has been living a story whose nature as history has been unfolded in analysis. She had *lived* unreflectively the story of a child besieged by her mother and mostly deserted by a father who liked her as long as she was competent. This competence theme she developed into the story of her life. Becoming reflective about it, however, she had concluded that it was an inadequate way to be living and so had entered analysis to change it.

The analyst has assisted her in the conscious reflective articulation of her story within the analytic perspective of the past reliving itself in her. As indicated, this *articulation*—that is, the analysis itself—has also been a story or history which in a number of ways has repeated the first story but which also has been a specific new history. The history of the analysis has been self-understood as a clarification and undoing of the first blindly lived story of the development of neurosis.

To grasp clearly this new historical development of understanding and living as constitutive of analysis is difficult unless two factors are kept in mind. First, analysis can be understood as a continual search for past history. Second, the process of analysis itself, with its drama of withholding, relevation, resistance, and transference, is itself a specific history, which understands itself as a new history of unblocking, releasing, healing, and widening of consciousness.

Thus, the story developed in successful analysis articulates a fundamental structure of *before* and *after* analysis. The before-analysis part is experienced within a specifically analytic theoretical framework. This part of the story has an inward horizon pointing to further exploration and deepening understanding from the viewpoint of the well-analyzed patient and his analyst. The after-analysis part of the story of the successfully analyzed patient is the carrying out of the analytic liberation into his life. This includes the living in the vision of truth provided by analysis, especially when that truth and that liberation are found again necessary as neurotic symptoms or difficulties recur.

*The ninth month.*   As Mary enters the ninth month of analysis she has had about 170 analytic sessions. She trusts her analyst to the extent that she can tell him when she experiences him negatively. She is very much at ease in the analytic stituation, moving readily on the couch, expressing even her tension, anxiety, anger, or half-baked crazy thoughts with little reserve or hesitation. Indeed, her language is occasionally coarse now, and four-letter words appear in moments of intense expression.

She dreams that she is reaching into her own vagina and pulling out yards and yards of penis. The analyst guesses that she is masturbating now, and she confirms his hunch. The dream interprets itself as a further confirmation of the general tenor of the analyst's interpretation about her wanting to be a man, the idea that she has frequently rejected being a woman and has decided that to have a man she must be a man. Mary realizes for the first time that she was literally a substitute husband for her mother, lying in her mother's bed in the place of the husband-father. Thus, it is not surprising that she learned to be the competent fellow to her peers. But even while these interpretations and understandings are developing for her, she is no longer being treated as very masculine. She now flirts more and is teased a little by men. Men open doors for her and ask her out, some who don't interest her and some who do.

She also dreams about men. "A giant man comes. He bends over me. I'm asleep and he awakens me. Am I naked? Is he? Maybe we're wearing nightclothes—but he takes me by the hand, and I'm very happy to go off with him." Here the analyst sees the awakening of her femininity and the wish for a giant man to come and take her. The giant man is her father, the first giant man in her life, and now she wishes really to be his little girl instead of the hard, competent, mannish woman she has been. The giant man is also the analyst, whom she wishes to take her by the hand and teach her about nakedness and sex. She dreams in series now—first, of having intercourse with her analyst; later, of becoming pregnant; still later, of having a penis; then, of being pregnant. She dreams of hunting for her little child who is lost; then she dreams again of being pregnant.

The analyst interprets this as a gradual moving toward the resolution of her "penis envy." She herself had wanted a penis and now moves toward accepting her feminine power to give birth to a child in place of having a penis. To have babies is becoming for her almost as worthwhile as to become a man. The analytic interpretation returns first to childhood and to her early childhood fantasy that her penis was not missing but rather was inside her. This was originally a compensatory fantasy in the light of her feeling inadequate, small, and helpless.

## THE DREAM LIFE AS DIALOGUE

The patient's dreams are seen to be constantly responsive to the process of analysis, expressing the quality of the relationship as well as whether or not they are sharply attuned to the direction of the cooperative unfolding of the analysis itself. Thus, Mary's early inability to dream was also an inability to participate cooperatively with the analyst in the unfolding of the deepest levels of analytic truth about her. Also, the patient's dreams frequently represent a direct answer, a confirmation or further drawing out of the implications and directions set in motion by the nature of the analytic interpretations. The latter, when effective, are followed by a series of dreams which confirm, comment, and elaborate within the horizon specified by the interpretation and indeed, usually in the language of the interpretation.

In response to the analyst's interpretation, Mary dreams of having a penis. In further response, she dreams of intercourse and then of having babies. The language of Freudian interpretation becomes the language of her dreams, which are then Freudian dreams. The landscapes of the world carved out by the analytic schemata also become the landscapes of her dreams. If an analyst frequently attributes penis envy to his women patients and very frequently the women respond to his care and understanding with a dream of wanting or having a penis, he is a good analyst.

Fostered by the experiential fact that dreams appear as givens in the adult's wide-awake world, the fact that the dreams appear to confirm and elaborate a Freudian vision serves further to amplify and evoke belief and faith in the truth of the analytic interpretations. The dreams, as inner psychic events, evoke concrete images and feelings, especially as relived in the analytic sessions. They help to make real the powerful, concrete, and lively truth of the world as constituted through analysis. The patient dreams and lives out the transformation of experience and provides the proof of the validity and liveliness of the transformation. She then adopts the analytic metaphorical language as the language in which to express the truth about herself. As this metaphorical language does express life, or a vision of life and of life experience, her life is in many ways assimilated to, and transformed by, this truth and this language.

*The tenth month.*   As Mary enters the tenth month, after about 190 sessions in analysis, she begins to date another man. She is less ambivalent and less totally enthralled by Jack than she had been by Bill. Indirectly she asks the analyst's permission to date, and he gives it with an interpretation. They both know prereflectively the pattern of circumlocutions necessary to achieve this communication in spite of analytic conventions. Hence, she mentions that she feels like a little girl asking for his approval, and her analyst smilingly, warmly interprets her as clinging to her father transference. She notes his approval of her dating and is pleased.

She remarks that her boyfriend is a large man whom she jokingly calls her "giant man." Again the return to the protective father is given as the analytic interpretation, and Mary agrees with little concern or anxiety as she is increasingly able to become a bit detached from her needfulness, to see it in analytic perspective. She can see that she may feel real dependency at times, but she is not so horrified by her need-fulness, by wanting comfort from a man, or even by the nagging, whining qualities that she sometimes manifests. Now she merely smiles and says, "There's mother again." Seeing, however, the potential danger of overdependency, she also makes it a point to have some social life outside her relationship with Jack.

*The eleventh month.* At the beginning of the eleventh month Mary has had more than 200 sessions with her analyst. A holiday period is approaching, and although her parents have invited her home for the whole period, she decides to stay only three days. It is one of the most dreadful experiences she has ever had. She experiences herself as "locked in the house" five minutes after she enters; she feels aban-doned and scared, and it is almost as if the rest of the world disappears after she walks into her parents' house. For three days she stays at home in a kind of paralyzed horror, watching her father and mother interact—her mother always slightly bizarre, out of touch, strange, a peculiar glare in her eye; her father helpless, retreating, cold, and dis-tant. No one in the house talks with or contacts anyone else.

Returning to analysis after the visit, she and Dr. R. interpret to-gether how she has relived her childhood, intensified and simplified, in the three-day stay. She had gone home unconsciously hoping against hope that it would be a time to be taken care of, to relax, to be made welcome, to feel at home. Instead, she discovered that there was no one to feed or take care of her, and this time she had experienced the full intensity of her deprivation and depression. "No one feeds you and you are depressed," her analyst says, because this is very like the depression and anger she had experienced when she had felt that Dr. R. was not taking care of her properly and when Bill had stopped see-ing her.

Now she had gone back to the origin of that repeated habit of feeling abandoned, uncared for, and unwanted, except as the bizarre husband-substitute by her mother. Riding a flood of feelings and associations,

Mary begins in a very lively but slightly histrionic way to talk about her mother's seductiveness, reiterating and beating at this again and again. She emphasizes the glare in her mother's eyes, the way she has of dressing with her blouse hanging partially open. The analyst notes only that Mary is overemphasizing all this, and he wonders aloud whether perhaps she is avoiding something. Deeply offended and hurt, Mary feels momentarily abandoned by him; but for the first time she looks clearly at her own father and his incapacity to support her.

The analyst points out that feeling hurt and abandoned in the analysis when he did not support her attack against the mother was a repetition of the experience she had with her father. It was her father who did not defend her, and now she feels undefended and abandoned by the analyst. She sees now for the first time in a *lively*, though somewhat more sober, less agitated way the real disappointment that her father was to her, how disillusioned she was. In a sense, she had no father. She had had a crazy, overintrusive mother and a weak, very occasionally supportive father. Until now she had had to pretend that he was stronger and more supportive than he actually was.

At this point, an opportunity for a very promising residency in Mary's field opens up in another state. With some ambivalence and doubt, Mary raises the possibility of going away, which would involve terminating the analysis perhaps prematurely. If she decides to take the job she will be leaving in a month. Again she is asking for approval from her analyst, but she herself wishes to go because it will advance her career, further her break with the past, and generally give her a fresh start. They agree to her termination at the end of the next month.

## TERMINATION: THE TWELFTH MONTH

The twelfth month is devoted to review, summary, and moving toward separation. Mary sees now to what an extraordinary degree her life had been a response to the hungry, openmouthed dependency that she was left with by her parents. Her life had previously been both in line with this dependency and a strong reaction against it.

Even in the final month of her analysis she overindulges slightly in eating and drinking, noting that she does drink excessively at times.

Now she easily finds a number of everyday ways in which she still tends to live out the ways of dependency, loneliness, abandonment, and shrinking from social contact. It is as if she still at times responds to her mother's injunction to be careful. Even in the kind of men she had found, she understands that she was seeking a mixture of the father she had never had and the father she had actually had. She was apparently seeking strong, vital, dominating men, who after all turned out to be rather malleable, manipulable, and nonassertive in intimate situations. Her father, too, had been competent and strong except within the family and in close relationships.

Mary now looks at the real homosexual trends in her life, which were expressed in the kind of girlfriends she had had. She can see now that she had developed a number of erotically tinged relationships with women, had selected dependent, disturbed women or girls younger than she whom she could support and be helpful to. In this way she had derived a kind of indirect homosexual gratification and had also lived out some closeness with women who were like her mother.

At the conclusion of her analysis, Mary summarizes: "I was kind of an orphan, but no longer. The analyst has been the 'good father.' He has taught me about the world and how to live independently in it. Now I am able to catch my nascent movements toward repetition in the bud, to analyze them." At the same time she has learned much of which she is not clearly conscious. She has learned certain specific modes of speech, tones of voice, characteristic phrases and gestures, a whole way of thinking-feeling which she has adopted from her analyst. She will repeat again but this time will repeat the better adapted things that she has learned from her "father-analyst." Now she can reason, understand, and disinhibit by putting herself again through pieces of analysis more or less independently.

Religion was barely touched upon in analysis, but she notes now that she is not very sure of her own views and suspects that religion had been pretty much a neurotic compensation in the past. She finds now that most of what is really meaningful in her life is that which was given meaning in the analysis and that most of what is not meaningful in her life is that which was in some way ignored, slighted, overlooked, or indirectly denigrated through the process of analysis.

BIBLIOGRAPHY

Boss, Medard. *Psychoanalysis and Dasein Analysis*. New York: Basic Books, 1963.

The opening of new worlds of affirmable life through the Dasein-analytic "why not?" as distinct from the analytic "why?" is part of the background for this chapter.

Ehrenwald, Jan. *Psychotherapy: Myth and Method*. New York: Grune & Stratton, 1966.

Ehrenwald's acute appreciation of the symbolic and transformative powers of new ways of understanding and speaking contribute to the background of this chapter's understanding of the power of interpretation.

Freud, Sigmund. *Three Case Histories*. New York: Collier Books, 1963.

These case histories, together with Freud's other cases and writings on therapy, serve as the basic ground of the present construction of Mary's case.

Heidegger, Martin. *Poetry, Language, and Thought*. New York: Harper & Row, 1971.

Heidegger's view of language as the "house of being," the "clearing within which man lives," and the space within which "history comes to pass" is reflected throughout this chapter especially.

# 5

# Jung's view
# of the patient

○─────────────────────────○─────────────────────────○

## JUNG'S COMPREHENSIVE INDIVIDUALIZING

Jung's theory strives to be both comprehensive and individualized, and the individualizing aspects of his thought make it difficult to give as schematically clear a description of his patient as of Freud's. For Freud, the patient's trouble is that he has too much repressed impulses having fundamentally to do with sexuality or aggressiveness. What needs to be done is to bring these particular contents into consciousness in a living and insightful way. Jung, however, does not believe that his patients are this much alike. To be faithful to his vision of patients as individuals means to ask, Which patient?

Jung agrees with Freud that the patient is divided into warring camps and is usually neurotic, which means that there exist in him two different areas of self-being. On one level of personality he has attempted an adaptation to the world. This conscious, adaptive, socially-oriented self—or, in Jung's term, this *persona*—is at the fore in his relations with the world. On the other side are the darker, unconscious aspects of his personality. Freud views the conflict as between certain

91

primitive impulses and a pseudomoral self, but the patient who enters into psychotherapy with Jung is seen as more radically split than this.

At its heart, the neurosis is understood by Jung as part of the individual's struggle to reconcile the apparently contradictory, opposing aspects of himself. Insofar as he is neurotic, he is not succeeding too well. The neurotic person has so excessively overemphasized some subaspect or subproject of his life that he has ignored other, equally important sides of himself. As a professor, for example, he may have so overdeveloped his intellectual and cognitive powers that the feeling, intuitive aspects of his existence are submerged, announcing themselves only in symptoms, strange moods, or in distortions of how he sees other people. These underdeveloped, as yet undifferentiated sides of his life, haunt his dreams and nightmares and appear in symptoms, dissatisfaction, unhappiness, tension, anxiety, obsessions, and so on. He has allowed important functions and contents of his personal life to lapse into unconsciousness and in so doing has left them in a primitive, inferior, and undeveloped state.

In Jung's view, however, what is to be found on the two or more sides of the divided personality varies from person to person. Jung agrees that sexuality-aggression and its repressions may constitute for particular persons—indeed, for very many people—a fundamental schism in the personality. Man can split sexuality and aggression off from the rest of his functioning, thereby create a sexualized unconscious, and thus develop characteristically Freudian problems for which he needs a Freudian interpretation. But Jung insists that this way of understanding is only appropriate to certain specific neurotic personalities at certain specific stages of their development, which radically relativizes the Freudian comprehension of the neurotic. Jung also agrees with Adler that the power drive and the striving for superiority may constitute a fundamental neurotic split for many persons. For such persons he recommends an Adlerian reduction and interpretation as a necessary way of understanding. Again, however, this understanding is seen as appropriate only at certain stages of their development.

At their core, the Freudian and Adlerian understandings of the neurotic personality are insufficiently comprehensive, according to Jung. They fail to include the variety of personality types, nor do they adequately encompass the variety of levels of personality development.

Personality, according to Jung, is shaped at its deepest ground by the fundamental attitudes which a person *is* in his relationships with reality, and these fundamental attitudes differ from person to person, race to race, culture to culture, from one time to another within the same culture, and even at the different stages of an individual's development. Each fundamental attitude requires a unique psychology developed in the light of that attitude.

Jung stresses that if you teach the wrong thing to the wrong person, he may march off a cliff, psychologically speaking; that one man's truth is another man's falsehood, at least in the realm of psychology. To suggest to an extroverted modern American salesman, for example, that he should participate more in the social world, shape himself more according to the social realities of his everyday life, is to suggest that he commit psychological suicide. It would be equally wrong to tell a hermit-monk to turn to his inner life for further fructifying insight and spiritual development. If this is true, it means that to adopt in relationship with patients any particular technical approach will kill a number of people psychologically; that which nourishes some will cause others to choke and die.

To approach a person who views and lives the world as a place within which to obtain satisfaction through the exercise of power (Adler's view) as if he were trying to obtain sensual gratification from the objects of the world (Freud's view) is to do him a severe and damaging injustice. The patient who seeks pleasure from such objects must be understood in those terms if he is to be reached and helped. To fail to understand his fundamental attitude, to distort it and imagine that it is another attitude, or to bias one's understanding in order to act as if it were the same attitude as that of the theorist-therapist is to falsify the reality of the patient, to injure him, and to alienate him from his own spontaneous life-modes.

The problem of correctly drawing out the person's fundamental attitudes is not the task of psychotherapy alone but is the fundamental task of any real education. Any given culture will be inimical to certain persons because each culture insists that man is a certain way or holds a certain fundamental attitude. The naturally contemplative introvert has a very difficult time in the United States and will probably, therefore, become a disturbed patient. Because he is strongly discouraged from developing his fundamental attitude, he is likely to be forced to develop a less natural attitude for himself.

## THE PATIENT'S CONDITION

All of this introduces a unique difficulty in answering the question, What is the matter with the patient according to Jung? Unlike most other personality theorists, Jung gives us back the question by asking, "Which patient, with what attitude or attitudes, at what stage of his development?" He allows further that the answer may correspond to Freud's answer, to Adler's or, to a whole horizon of theoretical answers, each of which will hold true for a certain number of patients with certain specific attitudes at certain stages of their development.

Nonetheless, there are some basic postulates to which Jung commits his therapy, among them the view that the patient is one who has overemphasized a certain aspect of his life or person and is bedeviled, as it were, by the underemphasized and underdeveloped sides of his personality. Jung views the patient as not allowing himself to be his *whole self* in all of his aspects and as not fostering his own total development to as great an extent as he should. These unrealized aspects of his personality manifest themselves in the form of symptoms and life difficulties of a peculiarly subjective, inner-personal, as opposed to situational, kind. Everyone has life difficulties, but these unconscious aspects of the patient's total self which are left unexpressed, unsymbolized, unrealized, and discarnate now take shape, announcing themselves in symptoms of all kinds and in all kinds of specific life-difficulties.

The man who has developed his rationality to a high degree, for instance, finds his feeling-life announcing itself in mysterious, irrational moods. He is suddenly dark and cloudy or angry at trifles. He is expressing himself at the feeling level in a strong, chaotic, undifferentiated fashion. This peculiarly subjective, inner-personal difficulty is not caused by his hysterical wife or his delinquent children (although his moods may cause his wife to be difficult and his children to behave badly). The patient's *fundamental* problem is that he needs to become more his whole self-being and to bring together the contradictory, paradoxical, apparently irreconcilable aspects of his total self.

But even this statement is relativized by Jung, who observes that to set such a task of synthesis, awareness, conscious contact, and self-realization for some patients would literally make them psychotic because they are too weak to stand it. Thus, Jung always adheres to the goal of self-development but within the limits that a particular person is able to realize. He modifies but does not really depart from his goal.

Jung views the patient, then, as one who has betrayed his wholeness in the interests of some subaspect of himself. It is the primitive, undifferentiated incompleteness of the personality that makes neurosis. These aspects announce themselves in particular mood susceptibilities, infantile ways, and other symptoms, and it is a fact that these dark and unrealized aspects *are* childish, neurotic, and blind. They may be thought of as inferior parts of the personality because they are inferior.

The intellectual professor who has developed his powers of analytic thought to a high degree of refinement is rightly seen by his wife as a kind of child, because such powers have little to do with the way he is with his family. At home with a sore throat, the great, wise, mature, balanced professor, who has developed in his life some marvelous concepts of balance and wholeness of personality, may not be so balanced; he may be a crybaby. Jung means that these undeveloped or dark aspects of the personality are literally inferior.

## PROJECTION AND OTHER SYMPTOMS OF NEUROSIS

One of the major tricks of the undeveloped personality is projection, which occurs when I attribute to other persons or objects that which belongs to my own character, impulses, and feelings. According to Jung, the most common projection is the projection of the unconscious and (by his definition) therefore inferior aspects of personality. Thus, projection serves to express the inferior aspects of the personality as well as to defend the person against his undeveloped side.

For instance, a woman who has a poorly developed masculine side, a poorly developed *logos* or thinking side, will frequently accuse men of arbitrariness, egocentricism, excessive sureness, and opinionatedness. She refers in this way to the thinking aspect of her own personality, which is poorly developed. This inferior side possesses her at times, fascinates her consciousness in an irrational opinion. It is she herself who suffers from undeveloped thinking and irrational opinions, and she holds them with fervor and conviction, absolutely sure that she is right. Unaware of this, she finds those whose masculine side is developed as irrational, arbitrary, and opinionated.

In Jung's thinking, the projection of one's undeveloped side onto others represents an attempt of the total personality to move toward wholeness and heal the split. The law of the total personality is to *be itself*. Within the Jungian schema this includes thinking, feeling, intuiting, and bodily sensing as basic functions. By *sensing* is meant direct bodily contact with the world as a form of knowing the world, which, unlike *intuiting*, does not grasp the whole in its knowing. These two reality-contact or knowing functions are balanced in the personality by the evaluative functions of feeling and thinking. *Feeling* involves evaluation of pleasure-unpleasure, liking-disliking; *thinking* involves a looking, comparing, mental seeing, and working over to order and articulate how things are. No matter which of these functions is better developed or more adaptively differentiated, each person *is* all of them. Every person is a feeling being, even if his feeling function is undifferentiated, unreliable, and primitive. Each person is also a thinking, sensing, intuiting being, whether these functions are well developed or not.

The emphasis on the law of adaptation, which is the normal basis for the conscious self, is such that every person is inclined to develop those sides which are already overdeveloped, with the result that the conscious, narrowed-down mentality tries to tell the total self not to be itself. Most persons are therefore split to some degree. Jung's idea is that the conscious *persona*, the adaptive being, insists on not being too inferior if it can help it. This principle immediately stamps the inferior functions as taboo.

The man who has overdeveloped the rational side of his life has a terrible time with his feeling side. He feels stupid, and is stupid, because his feeling side is an inferior function. Then he projects: "My wife is stupid; she has all those crazy feelings." His wife, on her part, may have a finely differentiated feeling sense, but she cannot think. She finds him irrational and opinionated, which he is not. They each

project onto the other the inferior qualities of their own inferior function, and this is the beginning and end of many marriages. In our
culture especially, where men tend to develop the thinking side and
women the feeling side, unfeeling blockheads frequently marry sensitive flowers and have a most difficult time communicating without
distortion.

The smaller self—the ego-self or *persona*—primarily follows the law
of adaptation insofar as it poorly understands it. The narrowed ego-self
has relegated much into unconsciousness but nevertheless does not
succeed in keeping things in control. For Jung, the lack of success is
due to the fact that the larger, mostly unconscious self, the totality of
self, is, like Freud's notion of the unconscious, a continuous active
process which breaks the narrow limits of consciousness and announces
to consciousness its imprisonment. By evoking or expressing itself,
this unconscious is already moving toward healing the split in the
personality.

By announcing to the blockhead of a man his irrational feelings, it
can teach him how important his feelings are to him and why he must
pay attention to them. Perhaps he has said all of his life that it is facts
that count, not feelings. Now his larger life tells him that he is wrong;
feelings do count, and if you ignore them you may literally be crazy.
Already, then, the obedience of the total self to the law that it must be
itself is such that it shatters the complacency of the adaptive consciousness.

The unconscious actualizes itself in the possessed moments when the
person is swept by a mood, an unreasoned emotion, a compulsion, a
tune he cannot get out of his head, a mode of speech he uses habitually
and meaninglessly, and, perhaps most importantly, in dreams. These
expressions of the unconscious are, in Jung's view, a movement toward
making real those aspects of the personality that have been relegated
to the darkness of unconsciousness and unrealization.

The difficulty with bringing back the unconscious side is, first, the
fact of its inferiority. The unconscious is comprised of undeveloped
functions, childishly simple, undifferentiated, unrefined aspects of the
personality that have been left unrefined and simple by being left in
darkness. The highly developed cognitive man, when approaching the
feeling-intuitive sides of life, finds himself subject to curious moods,

strange superstitions, crazy and mistaken hunches about people. In fact, he is seldom right in this area precisely because it is just a hunch. It is not the hunch which perhaps his wife has, for she has developed her intuition and can grasp the totality of another in the way that the other person presents himself.

For the scientifically trained psychologist or psychiatrist, intuition is relatively poorly developed. In their view, then, hunches are unreliable and defective because for *them* they are. The psychologist-thinker who declares the intuitive artist crazy is projecting. The truth is that he, the psychologist, is so weak and undeveloped in his intuitive-aesthetic dimension that *he* is crazy in this dimension and is unable to recognize the superiority of the other person in the dimension in which he himself is weak.

This is a common phenomenon between husband and wife. One of the basic difficulties in many marriages is that the wife is encouraged by the culture to develop her intuitive-feeling side; the man, to develop his intellectual and sensing dimensions. (These are the four functions that Jung talks about.) As a consequence, the battle between them becomes a battle of projections. The man says, "You, with your crazy hunches, feelings, and intuition, are irrational." The woman says, "You, with your crazy sex hunger, opaqueness to feeling, and coldness, are practically inhuman." Each projects onto the other the inferiority of a function that actually belongs in himself.

Freud and Jung both say that projection is from the unconscious, undeveloped side of the personality, so that it is the person's inferior aspects that will be projected. Freud sees primitivity as simply bad, but in Jung it is always seen as newborn and in need of development. To Freud, the onset of a neurosis is the return of the repressed; to Jung, it is the insistence of the undeveloped part of the personality that it be heard and realized.

## THE COLLECTIVE OR UNIVERSAL UNCONSCIOUS

Unlike Freud, Jung believes that the return of the repressed is aimed at the fulfillment of essential universal human potentialities and tendencies. It is not to be understood merely on the basis of the person's accidental, idiosyncratic history but is grounded on the deepest level of the submerged inner life. These deep inner levels have their ultimate reference point in the most fundamental human tendencies and in this sense transcend the particular individual involved.

Just as individual man carries part of the genetics of his race and of mankind in his sperm, so does he also carry within himself fundamental tendencies and psychic dispositions which belong to the human family, to his race, and to his individual family. These basic tendencies can be understood as akin to aptitudes or directional tendencies to engage in certain kinds of imagining ("image-ing"), symbolizing, and inter-personal relationships which are built into the human being on the basis of his being human and having a human body.

For instance, highly specific modes of masculine directedness to reality can be seen beginning in infancy to a greater extent in male than in female babies. This masculine directedness, which can be understood as a certain aptitude for relating to reality in the modes of conquering, or overcoming, reality, psychoanalysts refer to as phallic modes. In Jung's understanding, this masculine directedness to reality carries within it, already given in the body, the mode of femininity. That is, conquering carries within it, or beside it, an understanding of the mode of being conquered, of receptivity, acceptance, and complia-ance. The man's body tends toward the woman's body, just as the eyes call for a visible world and the teeth for chewing. There is already given in maleness a readiness to respond understandingly to femininity.

According to Jung, in the first blush of the infant's masculine di-rectedness a universal tendency is manifested—an archetype, a primor-dial mode or type of human being, which has been sung, spoken, and lived throughout all ages. This masculine tendency has been lived by man in neurosis and psychosis, as well as in heroic acts, in wars, in the building of monuments, towers, and churches, in the litanies to God the Father, creator and maker of the world. Thus we find that a uni-versal trend to move in a certain way, to image in a certain way, to feel the texture and sense of the world in a certain specific style is given in the human body-psyche. When a man deals with his wife, for example, by rebelling indirectly and neurotically against a subtle form of dom-ination, we have already at the deepest level of the man's unconsciousness an evocation of the primordial tendencies of the masculine mood and mode—the fundamental tendencies of the "hero-archetype" who fought through insufferable barriers to victory.

The Freudian would emphasize that such a neurotic man had had a dominating mother whom he now fights against in his wife, repeating in this way the forlorn and unsuccessful rebellion of his childhood. Jung admits that this may be true, and, if so, must be accepted and understood. But there is also a universal factor in such a battle between mother and child that echoes back into the deepest recesses of myth, folklore, and fairy tale—the hero and the dark all-powerful mother who engendered him locked in battle. From within the personality of the most ordinary middle-class patients emerge extraordinary symbols and images of being devoured, of birth and of rebirth, of coming from the mother, of being eaten by her, and of killing the great giant-mother. The symbols, images, dreams, and the husband-wife mother-child conflict have to be understood as expressions of fundamental archetypes.

Archetypes represent a tendency to imagine, symbolize, and move in a certain direction. The image of energy, for instance, is for Jung a very late manifestation of a very ancient archetype (i.e., energy: psychology-libido, physics-power) which is expressed in such sayings as "the earth is charged with the grandeur of God" and "he is a powerful personality." In earlier times it was "she is a witch and you can see her power." In modern times this is expressed in $E = mc^2$, which retranslates, "The world is charged with the grandeur of God." In other cultures, such as the Polynesian, it was expressed in the idea of *mana*, or vital "spiritual power"; in former times, in the notion of animal spirits or animal magnetism. These historical and cross-cultural comparisons lend support to Jung's notion of the archetype of power.

The point that Jung wants us to recognize is that man is a creature who throughout all ages and all times has imaged in this way and acted accordingly and that this is a most important factor in his life. If you try to do away with an archetype—if you say, for instance, that God is dead—the archetype will manifest itself in the most unlikely places because an archetype cannot be killed. God only changes to something else, and it becomes literally true that men can worship at the altar of Baal, or of self, or of psychological insight, or almost anything. Jung's point is that you cannot simply do away with the archetype of the engendering father and mother who are the psychic ground upon which our lives are cast.

## SELF-UNITY AS THE GOAL OF LIFE

Thus far, Jung describes the patient as a person who is fundamentally split into two or more sides which are at war with one another. He does not say specifically that on one side we will find the forces of aggression and sexuality but suggests that on the unconscious side there can be a great variety of psychic dispositions. For Jung, the composition of the unconscious is not as clear or as definite as it is for Freud or Adler. Jung tries to tell us that the patient has in the course of his life exaggerated or overemphasized certain aspects of himself to the exclusion of other important aspects and that these undeveloped aspects, which insist on being heard, now return to haunt him in the form of strange moods, neurotic symptoms, and other manifestations of incompleteness. This insistence on being heard is also an urge to fulfill essentially universal human tendencies, potentialities, psychic dispositions, and directional tendencies built into the human body.

What Jung stresses is that below the surface level of a phenomenon, below the Freudian or Adlerian levels, there still remains an underlying level. It is this level, below the idiosyncratic, accidental individuality of the patient's specific life history, toward which the specifically Jungian interpretation aims. It aims at the realization, symbolization, and understanding of life as universally human and toward the balancing of these fundamental universal trends and tendencies.

Thus, the development of the Self must be understood as the task of the person's total life. Most commonly, the first half of life, the first forty years or so, are dedicated to the development and actualization of the adaptive-self, the ego, in its attunement to reality. This ego, as Freud indicated, operates on the reality principle; that is, it is the person's effective way of handling reality. This is what is ordinarily meant when we use the pronoun I. But this adaptive-ego is not the total personality.

For example, when someone speaks in an organized and yet fairly free way, as in a lecture situation, it is possible to suggest that it is not only I-myself who am lecturing. That is, there is a way in which the lecture makes itself. I do not know what I am going to say next, but I know that I have neither spoken nor written this before. That ego which is oriented toward reality as rational is not exactly in command as "I" lecture or as the lecture is made. What, then, makes the lecture if it is not "I" (in the sense of my adaptive-ego)? It may be that the Self makes the lecture. In our ordinary life the reality principle or the ego "I" imagines itself to be the center, imagines that it wills that which is done. But a careful analysis of that which is done may show it to be repetition compulsion, which means it is not the ego but some aspect of the unconscious which does it.

In a decently organized lecture, a more profound integrated principle operates, so that it is a unity, a balanced centering between consciousness and unconsciousness, which makes the lecture. If, for example, a lecturer speaks in the light of a long historical tradition, he sometimes experiences the feeling that he would like to hear his own lecture because he has not heard it yet, that what he is saying comes from some source he does not exactly know. A kind of synthesis begins to emerge: thoughts get thought, integrations get integrated, syntheses get synthesized, connections are made which have never been made before. This is fairly typical of any extended performance of almost any cultural activity—dancing, speaking, playing, singing, and so on.

Thus, one may become aware that the center of one's personality is not really to be found in the conscious, rationally structuring, biased, excessively categorical ego-consciousness as Freud describes it. Freud says, "Where id was let ego be," and by ego he means rational consciousness in the usual Western sense. Jung shows that the ego is not the center of the personality. Freud had already begun to discover this truth but wanted to rescue man from irrationality and make ego-consciousness central.

Jung's direction was much more in keeping with the ascetic spiritual traditions of East and West. He says that this "I," which announces itself with presumptuous pride as the center of the personality, not only *is* not but *ought* not to be the center of the personality. Rational ego-consciousness is a surface manifestation of a much deeper total personality. It is only in the second half of life, when success in the world is no longer a problem, that it is possible to question the value of success and of adaption to reality and to develop the kind of philosophic, religious inward questioning that makes the Jungian style of interpretation especially relevant.

There are many persons who have never had social success, who have never been able to adapt easily to groups of people or individuals, who have had difficulty developing friendships, who are not popular. For such persons, paradise is a world of social ease. On the other hand, for the man who since childhood has been sociable and well-adapted and whom people liked, social adaptability is scarcely a value, since the fundamental thrust of personality is always oriented to the values of the not yet actualized. Therefore, a fair majority of Jung's patients (at least, in his later life) were successful, well-adapted people over forty years of age. Freud regarded patients over forty as generally poor risks for analytical therapy because they had become rigid and settled and would be very difficult to help by orthodox psychoanalytic therapy. A specifically Jungian mode is not even relevant for most people under forty.

It is interesting to note what these two men value concretely in therapy. Freud wants bright young people who seek to adapt to reality but who have inhibitions or blockages in their adaptation. Jung says that he will help such people to overcome their blockages; but what really interests him is when all of the adaptive blockage is finished and they proceed to the next level of self-development. There is parallelism here also in the levels of interpretation. The Freudian level is more individual, idiosyncratic, and accidental in quality, dependent on the vicissitudes of breast feeding and oral fixation which have to be worked through in psychoanalysis. Jung's interpretation is at a much more universally human level. Indeed, Jung adopts the person at almost precisely the point at which Freud would call him cured.

## JUNG'S THEORY OF COMPLEXES

Jung invented the term "complex" to describe the results of his word-association experiments, in which he discovered that the rapidity of responses to a list of words resulted in specific patterns of association and specific emotional responses, including very rapid responses in some areas of the word list (sex-aggression words, for instance) or inability to associate in other areas (mother-father-child words, for instance). The idea of complex was used to describe the constellating, or gestalting, of psychic contents and structures within the personality around central themes. A complex, then, is a kind of thematic field or thematizing psychic structure.

The most fundamental function of a complex is organizational. A complex is a unifying, simplifying gestalt which brings together an otherwise heterogeneous grouping of psychic events. Complexes are psychic structures which exist relatively independent of one another, may be conscious or unconscious, but are to be understood as semi-autonomous psychic realities—each, so to speak, a small subpersonality with a life of its own.

You may experience a complex in another person when you manipulate him. By doing certain things—pushing a certain button, as it were—you can make him go through a whole complex pattern of behavior. You can detect a complex in yourself when you go through a particular behavior pattern that was not chosen by you. Such behavior may occur even as your ego-personality stands off, observes you, and asks what on earth you are doing. The person who is "beside himself" with anger goes through a complex pattern of retaliatory behavior at the same time that he may have a background awareness of its irrationality. Compulsive talking in a social situation is a common complex for many people. That they try to control it but cannot is a typical manifestation of a complex, in which a certain suborganization of the personality leads a semiautonomous existence without our intervention.

Complexes are not necessarily neurotic or causes of blockage, however; every organization of the personality can be understood as a complex. The lecturer speaking to a group is a certain style of personality which differs from his nonlecturing self. The lecture situation elicits from me a certain constellation of behavior which is partly conscious and partly unconscious but which results in any case in a certain "lecture personality" for me. For example, although I am perfectly willing to be assailed by doubts under other conditions, I will not allow myself to be assailed by doubts when I am lecturing. If I do, I cannot lecture. Thus, my lecture personality is a certain organizational complex which does not admit all psychic phenomena equally. Social roles are therefore the external side of certain complexes. The conditions under which one's language becomes vulgar or refined, for example, depend upon a number of things. In a lecture situation, crude language is used only to make a point having some relation to crude language and taboos; ordinarily one does not use such language in lecturing.

As Freud and Adler indicated, the complex is an organizational structure within the psyche which has roots in the patient's individual life history. It also springs from the depths of the individual's psychic life and from the fundamental attitudinal structures and typical tendencies built into the Bodily Humanity of the patient. For example, the masculine sexual role is for particular individuals a complex which occurs under certain specific conditions. Within this moment or mood there is a certain horizon of activities, of verbal statements, of bodily movements which lead to an expression of maleness. This, then, has its roots (and this is generally true of most complexes) in the particular individual life of the patient. His style of masculinity is also rooted in fundamental attitudinal structures, such as that there is an introverted and an extroverted way of making love. Finally, there are the underlying archetypal structures which are built into the patient's being bodily human.

Some complexes may be easily exhaustible; they may form over a very short period of time around a theme only temporarily significant in a person's life and drop away fairly rapidly. Having seen a movie with a certain musical theme, specific styles of interaction, and a certain mood, a person will develop a small, somewhat conscious complex which may include melody, certain musical instruments, certain kinds of interactions, and a certain mood quality. All of this can be evoked together for several weeks after the movie. But this complex, an organized structure of psychic content that manifests itself in memory, mood, and imagery, will ordinarily be absorbed by more enduring organizational structures and thus will disappear, unless, of course, the movie is to form a significant moment of psychic structuring in the person's life.

## THE EGO-SELF AND THE REAL SELF

A complex of considerable scope and power in Western society is the complex already referred to by the use of the pronoun *I*. Ordinarily, for Western man, this complex—the ego—is mistakenly identified with the total personality and the authentic Self. Such identification is deceptive because the ego-self only deceives itself into imagining that it chooses, wills, feels, and thinks many things that are factually and actually gifts from the larger personality. This self-deceiving "I" usually wills very much in accord with what is done, which is very convenient.

To begin to understand this is to try to change some personal habit. The "I" decides that it is going to change and only then discovers that the true center of the personality is somewhere other than in itself. The timid person who attempts to be bold, the introvert trying to be extrovert, the sexually-driven person trying to be cool, the impotent man trying to sustain erection—all can testify to this truth. Try to will the simplest acts of your daily life and you may discover that the adapted ego-self is not the absolute center of the personality. The rational consciousness is not the most fundamental mover of personality functioning but rather is itself moved and, in moving, follows a deeper and more ancient music than that of rational consciousness.

There is, however, a fundamental archetype that can constitute a fundamental center to the personality—namely, that complex which unites or integrates all of the personality into a unity. This Self is a goal rather than a fact, a movement rather than a state. It is like salvation, which is not attained but always to be attained. This Self does not exist as an abstraction, however. It is experienced as a coherent, fluid, somewhat symbolizable movement toward unification in the personality, as an underlying continuity not only within itself but with mankind and with reality as a whole. This sense of continuity comes about because the emerging complex unifies and makes coherent a variety of complexes within the personality, moving them, as it were, into a single symphonic theme. It provides a sense of continuity with mankind because it includes, most importantly, the healing of the fundamental universal conflicts to which all men are heir and also resolves them in an irrational universal synthesis.

## SUMMARY

The neurotic or unactualized person is seen from the Jungian perspective as one who has relegated important aspects of his life experience to darkness and unrealization. Because he finds aspects of his personality poorly developed, unadaptive, or dangerous to self-acceptance, he suppresses or represses them, with the result that these sides of his life, these abilities, tendencies, or inclinations, remain in a primitive, undeveloped state. That which is neglected or tabooed can be virtually any content, inclination, or tendency; but in every case these suppressions mean also the suppression of relatively universal human tendencies built into the human being. These held-under tendencies have, however, a dynamism of their own. The archetypes do not rest; rather, the total personality obeys the law that it must be itself, and the neglected sides and tendencies emerge in various forms of maladaptive functioning. This emergence in the form of symptoms is a movement toward actualization. The personality naturally moves toward unification and integration through the action of an underlying archetype, which can only act fully when the person allows himself to be fully himself.

The narrowed ego-self will often disapprove of aspects of the total person and, by suppressing those bad, immature, or inferior sides, will also suppress the action of integration and unification that naturally proceeds through the tendencies of the Self. The personality must be freed from the narrow judgments of the ego-self for the development of that balanced integrative centering of the personality. In this way the real Self, or tendency toward wholeness in all men, can be brought to fruition.

## BIBLIOGRAPHY

Fordham, Frieda. *An Introduction to Jung's Psychology*. Baltimore: Penguin Books, 1953.

A condensed, less thoroughly systematic account of Jung's thinking than Jacobi's, though schematically clear enough to help guide a reader through Jung's thought. Chapters 2 and 3 describe psychological types and archetypes.

Jacobi, Jolande. *The Psychology of C. G. Jung*. 6th ed. New Haven: Yale University Press, 1962.

This highly condensed, erudite account of Jung's psychology viewed as a system is more logical, integrated, and systematic in presentation than Jung's own writings and may help the reader who finds himself lost in the Jungian labyrinths. Chapters 1 and 2 offer a general outline of Jungian personality theory.

Jung, C. G. *Modern Man in Search of a Soul.* New York: Harcourt, Brace & World, Harvest Books, 1933.

A clear, popular exposition of Jungian thought. Chapters 4, 5, and 6 offer a brief statement of Jung's theory of attitude types, the stages of life, and his view of Freudian thought. The chapter entitled "Archaic Man" also reveals the characteristic universalizing interpretation of human life.

_____. *Psychological Types, or the Psychology of Individuation.* New York: Pantheon Books, 1923.

An enormously complex, comprehensive historical approach to the subject of psychological types, including the history of thinking about types of persons, theological and philosophical disputes, periods and types of poetry, and the meaning of introverted and extroverted types. Difficult but rewarding reading for those seriously interested in understanding Jungian thought.

_____. *Two Essays on Analytical Psychology.* New York: Pantheon Books, 1953.

A provocative book written with literate simplicity. In the first three chapters of the first essay Jung develops his understanding of Freud and Adler. Chapters 4 and 5 introduce the questions of fundamental attitudes and the collective unconscious so essential to the Jungian interpretation of neurosis.

# The Jungian approach to psychotherapy

○ ———————————————— ○ ———————————————— ○

## TOWARD INTEGRATION

For Jung, every psychotherapy aims directly or indirectly at the development of more comprehensive complexes which will absorb the harmful complexes whose semiautonomous existences make the person prey to irrationality, fear, and anxious blockage of his life goals. The development of these more unifying complexes aim at making it possible for the person's feelings and thoughts to balance each other, so that wildly irrational moods are not met by a rigid, logical, perfection-seeking, machinelike thought process.

In Freud, this unification striving is manifest in the constant attempt to bring unconsciousness into consciousness and thereby to form a sensible whole. A new, differentiated attitude occurs in the dialogue between consciousness and unconsciousness, and the conflicts are resolved. This integrative activity can occur very fruitfully in the act of writing or of painting, when an encapsulated complex may break out and be reintegrated at a higher level. The question of how a psychotherapist can foster this integrative movement is the pathway of Jungian psychotherapy.

It is very difficult, however, to describe Jungian psychotherapy specifically, because Jung has been more discreet than Freud in detailing his psychotherapeutic procedures and methods. Jungian psychotherapy is radically less technical in its orientation and approach than Freudian psychotherapy. In the introduction to his autobiography, Jung says that only internal psychic events have any significance in his life and that external events pale into insignificance by contrast. This was his view of psychotherapy as well. He speaks of the spirit, intentions, goals, and aims of his psychotherapy, but he does not give the equivalent of Freud's technical recommendations.

The purpose of the Jungian analysis is to make conscious that which is unconscious and to bring into the open that which has been shut off. As already indicated, however, Jung insists that there is no one approach that is appropriate for all people. Many simply need sound advice and guidance in respect to a particular life difficulty. These are the people who traditionally went to the wise man, elder, or priest with a difficult moral decision or specific problem for some form of answer or clarification.

Jung also notes the need to engage in confession, usually accompanied by emotional release. People often need to share their dark side with someone, to unburden their souls, and while various religious forms of confession have satisfied this need for some, for others the situation is more complex. Some patients need to unburden their souls in an emotional reliving of experience. Jung's understanding of the therapeutic value of emotional reliving is distinctive in psychotherapy. For Freud, the patient must emotionally relive this release accompanied by conscious intellectual understanding. To him, insight made lively and real is the most fundamentally curative activity of the analysis. In such a view, reliving is a making real in order to kill off with intellectual understanding. Reliving has the additional advantage of providing a direct tension release, a reduction of strangulated affect.

Jung says that such emotional reliving is not therapeutic in itself. If it were, tantrums and other emotional outbursts would be curative; the popular idea that it is healthy to explode or to act out emotions would then be correct. But even a cursory knowledge of human nature indicates that this is not so. The most that can be said of someone who has outbursts is that he has outbursts. Emotional reliving depends for its effectiveness on the strengthening presence of the other, who *supports* the patient morally as well as intellectually. Only with this support is it usually possible for the patient to accept, own, assimilate, and integrate his unconscious sides.

Both Freud and Jung are aware of the need for another person to make emotional reliving curative. In Freud's view, the other person is needed to provoke the emotion through the transference and to lend his intellect to the patient. For Jung, the lending of intellectual strength is not primary in the relationship; it is rather the total personal support —the personal and spiritual presence of the wise guide, the friend, the good man—which makes it curative. The patient has disowned a certain content in his life, and the analyst's task is to lend him his total strength and courage.

The patient thus fortified will have the power to assimilate and integrate this complex into the larger sphere of his total personality and consciousness. Even with intellectual insight, emotionally reliving without this supportive personal presence tends to lead nowhere because the person has to have the strength to accept what he discovers about himself, to take a stand in relation to it, and to make a moral evaluation of his life by which he feels bound. In this way, the felt-insight or understanding is not mere intellectuality or aesthetics but provokes genuine fundamental personal transformation.

## SYMBOLIC SOUL MEETING

It is important to note that a specific therapist, regardless of theory, may provide just that curative support which Jung indicates as crucial. The emphasis on personal presence means that the therapist does not make himself invisible, as in the Freudian method; he faces the patient, because the whole process of psychotherapy involves a soul meeting, as it were. The therapist neither claims nor assumes that he has priority with respect to the interpretation of reality. He explicitly renounces his claim to superior technical knowledge in his relationship with his patient. Phenomenologically, therefore, his being up while the patient is down would not be consistent. He renounces only the claim of his professional and technical self; he does not give up claims that are part of his larger personality.

The therapist does not credit the patient's rational ego either. Understanding ego as the narrowed-down, rational, conscious self, he trusts the rationality of neither his patient nor himself. Patient and therapist sit together, walk and talk together, interpret dreams together, imagine together, and engage in a wide variety of activities in which they ask themselves what is the truth of the patient's life. Thus, the Jungian's therapeutic presence begins with the assumption that the merely rational, professional, well-disciplined self neither knows nor understands the pathway to cure.

The possibility of real help in the therapeutic relationship is seen to rest on the transformative power of symbols and on the radically irrational life of symbols that man is. A symbol is an image, idea, a sense of things, or a psychic organizer that directs, focuses, and gathers energy. It is by its very nature an integrator, bringing together diverse impulses, energies, thoughts, and actions into an underlying thematic unity. For Jung, this can first be seen outside of psychotherapy in the transformations that occur in natural development.

For example, an adolescent boy falls in love. A tremendous amount of energy and activity now organizes itself around his beloved. He is more attentive to his appearance, more serious, and begins to consider school somewhat more seriously so as to be worthy of his beloved. His sexual life, previously unfocused in diffuse fantasies and masturbation, is now centered on a more personally romantic-spiritual love of the girl who is the "special one." Often his masturbation ceases altogether without special effort. He no longer just hangs around; his total life has undergone a specifically meaningful transformation. The beloved light of his life becomes for him an organizer and integrator of himself.

Another common example of the transformation of a total life is the transformation of a girl into a woman or a boy into a man. Everything changes in the person, who now walks differently, talks differently, and approaches the world in a radically different way. The young woman takes up the bodily receptivity, understanding, and maternalism that characterize real womanhood and gives up the giggling girlish life. Real discussions now are possible as she has her own adult stance and no longer experiences herself as merely a child. Such transformations are not, and cannot be, accomplished by mere willpower or rationality.

Further, these transformations always have their roots in the universally human—that is, they are grounded in the archetypes of the collectively human. For thousands of years the transition of boyhood-girlhood to manhood-womanhood has been seen as a symbolic activity for which each society has specific forms. Initiation rites, usually of a relatively formal kind, have almost always served to announce, verify, and help to make the transition possible. "Today I am a man," the boy-man announces and the elders agree, thus shaping the symbolic truth of his manhood together. If he believes the rite and its implications, he will now be a responsible adult. His life will be transformed through the communal power of the 'felt-lived-imagined-symbolized' being a man.

Not all symbolic transformations have positive value, however. A man who has experienced considerable uneasiness, anxiety, and strong feelings of impending doom has a crisis in which it comes to him that he is the "Messiah," the "Chosen of God." This organizes and focuses his life. He now sees that he is being systematically persecuted by the minions of Satan, that this is the time of quiet suffering for him, that later on there will be the time of proclamation and resurrection. His feelings of helplessness are thus reinterpreted as a holding back of his great power. Every detail of his life is transformed; even his movements, his face, his eyes, especially in his way of looking at others, will undergo radical change.

He now becomes what psychiatrists see as a paranoid schizophrenic, which is also a symbolic transformation to be understood as an expression of underlying universal human motifs. None of the powerful symbols that lead (in this case, pathologically) to a transformation are of his invention. They are archetypal symbols which antedate even their historical Christian or Jewish expression. From the dawn of time, men have been chosen and sent by God to announce, profess, or bring his gifts. These heroic figures have typically undergone purifying trials or persecutions; they have typically seemed to succumb, to die, to be overwhelmed; and in the end they have reemerged from the darkness in triumph. Hence, in both normal and pathological development, symbolic transformations are grounded in motifs, dispositions, and tendencies that are universally human.

From the vantage point of therapy and the possibilities for therapeutic change, this understanding of man as organized, integrated, and brought to focus through symbols provides the ground for inducing personal growth and transformation. It is the therapist's task to foster the development of symbols that will transform and integrate the patient's personality in a healthy way. Each man has a story or myth that he lives out as his life. By overemphasizing the "good" or well-adapted side, the story or myth is inadequate to the life. It neglects important spheres of actual life and also does not appreciate its own universal structures. The story is therefore arbitrary, inaccurate, and inadequate to the truth of life. The therapist's task is to help develop a more adequate, comprehensive, and truthful life story.

## RECOGNITION OF THE SHADOW

According to Jung, the neurotic person has so overemphasized, exaggerated, and developed one side of his personality that he has left the other sides in a radical state of undevelopedness, immaturity, and inferiority. At some point the undeveloped side begins to haunt him in symptoms, irrational moods, obsessions, or other interferences. The first task of the therapy is therefore to develop contact with, understanding of, and symbolization of this shadow side of the personality.

Typically the neurotic person has already experienced inklings of this inferior side of himself. He is prey to disabling or very unpleasant symptoms which tell him that something is moving in his life against his clear wishes. Interfering with his desire to get along pleasantly with people is a mysterious moodiness, a whiplash tongue that bursts into sarcasm and alienates friends. "Why do I do such things? I have always stressed in my life goodwill and a pleasant approach to others. Now, even when I bite my tongue and don't say them, the most sarcastic, cynical, destructive thoughts occur to me."

In this case, a clearly pleasant, socially-adaptive self is interfered with by the emergence of a different complex. The dark, brooding, angry, cynical, sarcastic self that emerges in those moments when the patient is possessed by this mood is clearly the opposite of his ideal adaptive-self. The Jungian sees this as the emergence of the shadow, the side of the person that has been submerged in the interests of "getting along." Here, for Jung, perhaps the Freudian interpretation would articulate the shadow side as the way in which even the nice, pleasant self participates in secret aggression and selfish pleasure seeking. This corrosive form of interpretation, in which even the person's best side is reduced to sex and aggression, would be used only to help the person to restore a more mundane level of self-understanding. The ideal, considerate, pleasant, always altruistic self-image could thus give way to a more appropriately balanced view. If the Freudian schema is used, it is only in the interests of giving symbolic expression to a more adequate self-story. The intention to develop an adequate life-myth remains at the heart of the therapist's project.

It is a universal, human, archetypal tendency for man to have a shadow side. Human beings have always had a shadow side that expresses itself in dreams, myths, and fairytales. It is not merely a personal or individual possession but a collective one as well. As the patient begins to recognize and symbolize his own shadow, he realizes that both shadow side and its accompanying light side are universally human. In this way the dread of inferiority which comes with recognition of the shadow is experienced as a universal, belonging to mankind as well as to the individual. This realization reduces anxiety by giving sense and meaning to the conflict of the two sides and making them less personally reprehensible. The shadow is not experienced as unequivocally bad but is understood symbolically as an untapped lode, an area of the personality that has been too much neglected.

The therapist views the shadow as full of value—as a positive source of energy, a potential means to achieve balance in the person, and a rich area within the person which has not yet been allowed to actualize itself. To the degree that the person has neglected, overlooked, suppressed, and repressed his shadow side, he is relatively impoverished. The Jungian therapist therefore does not share in the shame, moral defeat, and unhappiness which the person feels when he finds himself prey to a shadowland of symptoms and life interferences; he rejoices in the person's movement toward wholeness and increased life-amplitude in the expressions of the apparently inferior shadow.

Thus it is precisely that sphere which the patient would prefer to overlook that the therapist views as positively valuable. He wishes to give weight and significance to this dark, undeveloped side of the personality and to bring it into consciousness so that it may coexist with the light side. This coexistence is expected to lead to the birth of a third term between the two which will reunify the personality at a more comprehensive level. If a man has overdeveloped an adaptive-self characterized by a tough, competitive, highly competent, unsentimental exterior, the shadow side will tend to be soft, yielding, and sentimentally awash with feelings.

The therapist, through an attentive, appreciative copresence to both sides of the person, awaits the reunification, not knowing exactly what the resolution will be. In the light of the therapeutic relationship, the patient dreams of women in a variety of ways. First, they are witch-like, spooky, fearful, powerful forms; later, soft, agreeable, still mysteriously powerful, romantic shapes; finally, he meets in one of his dreams the wise, serene, balanced woman who tells him that a man does not always need his armor. Thus gradually, by applying this to his life, he finds it possible to be a more kindly, fatherly man who appreciates the importance of tenderness and careful regard for others. In the image of the kind and just father which he now lives there is a symbolic integration of the heretofore exaggerated tough, unsentimental side and the shadowy feminine-feeling side. Both sides are now realizable in a balanced way.

## THE PRINCIPLE OF COMPENSATION

Within a Jungian understanding, the relationship of shadow to light is fundamental in the working of the psyche. Emphasizing, developing, or focusing one facet of the personality always leads to a compensating movement within the total personality. The exceptionally good or virtuous person is expected to have vicious and perverse dreams; the most stolidly affect-free person is expected to have moods sweep over him; the most totally pragmatic and reasonable person is expected to be assailed by obscure hunches and strange superstitions. The total personality, in following the law that it must be itself, always compensates one-sidedness in one direction with an equal or answering one-sidedness in an opposite direction.

Thus, the fundamental structure of the personality as a whole can be seen as a moving toward balance, wholeness, multifacetedness, and the fullfillment of all its multiple possibilities. In both the total personality and its subaspects, there is an underlying duality, a tension in opposition, a polarizing around an invisible center. Jungian therapy directs itself radically to this center through the progressive affirmation of both sides of the duality. If a bland, permissive kindness is a highly developed virtue, the Jungian pursues the aggressive, judgmental side. If a tender, warm kindness is highly developed, the Jungian emphasizes those areas in which a "don't-give-a-damn-about-anyone" attitude prevails.

By pursuing the opposite, the therapist resembles the Freudian, who also expects the virtuous side to be masking its opposite. Unlike the Freudian, however, the Jungian strives to give full weight to both sides. The kindness is not seen as a coverup of its opposite; rather, both are seen as equally valid yet incomplete expressions of the total personality. If the patient is cynically tempted to reduce his highest aspirations to the mud of Freudian interpretation, the Jungian will warn him against this arbitrary judgmental attitude. "Both the high and the low live themselves in you, both god and devil, kindness and vengeance, virtue and evil."

## AMPLIFICATION

From a Jungian viewpoint, the symbolic integration of masculinity and femininity, of aggression and care, of thought and feeling, of the universal and the individual is not achieved primarily by means of thinking, understanding, or explaining life. Such personal unification occurs spontaneously in the unfolding of the person in his many-sided, apparently contradictory personal expression. The stew of apparently irreconcilable elements is expected to contain its own principle of unification, which, if allowed to emerge, will restore balance and wholeness. The therapist wishes to intensify the stew of conflict as well as the emerging symbols of unification, and his immediate way of doing this together with the patient is through the use of "amplification."

Amplification involves the therapist giving himself, and inviting the patient to give himself, over to the emergence of rich symbolic meanings. The therapist attitudinally treats as "pure gold" something that the patient might shrug off as unimportant. Thus, a patient might speak of himself as tired, worn out, spent.

THERAPIST: Yes, you seem spent, and even now you are conserving yourself, not spending yourself, holding yourself back.

PATIENT: It's just a mood; I'm just kind of tired. It's not important, really.

THERAPIST: Even your not wanting to try to understand this mood is a conserving effort, a saving yourself from spending.

PATIENT: Yes, I can see that. I often do that. It's just like things are too much.

THERAPIST: You feel you have already spent too much and don't want to give. Are you spendthrift in some way?

PATIENT: I guess I do try too hard to be generous. My friends warn me not to be such a sucker sometimes, but I don't like to be tough, hard, or unyielding. There's so much nastiness in the world.

THERAPIST: It would be nasty to say no, but you can be too tired and that's all right?

PATIENT: Yes, damn it! I just get fed up with having to be so generous all the time.

THERAPIST: Is it just like spending and spending without end?

As this interaction develops, the therapist indicates that the compulsion to give, to spend on others, to be always the generous one, gives rise to a countertrend in the personality, a movement toward self-preserving and conserving. "There is a point at which giving, especially compelled giving, becomes giving yourself away, losing yourself. At that point you rebel and restore the balance." The therapist inquires, "Don't you also find yourself positively ungenerous, stingy, holding out sometimes? You would almost have to." In response, the patient elaborates his stingy side, his ungenerous thoughts, his holding out, and secret selfishness.

While he does this unfolding with hesitation, shame, and doubt, the therapist is fascinated by the unfolding complexity. "But you also are just simply generous sometimes, yes?" the therapist asks. The patient elaborates those rare occasions when generosity and pleasure unite, when giving is also receiving. "Curious," the therapist observes, "isn't it, that when you are getting, taking pleasure, and being perfectly selfish, you are happily generous. In those moments you are most saving and most spendthrift all at once."

"But, in those moments I don't have to try. It just happens."

The therapist responds strongly, "You give up your puny rational trying for something far finer, yes?"

Even in this rather commonplace, undramatic example, a considerable life transformation has been effected. By giving intense interest and attention to an apparently insignificant mood, a theme of genuine importance has emerged. Further, the patient has been convincingly taught by the evidence of his own life the principle of irrational unification as the proper mode of living his life. In the process there have been several reversals of valuation: the selfish, stingy side has been seen as preventing a foolish compulsion, as a saving of self, and a preserving of sane balance; the generous, rational side has been seen to be too narrow and puny and as inadequate for life. The fine value of a careful nurturing of the total personality is forcefully affirmed throughout.

By seriously seeking to penetrate the inexhaustible depths of meaning given in a specific motif, that image-thought-symbol assumes intense meaning in the person's life. If the patient believes in the possibility of being helped and really seeks to improve his life, he will begin to dream. The therapist has told him, "We already have some hint of a solution to the dilemma of giving too much and being too stingy, but it is not clear to you or to me as yet. Perhaps you will dream of it. Pay particular attention to your dreams, as they may suggest the right direction for us to follow."

The patient would probably dream something about the problematics of giving and taking. "I am walking up a hill toward a park bench, and there is a beggar there with a tin cup. Just as I am about to drop some money in his cup, pretty much automatically, I notice that there is already an enormous amount of money there." Further dreams around the themes of giving, taking, generosity, and stinginess would naturally evolve out of the interest and attention that both patient and therapist are giving to this theme. Amplified through a number of therapeutic sessions, the myth of giving and taking would take on increasing intensity and meaning. The symbols of beggar and rich man, lord and slave, mighty and small would become for the patient genuine preoccupations. The whole world and his life in it would be filtered through the lens of this unfolding symbolic problematic, until his thinking and feeling begin to participate in the unfolding, mythic, believing consciousness. His manner of tipping in restaurants, his feelings when he pays for things, his *giving* thanks to someone or *paying* attention, his listening to songs about falling in love and *giving* everything—all would participate in intensifying and vivifying for him the central myth he is developing. Noticing these things in his life, he would become selectively attuned to the themes dealing with giving-taking.

The Jungian typically makes great use of dreams. In the course of a single session the therapist may keep circling back on the dream, using its images and language, showing that the dream has already said what is now being resaid. The patient complains about being slighted, and the therapist responds with the dream image of the "poor beggar."

"Well, yes, there is something greedy in me. I do want everyone to appreciate and extol me." "So," the therapist says, "no matter how rich you are, you are always the poor beggar and yet always also the generous giver."

In this way the dream takes on a weight and significance. Both patient and therapist lend themselves to an attitude of expectancy, a hovering attention to the dream as the mysterious "speaker" who will tell them answers needed for life.

### The amplified dream

Dreams are more reliable and truthful than any rational statement; a dream cannot lie. Further, dreams are announcements from the unconscious sphere, which is a larger and more comprehensive basis of the personality than the rational ego. Ordinarily, they are compensatory or complementary to the patient's conscious attitudes and projects, representing, or speaking for, the "other side." If the striving for unification and actualization of all sides of the personality is understood as the fundamental goal of therapy, it is clear that the dream is very much at the heart of psychotherapy and, in a special way, the pathway to cure. Jung says to his patient, in effect: "You and I are two sensible, fairly well-adjusted, well-adapted human beings who have sufficient strength to get along fairly well in the world. Let us give fully our attention, sympathy, and intelligence to a comprehension of the much neglected and yet centrally important statements from the underworld of your total personality. Let us listen to your dream world and concentrate on it."

Jung's attitude toward the dream world differs sharply from Freud's, whose basic method was to ask a person to associate mentally to each element in the dream. The dream was understood to be composed of, or caused by, the areas associated to; by hooking these associated elements together, the dream's meanings emerge. Jung says that associating to a dream or a newspaper story will always have the same result: you will discover the patient's complexes. Following the association method, you will always find the meaning of the dream in its relation to certain pervasive complexes of the person. The dream itself will never be understood in this way, because the *dream means what it says.*

It may be that relating the dream to complexes explains something about the dream, just as relating a lecture given by a person to some of his complexes may explain something about the causes of the lecture. But neither the lecture nor the dream can be properly understood in this way. Both are a speaking and are in a language. The speaking means what it says and is never obscure, although the language may be difficult to understand.

The basic method to use in understanding a dream is to *amplify or expand its meaning.* The first thing that must be done is to make an exact specification of the dream images in order to make the text of the speech clear. The complexes revealed when the patient begins to associate represent part of the patient's current situation, which must be taken into account. First, however, the dream is taken *exactly as it is.* The patient is asked to amplify the meanings of the elements, then to define the images more exactly—their colors, shapes, and positions—and finally to specify his own position and attitude in relation to them

The dream is a small myth or story and must be understood as such. The patient is invited to tell the story repeatedly, to revivify it, to take the dream seriously, to brood over it, reflect on it, reimagine it. Patient and therapist join together to unfold the concrete meaning of each element of the dream and its interconnections. They keep repeating the dream, recasting it in a different language, and seeing it again and again until it yields its clear intention. Both train themselves to read the dream correctly so that its elements are woven into a single text which the dream speaks with limpid clarity.

An ideal reading of a dream makes sense in the same way as a proper understanding of a difficult philosophic text. All the conjectures and previous approximations to the meaning fade away, and the reader stands in the light of a genuinely perceived understanding. The penetration is to what is given in the dream-speech itself and is self-evident, not requiring theoretical explanation or justification.

Thus, a patient dreams of being in a biology laboratory, involved in a regeneration experiment on some large hydra. Her job is to cut the hydra in two. Although she does not know how to do this, she bends over them with a knife and finds that there is actually an appropriate cutting place as if marked on the body of the hydra, so that she is able to do the job. In a properly Jungian interpretation, the dream is carefully amplified to read in part:

"It is very important for me to move toward biology (body understanding) in a lived-sense, as my body is of special significance to me now. This undifferentiated, essentially asexual creature (which I have been) needs to become more differentiated in order for the regeneration (therapeutic transformation) to occur successfully. While I am anxious about my ability to regenerate, the dream suggests that there is already a mark on the body that will make the transformation somewhat easier than I would expect. I can count on my basic femininity, therefore, although there is a specific two-sidedness involved and a work is necessary. The work involves cutting or separating but along a line already present. The fact that it is a hydra—a very low-level, relatively undifferentiated creature—suggests that I have just begun on this task."

The therapist and patient go back and forth reading the dream together, both using their understanding of images, symbols, and of life to elucidate its mythic, symbolic structure. The relation of the dream to the patient's concrete life and everyday situation is clarified; more importantly, its relation to the general direction of the patient's total personality is elaborated. Thus, in the example above, the patient's bodily being is generally affirmed as worthy of attention and work. At the same time, the dream comes to mean, very concretely to the patient, that she should study and learn more about sexuality from books, that she should move toward dating now, and that the regeneration experiment (therapy) is working properly even though she does not know how. This is a concrete relief to her from the anxiety and concern she has felt about her own development.

As she elaborates the meaning of the hydra, she experiences its having two arms as referring to a greedy, hungry, grasping nature. Her fantasy of the hydra is that it constantly reaches out and stuffs things into its mouth and that the operation which she had done had involved the area of the hydra's mouth. On continued reflection, it becomes obvious that the dream operation would temporarily destroy the mouth while leaving the grabbing appendages intact. A certain aggressiveness, not passively pampering her own needs for comfort, seems indicated as the proper path for her self-development. She and her therapist together work out this path, using the dream and its "reading" as a basis.

At a certain point both therapist and patient come to a sense of the fulfillment of the dream work. Later perhaps the dream will be tied into a whole series of dreams, and parts of it that were difficult to understand will become clearer. There is a genuine moral seriousness of purpose involved in the pursuit of the dream; understood, it will serve to guide the life of the person in many concrete ways. It may mean studying a certain area carefully or taking up an artistic interest, but even more radically it means changing attitudes.

In the Jungian context, a dream that suggests a change in attitude also accomplishes some of that change. If the amplification suggests "don't worry; things are going well," the patient actually relaxes and is less inclined to worry. If the dream suggests that sexual problems are being exaggerated and that questions of ability ought more importantly to be considered, the patient moves toward doing the work of amplifying within the areas of competence and ability. In this way the patient's field of attention, understanding, focus of interest and feelings shifts in accordance with the developing stories, or mythic, symbolic structures that are elaborated in the therapy.

## Amplification versus explanation

To regard a dream as expressing a story that needs elaboration and amplification in order to be clearly understood is very different from regarding a dream as expressing underlying causes or hidden impulses. The story, with its implications for life, invites a lively participation between patient and therapist, in which both strive to uncover and expand its meanings. Because both have access to the meaning of the dream, it is relatively easy for them to cooperate in the common task of elucidating the dream or other expression of the personality. The dream is not to be boiled down to its underlying causes or impulses but to be enriched, amplified, and helped to speak to the patient's life. The therapist is therefore not the expert, and the patient is not reduced to data in need of interpretation. Rather, the patient is a rich source of meaning and symbolization in his own right. In principle, every meaning that the patient gives a dream or any other event is a valid meaning, even though it may be momentarily one-sided or inadequate and may need considerable elaboration to express itself fully and be integrated into the personality.

This differs distinctly from the orthodox psychoanalytic emphasis on the invalidity of the patient's meanings and the corresponding elevation of the meanings given within analytic theory. In orthodox Freudian analysis, the patient is data to be understood; meanings which arise from his natural life, from his unrealistic evaluations of himself or his dreams, are seen as *essentially* mistaken. The real meanings correspond to the underlying causes (impulses), which are expressed only in the purity of analytic theory and insight. Truth belongs to the analyst—to the patient, only insofar as he becomes "junior" analyst.

Explanation, a reduction to underlying causes, is experienced by the patient as an "addition to" his life. Alongside his usual thematizing consciousness of himself, he elaborates together with his analyst a schema of interpretation which lives itself out within a critical, evaluative, judging consciousness. Thus, alongside of his "mistaken" understanding of himself as generous, the patient comes to see his underlying domination motives, his aggression, and his reaction-formation against his selfishness. This explanatory consciousness becomes, in the well-analyzed patient, a dominant mode, though he still retains his everyday understandings of himself. Consequently, explanation and reduction to causes exist, alongside and in addition to his everyday understanding, as a kind of commentary on his life. Orthodox analysis thus brings about a duality of consciousness; one side is the 'living-of-the-story-of-my-life'; the other side is a critical, evaluative, explaining reducing-to-causes. The analytic consciousness is always undoing the validity and value of the everyday-life consciousness.

Jungian amplification, elaboration, and intensification of meanings are experienced quite differently. The meanings that arise are taken from the already speaking, sense-making, symbolizing activity of the patient. In fact, the patient is helped to see that his making sense, his symbolic self-expression, is deeper than he had realized. Every symbolic expression of the patient is, in principle, to be treated as a valuable text; thus, the patient, especially in his dreams, fantasies, images, and myth-telling modes, is taken with the utmost seriousness as being a valued speaker of life-truth. Instead of denigrating his unconscious and its symbolic products through reduction-through-explanation, the myth-telling unconsciousness is treated as a fundamentally wise, ennobling, balancing spirit for good in the person. Thus, the fundamental fear of being stripped, made naked, ashamed, and unworthy, is radically transformed by appreciating the value and truth of the patient as mythmaker.

*The dream of a soiled coat.* The difference between amplification and explanation can perhaps be expressed by an example in which a young woman reports to her Jungian therapist, "I have hardly any dreams today, just a snatch of one that didn't seem important."

The therapist replies: "Maybe so, but let's see. You have been telling me a great deal recently about your relation with your father and with your new boyfriend. That you are frightened of them in some way is clear. Last time I suggested that you dream on it. Perhaps you have."

The patient describes a short dream in which she had difficulty putting on a coat that she liked. Finally she had struggled into it and then discovered that it was soiled along the bottom. Being new in Jungian therapy, she still expects the therapist to be a reader of secrets to which she has no access. As the whole area of her relationship to her father and new boyfriend is emotionally charged for her, she is afraid of what the therapist will find out. She hesitates to tell her dream, afraid to be found out or revealed without her own knowledge and consent.

If the therapist moves toward the arcana of Freudian symbolic understanding, in which the pleats at the bottom of the coat represent the vagina and the fear of becoming a dirty woman holds her back from growing up and accepting her bottom, this would fulfill her fear precisely. It would show her the expertise of the therapist and her own ignorance. In some way she would recognize the truth of the therapist's interpretation, but it would be a truth alongside her everyday understanding of herself. If the therapist invited her, in Freudian fashion to associate to all the elements of the dream and then constructed an interpretation from the blockages as well as the associations, this could still be a truth alongside her life.

The Jungian wants to say, in effect: "Let's explore, elaborate, and amplify the meanings together. The meaning is not hidden or obscure; we simply have to work to read it in the dream itself." He might then say to the patient: "Well, a coat is something you wear, a way of showing yourself to others, a way of expressing yourself as a woman. It may also be a shelter from the rough elements, but I do not yet know what it is for you in your dream. Tell me the meaning of the coat to you."

The patient explains that the coat is one she has recently bought, although her parents had objected to it as too expensive and fancy. In the light of his recent understanding of her as involved with men, the therapist asks, "Both your parents?"

"No, no really, just my father," the girl responds. "He always objects when I buy something, even though it's with money I earn."

She says further that she had especially liked the coat because it broadened at the bottom and was pleated. It leaves her body free to walk or run without hindrance. When she whirls round, it flares like a full skirt. As she describes it further she has a developing sense of her own involvement with the coat and its meanings—not a developing sense of a critical, careful, explaining consciousness but rather a developing enrichment of her everyday life in its fullness of meanings.

The coat takes on an amplitude of meanings: as decorative, feminine self-expression; as herself as distinct from her father; as a growing sense of freedom and happiness about her body and its self-expression; as something she is just struggling to develop and grow accustomed to. All these meanings grow simply and spontaneously out of her own life-understanding of herself as growing, maturing, and developing. The patient becomes increasingly involved in the unfolding of the dream meanings, all of which are taken as valid amplifications of the actual meanings of the dream's story. The dream matters because it is rooted to life through lived symbolic meaning and is itself myth and symbol maker.

Freud's idea of "hovering, unbiased attention" cannot be unbiased, because the categories of the Freudian unconscious are pregiven and preknown by the therapist. The Jungian and his patient, in contrast, both assume an attitude of expectancy in relation to the inner depths. Neither possesses the truth, but both wait to come into possession of it through the oracle of the dream, the fantasy, the hunch, the intuition, the image, or the change in feeling tone. The patient learns this trustful waiting from his therapist, responding to a series of typical injunctions, such as: "Dream on it," "wait and see where that goes," "make it more full," "amplify that more for us." Both therapist and patient exercise a hovering attention in which they expect something to emerge other than what they already know.

## THE GENERAL ACTIVITIES OF THE THERAPIST

While the Jungian therapist expects something as yet unknown to emerge from the patient's inner world, he also has a theory and guidelines which help him to know what is likely to unfold. The Jungian awaits the emergence of a symbol of unification. Each time the patient stresses one side of his life, the Jungian knows that there is a compensatory side and that the two come to some sort of potential unification in a third term, a symbol. The symbol is an act, a fantasy, an image or an idea which brings together divergent elements, and unifies and transforms them. These symbols cannot be arbitrary, or they provoke a new schism in the personality. Thus, Jungians object to routine, nonindividuated Freudian, Adlerian or other theory-laden styles of interpretation on the grounds that they are arbitrary, theoretically constructed symbols which are not carefully tailored to the specific patient and his specific unfolding life. As the symbols are expected to emerge from the inner depths of the patient's personality, dreams and their interpretation are uniquely suited to this project.

Jung does not limit himself to any one method of approach, however. Good sound advice which helps maintain a healthy adaptation to reality is sometimes seen as appropriate; confession and catharsis are needed at other times; corrosive reduction and interpretation on the Freudian or Adlerian models are also useful at times to prevent excess self-inflation or self-idealization. All of the therapist's wits and understandings of reality are necessary to help him guide the developing personality of his patients wisely. It is his wisdom in respect to symbols, myths, and the stories of mankind, however, and his assistance in their concrete transformative unfolding in his patient that are the specifically Jungian aspect of his intervention and help.

The Jungian is a specialist in symbols of transformation as universally lived in mankind but more particularly as applied and developed within the life of specific individuals. The amplification-intensification of meanings and symbols has been seen to be the fundamental activity of the Jungian with his patient, the primary assistance he provides in the unfolding of the personality, together with the assurances that come from having a wise and knowledgeable guide to spot pitfalls and point to the surest route.

## The method of active imagination
Jung employed the method of active imagination for the amplification of meanings and encouragement of symbolic unifications. In this

method the patient is invited to engage in fantasy in the therapy situation, to complete a dream, or perhaps to tackle a feared situation. Ordinarily the patient will close his eyes, as this helps the imagination to flower. An intense involvement in the fantasy is strongly encouraged, and the usually facile slipperiness of fantasies is discouraged. In ordinary fantasy the patient is not helped to deal with difficulties or problematics. As soon as an image becomes difficult or produces anxiety, it is laid aside, however important it may be.

In the method of active imagination everything is done to encourage the development of a "life-death" interest in the unfolding fantasy. First, the therapist selects for the fantasy a dream or image which has already been seen to be of crucial significance to the patient. Perhaps it is chosen from a frightening dream or from a dream that felt important, perhaps from a repetitive fantasy that the patient has had throughout his life, or perhaps from a recent thinking which involves themes already seen as critically important to the patient. In his own belief that the symbolic unfolding of life is of central importance, the therapist treats the movement toward fantasy as very serious. "Perhaps we can really move toward resolving this fear you have or come to a really new understanding. It may be difficult for you to persevere, but I will be here to help you." Thus, the patient is told that the imagining is important, has serious possibilities for benefit, and may be frightening or difficult. In all of these ways he is encouraged to enter the fantasy with a genuine responsibility and moral seriousness of purpose that departs strikingly from mere intellectuality or aesthetic imagining.

The implication of this is that slaying a dragon in the imagination is, when done seriously, fundamentally equivalent to slaying it in life. The power of the symbolic as real, significant, crucial, and transformative is thereby affirmed throughout the method of active imagination. In Jungian therapy, the dream, when treated as oracle and speaker of significant truth, is believed to effect life transformations in behavior, attitudes, and focus of attention. The development of "waking dreams" through the use of the active imagination is transformative in the same way.

A patient, for example, has a horror of bodily life learned in his early childhood. He dreams of approaching a young woman whom he likes, and just as he is about to embrace her she turns into a dragon, at which point he awakens. In the method of active imagination, the patient will be encouraged to close his eyes and complete the dream. Under the pressure of anxiety, he may want to go through it rapidly, but the therapist slows down the action. Each moment of the dream, each image, feeling, and thought as it leads to the embrace, is focused and developed. The patient relives the new waking dreaming even more intensely than he did the night dreaming. Further, as he enters the virtual trance of active imagination under the therapist's guidance, the question of what will happen, how he will deal with the fearsome dragon side of woman, becomes critical to him. He is actually frightened now as in his mind he approaches the attractive young woman to embrace her.

The therapist encourages him: "Go ahead, we will find a way. In your life so far you have always stopped here. Now you are ready for something different." The patient hesitates, screws up his courage, and reaches in fantasy for the lady-dragon. The dragon opens its mouth to bite him, and this time, instead of running away, he commands it to close its mouth, indicating a willingness to force the closing if necessary. The dragon changes into a nagging, critical old hag. Momentarily the patient is engulfed by a movement toward apology and withdrawal, but now, in the therapist's presence, he feels a surge of ability and power. The dragon-hag then turns again into the young lady, whom he hugs and walks off with hand in hand.

After coming out of the waking dream, he and the therapist discuss it and recognize that a change is in process. The fear he has felt toward women, toward sex, and toward criticism by others are all seen to be partially resolved. Both he and the therapist look optimistically to further developments and deepenings of this good beginning. The therapist may remark that this beginning is too easy and suggest that much more work needs to be done. Nonetheless, it is through such symbolic fantasying, imagining, and symbolic transformation that the patient's eventual freedom will be attained.

### The use of creative activities
In accord with his general distrust of the merely rational and his appreciation of the richly symbolic irrational principles of unification, the

Jungian therapist characteristically encourages creative endeavors on the part of his patients. Mere talk, fantasy, dreaming, association, understanding, and insight are insufficient for life transformation. The natural ambience of symbolic transformation is the creative imagination, which is linked to actual life through creative, concrete symbolic expression. In this way, also, imagination is taken with total seriousness and held before the mind's eye steadily and forcefully so as to provoke and reemphasize the symbols of unification in the patient's life.

To the degree that the Jungian therapy is transforming the patient's life, his dreams, fantasies, and imaginings are all moving toward a mythic universal format under the steady encouragement of the lively therapeutic view. The patient makes this all his own by concrete application to some form of art. By brooding over a painting, painting a dream image, writing a story from a dream image, or composing music, the patient expresses radically, and lives out his growing faith in, the fundamental significance of the irrational-unification principle. He expects his painting to produce unification and it does, as he takes it with great moral earnestness as contributing to his enrichment and transformation.

In the Freudian resolution of neurosis, the rational side of personality becomes the mediator between the different interests of the total personality. Sensual, intellectual, social, and work interests are all balanced by the ego in the interests of a reasonable adaptation to life. Thus, the person does not suppress his aggression and sexuality to such an extent that he has an outbreak of neurotic symptoms, nor does he live them out to such a degree that he suffers too much guilt or social shame. Through rationality, he moderates the claims of his conscience, his body, and his society.

Jung's idea of synthesis and unification resembles the unification of a work of art, because the making of art requires that a great variety of forces, complexes, and subaspects of the personality come into unified harmonic interplay. Typically, an art work has form, feeling, and a certain concrete sensual element; it carries out an intuition, requires the development of concrete skills and their reasonable use to express or make effective the intuition. All of these aspects come together not according to rational principles but according to some expressive unity.

Thus, artistic production, active imagination, and dreaming are all forms by which the irrational principles of unification are lived out by the person and become central foci for the workings of Jungian therapy.

## THE DEVELOPMENT OF THE ARCHETYPAL SELF

The spontaneous unfolding and unification of the person's life through symbols is seen in Jungian therapy as both individual and universal. At every step of the way, implicitly and explicitly, the therapist points to the collective universal trends in the person's life. His individual conflicts are seen as representative human conflicts, and their resolutions are seen as both belonging to him and yet superior to him. The union of opposites through the emergence of the unconscious symbol-making power is also seen as a generally human process.

The patient and therapist enter into a remarkable attitude of religious reverence and respect for the unfolding unconscious. The spontaneous symbol making of the total personality is seen as providential, as intending the unification of the person. The person's life must become a tuning into and following of the wisdom of the deep underlying unity which he is. All of the approaches and techniques of the Jungian therapist are in line with this goal of unification through symbols. A hovering over the symbolic manifestations of the personality with a richly expectant attitude fructifies and enriches the symbol-making powers of the person.

To whatever degree is possible, depending on the person's readiness, stage of life, and adaptive strength, the Jungian therapist bends his efforts toward the development of the Self. The Self is precisely the archetypal tendency of the personality toward unification and is always implied in the third term which connects, unifies, and synthesizes the apparently irreconcilable sides of the personality. The Self is that unity to which all mystical traditions refer when they suggest doing away with the narrowed ego as the center of life—"Not I live but Christ in Me." In the Eastern traditions, enlightenment has also meant doing away with the petty concerns of the ego as central—"Neither my success nor my failure moves me any longer." Thus, the ego, with its concern for power, success, and manipulation, takes second place to a more inward self-dwelling. This inward unfolding unification of personality is viewed by the Jungian therapist as a 'god-in-us'; it is a transcendent presence belonging to, and yet greater than, the patient, having its ground in the collectively human.

It is not surprising that with this movement toward an attitude of philosophic-spiritual self-dwelling Jungian therapy is especially suitable for persons in later life who seek to find meaning outside the folds of traditional religious communities. In the first forty years of life, most Western persons are too preoccupied with making their way in the world to seek the larger self with its accompanying relativization of work, power, and success values.

The Jungian therapist moderates his expectations with younger persons, though he does not give up his goal. The goal remains a virtual pantheism of the unfolding psyche, which, as the god or Christ in us, ought to have directive power over our lives in preference to the machinations of our little egos. The in-dwelling of the spirit of truth in us is the Self, that movement toward unification which ought to be our center; and this Self is lived in the depths of the collective unconscious as a kind of seed requiring attention and care. The patient is thus encouraged to turn toward himself, understood as that universal transcendent Self, and to make this the center of his life.

Finally and fundamentally, the Jungian quest is a religious one, in which conversion through the acceptance of God is the fundamental curative power. The god which is accepted, while it may be expressed in traditional theistic language by some patients, is fundamentally an in-dwelling god, a kind of natural spirit within the universal psyche of man. Obedience to this natural spirit, which unfolds itself in symbols of unification, peace, and religious reconciliation, is the fundamental goal of human life. "I have now found a peace beyond mere rational understanding, a sense of harmony with myself, other men, and the universe. It works within me mysteriously, and I can count on this unfolding, trust in it, rest in it, and follow its directions."

## BIBLIOGRAPHY

Ehrenwald, Jan. *Psychotherapy: Myth and Method.* New York: Grune & Stratton, 1966.

A comparison of Freud and Jung, with Jung presented as mytho-philac and Freud as mythophobic. Ehrenwald's discussion of doctrinal compliance—the tendency of the patient to agree with his therapist's theory—serves to explain generally that which is described in more detail in the present text.

Jacobi, Jolande. *The Psychology of C. G. Jung*. 6th ed. New Haven: Yale University Press, 1962.

Chapter 3, which comprises more than half of Jacobi's book, systematically describes the practice and applications of Jungian theory.

Jung, C. G. *The Integration of the Personality*. London: Routledge & Kegan Paul, 1940.

An overall view of Jung's thought focused on the development and actualization of the person as a whole, with case materials, dreams and paintings by a patient, and their interpretations.

_____ . *Modern Man in Search of a Soul*. New York: Harcourt, Brace & World, Harvest Books, 1933.

A clear statement of Jungian thought. The first three and last two chapters concern themselves with the practical issues of psychotherapy, focusing on openness of interpretation of symbols in terms of their universal and archaic themes.

_____ . *The Practice of Psychotherapy*. Bollingen Series 20. New York: Pantheon Books, 1954.

Part 1 of this work offers a series of clear, readable essays laying out the general approach of Jungian psychotherapy. Part 2 is more specifically directed to technical therapeutic problems. Part 3, a complex, scholarly, literary-symbolic interpretation of transference, is based on ancient alchemical texts and symbols and is very difficult to grasp.

_____ . *Two Essays on Analytical Psychology*. New York: Pantheon Books, 1953.

Chapter 6 gives the characteristic Jungian therapeutic approach and interpretation in a clear discursive style that makes his meanings fairly accessible to the nontechnical reader. In "The Relation between the Ego and the Unconscious," Jung continues his discussion of the collective unconscious, focusing on the therapeutic problem of individual development.

Van den Berg, J. H. *Different Existence*. Pittsburgh: Duquesne University Press, 1972.

Van den Berg's critique of the traditional ideas of projection and the unconscious, as well as his call for the development of a more social understanding of the therapist-patient dialectic, greatly influenced the development of the present text.

# 7

# Mary's case
# continued

○ ——————————————— ○ ——————————————————————— ○

Because the description of Jungian psychotherapy is thus far even more lacking in concrete detail than was the general description of Freudian psychoanalysis, the need to concretize the Jungian approach by describing a case in therapy is critical. The Jungian dialogue, as already noted, always lives itself out between a specific therapist and a specific patient. To pursue our ongoing phenomenological analysis of psychotherapy, it is necessary to look again at Mary's case, this time as it emerges in the context of Jungian psychotherapy.

## REINTRODUCTION

Mary is now thirty-eight years of age, a medical doctor who has changed her specialization to psychiatry. She consults at several hospitals, works one day a week at a local university seeing students, and also has a small private practice which varies from supervising the use of tranquilizers with some long-term mentally ill patients to intensive 137 psychotherapy of a modified analytic variety. While she considers her own analysis to have been successful, she is still dissatisfied with her life and with much of her psychiatric work. As she knows, some of this dissatisfaction arises because she lives by herself. Though she would like to be, she is not married and her prospects for finding a suitable husband are not good. As she sees it, however, her dissatisfaction has deeper roots than this. In some way, the purpose and meaning of her life are at stake.

"My life is satisfactory for the most part," she says. "I have very few really bad moods, don't often get depressed or really unhappy. My few remaining neurotic remnants are well controlled, hardly worth mentioning. However, I still feel too rational, too much competently in control. That's partly the hazard of being a competent professional woman, but even my lack of moodiness is almost too reasonable. It's almost as if I'm serving reason as a kind of god."

The various cults of self-expression—of "being yourself," "being spontaneous," "being fully in touch with your feelings"—appeal very little to Mary, who regards them as unbalanced, one-sided expressions of important aspects of life. Self-conscious spontaneity has had little effect in her life, and striving to be more emotional she would experience as artificial and unnatural. Nonetheless, she is dissatisfied. She finds her life too small, too reasonable, too busy, too irreligious, too superficial, too pragmatic, and too easy. "There seem to be no goals worth striving for," she says. "I can't get excited about making more of a professional success or making more money. It's almost as if I need to be more religious, but I don't know how. And it seems to me that the church is no real help, though I still go fairly often."

As part of her search for a greater sense of fulfillment and a deeper linkage with God and life, she begins to read some existentialist writers, whom she finds interesting but mostly morbid. By chance one day she comes across Jung's *Modern Man in Search of a Soul*, whose title strikes her as perfectly expressive of her plight. She is so modern and enlightened that she has somehow in the process lost her soul. As she is just entering that "second half of life" which Jung indicates is a time for genuine self-development, she finds the book interesting. Perhaps Jungian therapy could help her. But her professional friends discourage her: "Jung is too mystical, too unsystematic. They're a rather queer, arty bunch," and so forth.

The prejudice against Jung expressed by her more analytic colleagues intrigues her. None of them reveals a genuine understanding of Jung's thought; rather, they condemn it out of hand. Paradoxically, their remarks confirm her impression that Jungian thought and practice is something special, something more spiritual, a more ample style of thought beyond mere reasonableness. Delighted to discover that there is a Jungian therapist in her city, she decides to go, although she is somewhat deterred by the fact that he is a psychologist rather than a psychiatrist. Her familiarity with psychologists has led her to believe that they are for the most part rather weak people who concoct elaborate methods for evaluating patients but hem and haw when asked what they really think.

Nevertheless, she makes an appointment with this Jungian therapist and, in her first telephone contact with him, finds him different from the usual therapist. He laughs uproariously at her account of the prejudiced descriptions she has heard of Jungian therapy. In fact, he is thoroughly unbusinesslike and appears pleasantly unprofessional. He suggests that they meet on his farm and promises to send her a map so that she can find it.


## THE FIRST MEETING

Mary arrives at her first appointment a half-hour early on a Saturday afternoon. As she comes up the long dirt driveway, at the end of which stands a cabin farmhouse, she senses how totally urban she has become, how out of touch with the natural, and wonders to herself what sort of person would have a log cabin like this. Her other analyst had been an urban intellectual and bookworm, occasionally attending plays and symphonies. This Dr. M., the Jungian, seems a different type. She wonders whether the setting is connected with his following Jung or whether it is just a personal eccentricity.

She is greeted by a man in a wool plaid shirt, who, ambling along with a large Irish setter, invites her to walk with him as she is early for her appointment. Following the usual social introductions, they walk silently for a few minutes. He then says, "Enjoy the woods here; they're meant for you and me," and there is something in his manner, in the way he walks, in his being at home on his farm, that appeals to her. It suggests to her a link with nature and perhaps with God.

Everything in the house also seems attuned to nature: the wood surfaces, both rough and polished, everywhere; the large hand-woven American Indian rug in the center of the living room; a round table cut from a huge tree, exhibiting the tree rings and supported by thick wrought iron legs. Hanging just above the stone fireplace is a circular drawing; she stares at it for a moment and is told: "That's a sand painting used by Navajo medicine men for healing the sick. The patient sits in the middle of the painting, or lies there if he cannot sit. I understand it's a good therapy." In his office there is another Navajo rug, a leather couch with a rough-hewn wood frame, several chairs, a long table against the wall with a typewriter and some archeological artifacts on it, an array of paintings on the wall, and some other paintings on the floor against the wall.

As Mary sits down in a comfortable leather chair, the therapist places his chair directly in front of her, quite close, and asks, "Well, what brings you to me?" She outlines the kind of dissatisfaction she feels with her life and her hope that she can add dimension and depth to it. In an attempt to uncover her areas of strong development and of weakness, he asks several pointed questions about her religious life, her aesthetic interests, her reading habits, her workday, and her leisure activities.

"You are a thinker," he says, "something of a rationalist and a pragmatist in your life style. But you sense this is not enough. Also you have emphasized the senses in your life, the palpable, the material. That is understandable from the little you tell me of your very disturbed mother; to have been intuitively tuned into her world as a child would have been to have delivered yourself over to her madness. By emphasizing the observable, the commonsense clearness of thinking and simple concrete perceiving, you made an area of clarity and control for yourself.

"However, all of this has also had an unfortunate result. Your psychic life is correspondingly impoverished. Your commonsense reasonableness is also a prison that cuts you off from God and from the depths of your own self. The question for you and for me is how you can come to a more balanced unified wholeness, not so much based on the tyranny of a narrow reasonableness."

Mary is greatly impressed by the degree to which his general diagnosis agrees with her own sense of where she is. Although he speaks rather casually of her one-sided emphasis on reason, common sense, and the clear and orderly, she is not insulted or upset. She senses that her undevelopedness is an integral part of her life story; already she vaguely intuits that her life is a coherent unfolding. Her readiness to experience herself as an unfolding of new life potentialities is precisely what has attracted her to a Jungian therapist, and she already finds herself oriented by him toward the fulfillment of what she has not yet allowed herself to be.

## "In the dark water with a dolphin"

Mary responds enthusiastically to the therapist's description but admits that she is puzzled about the answer to her dilemma. "I really don't know how to develop my depths," she says, "though I obscurely sense my deficiencies. What is the pathway out? Do you see it, and do you think you can help me?"

"Let me show you how your question is directed by your own narrowness," Dr. M. responds. "You tell me that you *sense* your deficiencies. Further, you ask me whether I *see* the way out. Finally, you direct yourself to what I *think* about my ability to help you. In answer, I must say that I don't *see* the way out but that I *intuit* or *hunch* that together we can find a way out. We need an oracle, a guide who knows the depths of your inward life and can direct us.

"My expertise," he adds, "is that I know and have personally experienced many such journeys, most importantly my own, which is still ongoing. But this knowing of mine, however adequate or deep, is not yet an oracle for you. We must find a way to listen to you. From your previous analysis you know how valuable dreams can be for uncovering the hidden—that which lives itself out in darkness. Let's ask your dream life to speak to us. Tell me your most recent dream."

"I had a dream the night after I first telephoned you," Mary replies. "It's the first one I've remembered in a long time, and it's rather vague to me. The dream opens with my being on a small raft in the ocean or a great lake. Land is nowhere in sight and I don't know where I am, but I know that I'm lucky to be on this raft as there was a storm and I'd been swimming unaided. Apparently I came across this raft to keep me afloat through the storm, and it's very neatly made of some kind of plastic stuff. It looks like it's gradually disintegrating now, like gently crumbling, and I begin to worry and to feel lost. The water is very dark, the night is very dark. There are some fearful fish in the ocean, and that's part of what worries me—the unfriendly forces that could come and destroy me. I see what at first looks like a shark, but then I discover it's a dolphin. It looks at me and I have the feeling it's communicating with me, that it knows my plight and wants to help me. I start to follow it by paddling, and then I wake up."

"Your dream is very interesting and, I suspect, very important," Dr. M. responds. "It came on the day that you had decided to embark on a new life-fulfilling enterprise, your new therapy. It seems to me that it expresses your life situation quite well, though there's also much that I don't understand in it. Perhaps if I tell you the dream as your story, you'll understand it yourself in a new way.

"Your history has been one in which you lived for a very long time in a dark and chaotic world. You found for yourself a way of staying afloat and safe, first on your own and then with your former analyst. However, this way of staying afloat now seems inadequate; it's crumbling and disintegrating. The dream suggests further that you will have to swim in this ocean, this dark chaos, with guidance from neither the heavens nor the earth; there is, however, some friendly, intelligent animal that will serve to guide you. That is a very cursory reading of your dream. Does it make sense to you?"

Mary finds this reading very convincing, though she wonders aloud about the meaning of the dolphin-guide. The therapist returns this question to her, suggesting that by telling him what a dolphin is like, this will illuminate its meaning. On reflection, Mary realizes that the dolphin is intelligent, knows the underwater world, is reputed to have a language with which it communicates, is warm-blooded, and nurses its young; in fact, of all the creatures in the sea it is the most human, even breathing air. "Are you the dolphin?" she asks. The therapist admits that this is an attractive thought and probably one level of appropriate interpretation.

Dr. M. suggests strongly that a warm-blooded animal that is comfortable in the water is a perfect opposite of Mary's conscious self. Consciously, she is the more cool-blooded one who hangs onto her little raft of reason. Swimming in the dark chaos of the sea and knowing her way there is something she cannot consciously imagine, but the intelligence and sympathy of the dolphin are not so foreign to her, since even the dream indicates a bond of understanding between Mary and the dolphin. The very fact that she is attracted to a Jungian therapist, having been warned of the unreasonableness and mysteriousness of the project, again suggests that the dark, intuitive, aesthetic sphere is not as alien to her nature as she has imagined.

Two-and-a-half hours later, Dr. M. mentions that although he often meets patients in his city office, for their first meeting he had especially wanted Mary to come to his farm—"to balance your reasonableness with a bit of nature," he says. They arrange to meet twice a week for a while; meanwhile Mary is asked to write down all her dreams.

## INTRODUCTION TO DR. M.

Dr. M. is fifty-three, a slender man with a lean ascetic face. Before embarking on his academic studies, he had seriously considered becoming an artist. Although he still paints as part of his self-expressive activity and to assist himself in self-development, he had abandoned the idea of art as primary in his life out of a vague intuition that it would be bad for him, cutting him off from people too much. Now, having grown in self-knowledge through having been in therapy and by being a therapist himself, he realizes that, for him, being an artist would have been psychically very dangerous. His youthful pleasure in his gifts, in his intuitive ability to see beyond what most others could see, had bordered on dangerous self-inflation.

He is happy that he did not have to live out the megalomanic pride of the self-declared genius. The humbling discovery that he had been fortunate to make through an archeologist-historian teacher was that his own naive insights had roots even in the prehistory of mankind.

His own therapy—first in Freudian analysis, later in Jungian therapy—had even more deeply impressed upon him that his gifts were expressions of a common heritage. From the beginning of time man has attempted to express his life and vision, to capture it, express it, and immortalize it in song, poetry, myth, religion, painting, and so forth. Hence, he was but one in a long line, a concrete individual embodiment of the collective psyche.

At this point in his life, he experiences himself as in the line of spiritual guides, wise men, ascetical-mystical writers, and ancient philosophers who regarded philosophy as an actual guide to the good life. With his patients he mostly finds himself in the role of guide through the unknown. He relishes this role at times, though he knows that his desire to be mystic-seer can lead to self-inflation, pride, and to harming others. For self-balance, he reads a variety of profound thinkers, especially those of the East. He is also fortunate in having an intelligent wife, a down-to-earth, practical, earthy midwestern girl who moderates his flights with her concrete, pragmatic sense of the obvious. He consults with her regularly on his cases, especially with regard to the women he is seeing.

The lean cast of his face and body, together with the intensity of his intuitively tuned presence to reality, give him at times the appearance of an inspired man. He lives out a paradoxical combination of peacefulness and intensity. He also speaks with conviction and authority. As he says: "If I speak only from myself, my words are nothing at all. When I speak as rooted in mankind and a more universal wisdom, then there is a real speaking."

## THE DIALOGUE

During their first few meetings, Dr. M. and Mary get along well. She finds him warmer, more expressive and enthusiastic toward her than her former analyst. She also finds him somewhat mysterious and a bit spooky but is not put off by this, however alienated she would once have been by anything even slightly illogical or mysterious. She realizes, of course, that she is now fed up with the merely rational. Somehow, the way in which he speaks evokes for her a sense of the spiritual, a wisdom that moves toward natural harmony with oneself and the universe. This is exciting to her. She already has a sense that this is close to what she has been seeking.

She has entered therapy this time not to find explanations but to be helped to live more amply, and she already finds this beginning. Being openly guided instead of being thrust back on herself is pleasant to her. The therapist's judgments are there for her to see, his intuitions are openly expressed, and she is allowed to participate in elaborating or disagreeing with them. Yet there is much more than this. The therapist is at home and peaceful in these irrational waters, and it is his reverential attitude toward the unfolding of mystery that appeals most to her.

For his part, Dr. M. finds Mary highly responsive to precisely what he has to offer. He likes her, finds her a bit square and overrational perhaps, but this gives him a happy sense of authority with her and a sense of being able to be of genuine use to her. In many ways he sees himself as compensating her one-sidedness. She is a rational thinker; he is more intuitive-aesthetic. Feeling is more primary than thought for him, and intuition is more fundamental than sensation. Thus, they are balancing opposites, and within his Jungian understanding, he sees this complementarity as leading to the most fruitful kind of collaboration. In response to her, he already finds himself being more reasonable and thoughtful—a good development, as this is the area in which his own life is relatively less developed.

On the everyday level, emotionally hysterical people do not appeal to Dr. M., who prefers rational types, even though his work involves letting them into the more mysterious, intuitive realms of experience. Mary's commonsense seriousness also appeals to him. She is willing to work, is attentive, listens carefully, and is in all these ways an ideal patient. That she already appreciates and tunes into him is very gratifying. In short, they like each other.

## Finding Mary's type

The Jungian perspective holds that every person belongs to some natural type and that to live *amply* in accord with that type (that is, not one-sidedly) is the person's proper life style. Although this underlying type undergoes all sorts of life transformations, the idea of type suggests a fundamental unchanging core to the personality. This question of type is not a theoretical question. The therapy must take careful cognizance of the kind of person the patient is so as to be fittingly attuned to him. Only by carefully establishing his fundamental underlying natural bent can the therapy move effectively toward an adequate expression of his whole life in unity.

Mary is not only apparently rational and sensation oriented but her mode of living in accord with external conventionalities suggests that she is also a natural extrovert. She takes her cue from the world and adapts rapidly to a situation. Indeed, the very speed with which she assimilates and is able to move with her Jungian therapist is an indication of her extroversion. Finally, the fact that she had found the Freudian approach fruitful, which is an extroverted-sensation-thinking approach to reality, suggests even more firmly that her natural type is extrovert-sensation type with thinking as primary auxilliary.

The problem of natural type is not so easily disposed of in Mary's case, however, because the typology already done applies primarily to her adaptive-self, the *persona* she shows to the world. Intuition and feeling had been dangerous for her to develop in childhood because they would have opened her to full psychic contact with the extraordinarily destructive, hypochondriacal, fundamentally insane world of her mother. Thus, partly by minimizing intuition and feeling as functions, Mary was able to retain some semblance of normality in her life. Her extrovert mode of moving into the world with apparent confidence and competence, of not shrinking from contact with objects or persons even when they are new, was also a necessary part of her psychic survival. Without that combination of commonsense rationality and confident approach to the world, the dark chaos of her mother's disturbed world would have overwhelmed her. All of this suggests that her outward type is primarily a defensive response, and that perhaps her natural bent has never found fulfillment.

The radical distortion of a natural bent typically manifests itself in signs of a very severe pathology, which is not manifest in Mary's case. She has developed remarkably well within a fundamental commonsense extroversion, and she is a good thinker. In spite of the powerful pathological influence of her mother, Mary apparently is not and has never been severely disturbed, suggesting that those modes that were needed for successful adaptation to the world and successful defense against the mother had been Mary's natural bent from the beginning.

In balance, then, although there has probably been some exaggeration of the natural type on the basis of defensive need, Mary is overall to be understood as extroverted, sensation and thinking oriented, a diagnosis of type which rests on the judgment that she is not severely disturbed. While it is perfectly clear that she is not very disturbed from an everyday commonsense viewpoint, it is less clear from a sophisticated Jungian perspective. The fact that Mary's mother was a mental patient for a time could lend weight to the idea that Mary has an underlying potential for very severe disturbance. The Jungian theory always takes hereditary factors into consideration; further, the mother's early influence may still be there, sealed off in the unconscious.

Finally, by suppressing the development of her intuitive feeling functions and denying her introversive trends, Mary may have deeply weakened her personality in such a way as to make it prey to an overwhelming invasion from the unconscious. Perhaps her developing interest in the Jungian approach, her concern with religion, God, and the meaning of her life, can be understood as the beginning of the development of a paranoid-schizophrenic transformation of her life. This judgment suggests a completely different therapeutic program for her than the judgment that views her as a basically healthy, well-adapted, though one-sided person. It suggests that her basic type was radically distorted through her life history, that she may well be more of an intuitive-feeling type, and that at this point in her life a therapeutic attempt to develop her psyche amply is foredoomed to failure.

On the basis of this judgment her therapist would try to help her to rationalize and dismiss the rising of the unconscious, perhaps using the Adlerian interpretation to assist him in this corrosive rationalization of her religious quest. "You are still striving to be the special one, the favorite only child; you search now for mystical presence as a way of being exceptional. Give up this egoism and work with others to be of use to them. There rests your real gratification and whatever there is of real happiness for you in life." In so doing, the therapist would be giving up the Jungian therapy as inapplicable to the patient because of her psychotic potential.

## Mary's suitability for Jungian therapy

In order to see a strongly negative evaluation of Mary and the possibility of her rejection as unsuitable for Jungian therapy, let us suppose that she were in the hands of Dr. B., a Jungian therapist different from Dr. M. Dr. B. is a quiet scholarly person who, after some years as a student of physics, became a student of psychology, in which he obtained his doctorate. Having sought help from a Jungian therapist, he finally became a Jungian therapist himself. His own type is sensing-thinking, like Mary's; but in spite of his theoretical understanding of type psychology, he greatly distrusts successful extroverts. He is himself a naturally cautious introvert who always hesitates before involving himself with someone or something, always pondering the worth of something before committing himself to it.

At his first meeting with Mary, he inquires in great detail into the way in which her mother was disturbed. Noting that religion was one of the mother's preoccupations, he views Mary's developing religious interest suspiciously. In addition, he regards her superficially social competence as a thin veneer; she is obviously afraid of him. If he is to embark on a course of Jungian therapy with her, the real question is how strong she really is. Partly to test this and partly as an expression of his distrust of her, he is rather silent and frowns frequently during their first several interviews. Although she cannot tell what he is thinking, the atmosphere of distrust and lack of openness between them makes her frightened and dubious of the whole Jungian enterprise. It seems to her that he reverses what she says, always treating her judgments as superficial, carelessly thought out, banal, and unintuitive. He is not unpleasant, but his heavy mysterious reserve causes her to feel negated and afraid.

During their third meeting she tells him her dream. She had felt good after she had had it, but now she experiences a sense of darkness and pessimism.

"Shortly after we arranged our first meeting, I had a dream," she says. "It's rather scattered and unclear to me—I mostly don't remember my dreams. In the dream I'm on a raft just barely big enough to keep me afloat. I'm frightened, and I see that the raft is crumbling, disintegrating. The sea is choppy; big waves swell up around me. I don't know where I am; there's no land in sight. I have a vague sense that I almost went under, almost got swamped in a big storm, but was lucky to find this little raft.

"It's made of some kind of plastic—very well constructed—but still it's that kind of foamy plastic stuff that doesn't have much strength to it. The night is dark and the water is black. I'm lost and scared. I see a shark—it's swimming around—and then I see it isn't a shark. It's a friendly dolphin, and it looks at me as if it understood, and I start to paddle after it to follow it. It's going to take me to land."

To Dr. B., the dream indicates clearly that Jungian therapy is unsuitable for Mary. It indicates that she has survived the chaos of her life by constructing an artificial principle of buoyancy, that she kept afloat on a "plastic raft." It seems to point further to the disintegration of that way of staying afloat and ends with (to a discerning therapist) a virtual admonition that Mary be encouraged to find "safe dry land." The task of Jungian therapy, which would be to plumb the depths of the psychic life and integrate them into the personality, seems contraindicated by the patient's dream. The intelligent creature that knows the depths, the dolphin, does not lead her to explore the water but rather leads her safely to land. Hence, encouraging Mary to pursue concrete social enrichment goals is indicated; even her religious interest should be directed toward being with others. Perhaps work with religious youth groups would satisfy her need for vocation and purpose and at the same time keep her on conventional "dry land."

## The problem of objectivity

The constitution of Mary's pathology, as well as her suitability or unsuitability for Jungian therapy, is grounded on the dialogue between her and the particular therapist involved. Even the establishing of her natural type or lifestyle and the dream-illuminated diagnosis of what she needs in her life to retain, or attain, balance vary with the particular therapist. In one sense, this is not remarkable, because the Jungian approach assumes that there is a meeting of two persons whose subjectivities blend together. At the same time, the apparently objective reading of the dream, which is regarded as the true oracle, the speaker from the patient's unconscious, is cast into doubt by this variability. The attitude that the Jungian therapist teaches his patient is a reverential respect for the objectivity of the psyche.

Because dreams are diagnostic, as factual as a urine test or physical assay, both patient and therapist turn to the dream as true speaker. The dream tells *its* story, and the intention in relation to understanding it is to allow it to speak. But *it* does not speak; persons do, and in so doing they are giving to dream speech a certain oracular weight. The therapist and patient together grant this high level of validity and trustworthiness to the dream speech, and it is precisely this conviction of the dream's extraordinary trustworthiness that gives it its power. *Its* power is, in fact, *our* power to grant the dream credence within a Jungian context. Both patient and therapist forget the source of the dream-validity and attribute it to the dream as objectively given.

In principle, this is the same problem of objectivity that was encountered in the description of Freudian analysis. The analyst carefully constitutes a situation within which the analytic interpretation will have convincing power for both partners in the therapeutic process. He constitutes this situation, with many explicit and implicit agreements with his patient, in such a way that reality will show its face as the past repeating itself in the present. Further, the patient is encouraged to be irrational and infantile, placed in a relative social vacuum, and is then found to be irrational, infantile, unsocial, and self-absorbed by the analytic interpretation.

In the same way, the Jungian's power of conviction is lived out in the direct way in which he confronts the patient's apparently irrational inside depths, dream life, and other side. He suggests, evokes, and co-constitutes together with his patient the *oracle* by reference to the dimly known, poorly understood, not yet developed. The patient comes with an admission of need for increased life-amplitude, hoping that such increase can be found with the therapist. The therapist points consistently to the darker fringes of the patient's experience, and this is especially convincing to the patient if the therapist shows a skillful adeptness and fluidity in grasping the dim borders, the mythic structures, the shadow land already partially available to the patient. This amplitude of the therapist is, of course, a concrete amplitude of human life.

The therapist has only himself and the world he knows to bring to the patient; together they must constitute a field within which the patient's life-amplitude may be increased. Faith in the dream as oracular and a virtually religious sense of the underlying objective psyche is the Jungian's faith, which he directly and convincingly teaches to his patient. For it is true that what the patient needs is hidden, unrealized, still unkown, and only dimly adumbrated in a shadow land.

## A DREAM SERIES

Mary continues to meet with Dr. M. twice a week and finds herself having a series of dreams with an obvious underlying thematic unity. Her second therapy dream is in direct response to her therapist's interpretive image of "swimming sinuously in the ocean." She is swimming in moonlit waters, at first happily and playfully, but later she becomes anxious and wonders whether she will find her way. In a later dream, she dives down into the water and finds there a huge fearful octopus. Going into the ground, under the earth, also emerges as an image in her dreams. She finds herself in dark underground caves illuminated by an eerie luminescent light, where destructive frightening animals abound. Images of entrapment occur, reminding her of her feelings toward her mother. The most frightening animals are undifferentiated bloblike creatures that threaten to absorb or suffocate a person.

During this period of several months, Mary finds herself wanting to spend more time alone. Some of that time she spends trying to understand her dreams, reliving them in her mind. Her friends notice that she is self-preoccupied at times, more brooding and worried than before. During the day she lives with her dreams, dark images of which occur to her in the midst of her social conversations. More strikingly, she finds that many of these images are meaningful in her own work as a therapist. She finds herself using images of the octopus, the bloblike, jellylike threat of suffocation, the dark, and the underground in her work with her own patients. It seems clear to her that these struggles she is having are universal ones: the struggle of dark and light, the earth and sky, coming to terms with one's fear of the dark unknown. These mythic images, partly garnered from her dreams, have been amplified and given further meaning through her work with her therapist and her daily meditations.

In a way, the world of dreams is becoming for Mary the fundamental reality. As oracular utterances from the depths of her fundamental being, they merit the same kind of attentive care that she has heretofore given only to her work. In her previous analysis, dream images sometimes took on significance and life, but now it is almost as if a reversal of values and emphasis were taking place. It is to the dream world that she turns to find the fundamental, real, objective guide for her life. Indeed, the dream world and its unfolding as a story *is* the story of her life in its development. It is *the* drama of her life. Not the outer world of accomplishment and recognition but rather the inner unfolding of the landscapes of the mythic dream world are becoming increasingly the real.

If you asked her what was happening this week, Mary would tell you about the development of her dreams, emphasizing that it was her dreams and their unfolding that was significant; the therapist would be seen only as a kind of guide to this objective unfolding of the psyche. His power as co-constitutor of the dream world and its significations would be evident neither to her nor to him. There is indeed a level of human objectivity—that is, of intersubjectivity—in what he does. To exactly that degree to which he is faithful to being a Jungian, his work as therapist is not merely an expression of his own individuality. It is the expression of a whole culture, a whole orientation to reality, which has been developed communally.

## The therapist in the dream world

In discussing orthodox analysis, it was indicated that the patient's world of dreams in therapy is a response to his therapist and to the therapy orientation. The Freudian patient dreams Freudian dreams; the Jungian patient, Jungian dreams. This should lead us to neither a cynical denigration of the use of dreams in therapy nor to diatribes against arbitrary interpretation. The patient's dreaming, waking life, and unfolding sense of his own history is, and ought to be, inextricably bound up with the unfolding of the psychotherapy. The dreaming, the reporting of dreams, and interpretation of the dreams is done within a certain specific human context. It is pointed to the therapeutic interaction, which is always a concrete situation between two persons. Thus, the therapist is always implicitly implicated in the patient's dreaming. The patient dreams for his therapist.

However, the sense in which the therapist becomes a figure in the dream world has a special aspect in Jungian therapy. Since the dream is taken as the real, valid, true oracle of life-meanings for the person, the significance of the therapist as influence, power, and valued person is also assimilated to the dream world. The therapist appears typically in ways that express his closeness to wisdom, to proper life-guidance, to balance, and to the development of harmony and wholeness. He appears typically in dreams *in the guise* of incarnating some general life-principle—as guide, warning voice, witch, magician, or old wise man, who indicates by word or action which direction must be taken. Signs that indicate the proper direction—transformation rituals in which an animal becomes a winged spirit, for example—all express the therapist's guiding activity. This assimilation of the therapist's concrete actions, speech, and tendencies is toward a universalizing, mythic figure, the wise guide to the underworld. Depending on the therapist's particularities, the image is likely to express rather clearly his directions, inclinations, and encouragements—in short, his approach to the patient.

The appearance of the therapist as a background in Mary's dreams is fairly evident. The very direction her dreams take, toward the depths of the ocean and the innards of the earth, are directions her therapist has indicated as necessary for her proper development. In this early part of her therapy, however, her therapist is not yet an active figure in her dreams. She continues to dream of entering the bowels of the earth, an increasingly luminous, warm, even hot place. The shimmering light and heat sometimes seem too intense to her, as if she will be scorched, overwhelmed, burned. She wakes up literally hot and perspiring. Her therapist has been suggesting that she become more active in taming the fiery depths of her unconscious life. Perhaps she should take up some form of drawing or painting to try to express these dream images and bring them more fully worked-out into her waking life.

Shortly after this, Mary dreams of reaching the end of a long fiery tunnel. There is nowhere to go, and she feels increasingly frightened that she will be consumed by flames and heat. At this moment of impasse, an authoritative voice says, "Cool the walls," indicating a muddy pool. As Mary daubs mud on one wall of the cave, a circular figure emerges with a fiery dragon in the center, very like the sand painting she had seen in Dr. M.'s house but with a dragon added. She is relieved, feels calmer, less hot and anxious. The dream ends with her continuing to daub mud on the walls while more and more figures emerge in her mud painting. The oracular dream voice that says "cool the walls" reflects and expresses rather precisely her therapist's suggestion that she paint to help cool the hot depths of her unconscious life.

## THE USE OF ARTISTIC PRODUCTION

Within the Jungian experience, transformative integrating symbols bring outside and inside, high and low, earth and gods into symbolic unity. Darkness and light, consciousness and unconsciousness, sleep and waking are primary dimensions of this symbolic unification. The Jungian wishes to bring the mythic life of dream sleep into waking conscious life, and this is most naturally done through art work in which the unconscious synthesizes with consciousness. To paint is to handle the world consciously and adaptively but with respect to an inner horizon of inexplicit meaning. Painting expresses and tames, releases and yet gives form to, the still chaotic strivings of the unconscious life.

Mary begins to paint for the first time since early grade school. At first she tries to finger paint, moving as close as she can to the dream image of daubing mud on walls. Her therapist has encouraged her in this, also suggesting that she should try gardening to get the feel of muddy soil and growing life. Although her urban life offers little opportunity for this, on the few occasions that she does some gardening at a friend's house she finds it relaxing; images of planting and watching the growth of crops enter a few dreams. She continues to paint and, after a few weeks of finger painting, attempts to use a brush. Her paintings are crude but expressive, and she uses motifs from her dreams as their basis.

At first the painting is hard work because she feels self-conscious and incompetent. She is relieved when her therapist does not judge her paintings as art, and she learns in the process some additional principles of dream and art interpretation: that in paintings and dreams alike, the earth, the passions of the flesh, darkness, and a downward direction often go together; that an upward direction, light, the spiritual, and the reasonable also go together; that images toward the right side of a painting or dream often stand in some special relationship to the future, to the "right road to take"; that the left side often stands for the past. This learning does not occur abstractly, it occurs in the context of her therapy and her struggles with her life.

At first her paintings are dark, with emphasis on the downward side, on exploring and articulating the darkness of the earth and of fire within the earth. Almost in direct response to this one-sidedness, she tries to paint some that include sky, stars, and a differentiated upward direction, but she sees that there is, for her, an empty conventionality in this upward movement.

In one of her paintings she notes that "even the stars are like those in a child's picture book." It occurs to her and to her therapist as well that the direction of spiritual upwardness has been lacking—literally, not yet developed—in her life. For much of her life the principle of rationality, of good adaptation to a businesslike world of work, had been her "up-rightedness." Her early flirtation with religious work, while expressing some specific spiritual longing, had moved totally toward a kind of social-work group approach to religion. During her college years she had worked as an assistant youth minister for a short time.

Her therapist now inquires directly into the practice of her Christian faith. She seldom prays, although under the Jungian influence she has been regularly meditating on her life, and some religious themes have emerged in her thinking of herself. Because Mary and the therapist are both alerted to this undeveloped area in her, they emphasize this direction, which intensifies her attention to the liturgical and ritual elements in her church. She is more keenly aware of the meaning of saying the creed, the degree to which it means an offering of self to God. Partly this increased awareness of the liturgical aspects of methodism leads her to recoil, reminding her of the empty way in which she has lived out her conventional religious life. Also she dislikes the idea of "giving oneself over to God or anybody." She is now, however, looking more alertly at the liturgy, seeking to connect herself with it.

One day she is angered to find herself impulsively drawing a small cross in the upper left-hand corner of a dark, nearly black painting with red fire underneath. In entering Jungian therapy, she had sought something spiritual, but the cross in her painting makes her realize how much she fears and actually hates her Christian background. The cross means for her all of those horrid, frightening, nonsensical lectures about sacrificing and doing good that her mother had directed at her when she was a child. It was connected with "honoring thy father and thy mother," a precept which had aroused profound guilt when she had detached herself from her mother in the interests of self-preservation. In her more psychotic moments, Mary's mother had talked about the blood of Christ, giving blood, giving her all in sacrifice for children. These rambling insane-religious talks had come to mean for Mary the onset of domestic disorganization and the terrible ordeal of arranging to have her mother hospitalized again.

## RELIGIOUS DEVELOPMENT

At the next session, Mary is angry with her therapist. She recounts a brief dream in which he had appeared as stern and demanding as "an Old Testament prophet." Dr. M. inquires whether he seems different to her in person than when she thinks of him or imagines him outside the therapy hour. The fact that he has remained unruffled, interested, lively, and undefensive while she has been attacking his therapy impresses Mary. She sees vividly that he is warmly interested in the meaning of the cross and the Old Testament prophet role and that he is obviously pleased at this new development in their relationship, as well as in the unfolding of her psychic religious life. Hence, she reflects on her way of imagining him outside of therapy and realizes that when she was away from him, he seemed uncanny to her, witch-like, magicianlike. Once or twice in passing, she had imagined him having a golden halo; on another occasion she had imagined him as a witchlike yet kingly person brewing a sacred or evil potion.

"How very odd that I would see you like that," she says. "That's not at all the way you are with me. I guess it's just that I was always scared as a child that some powerful godlike person would condemn me for who I was. You know, I always had trouble looking at my mother when she was crazy. There was something about her eyes when she talked of plots, counterplots, or Jesus Christ; there was a kind of fanatic glaze, a kind of inspired intensity about her. It really used to frighten me. She was so absolutely sure, so certain, so intense, and then the next moment she would just be scared."

Mary glances briefly at Dr. M., who is sitting close to and directly across from her, seeking his reassuring warmth. She is startled to find him intense and inspired but also gently concerned. He is almost bending over her, or so she feels, tending to her as a good parent might tend to a frightened child.

The session ends with Dr. M. reassuring Mary and stressing that all these images—of the sacred, the holy, the cross, the intense inspired eyes, Jesus Christ, the Old Testament prophet—belong to her. They are also a collective gift of the psyche, aside from the peculiar ways in which her mother may have taken them up or even the ways in which he reflects some attributes of inspiration or religiousity. He suggests that she read those sections of Isaiah in which the prophet varies from angry deliverer of judgment to consoler, promiser of tenderness and mercy. His basic message is that she should allow these religious themes and images to develop in their own unhurried way. They belong to her collective unconscious and can be good life transformations of experience, which unify and give direction to the person.

In the following weeks of regular sessions, Mary comes to see that her projection onto Dr. M. of uncanny, spiritual, and even demonic attributes belonged to the development of her own psychic life. It was not his witchlike, kingly, or prophetlike presence to which she was responding but rather to her own need for a prophet, king, or spiritual leader. The response of her unconscious had been to lead her back first to the cross and to Christ. The direction of this unconscious flow toward religious life was still unclear to her.

Looking back over the developing story of her therapy, Mary could see that she had first been concentrating on the development of the dark, bodily, chaotic side of her life. Already she felt more alive, more in her body, more amply present to her life of 'being-with-others'; the enrichment of meaning of her everyday life, her meditative presence to herself and her dreams, even the brooding and worrying, had increased her concrete sense of life-amplitude. She is now more intuitive and more in touch with her own emotionality. She has developed a more vivid, mythic style of speaking, and this has put her more in touch with the affective dimension of her life. She is now more emotionally expressive than she has ever been.

## The assimilation of religion

It should be noted that there is no discussion of the truth or falsity of religious claims; neither is the patient encouraged to enter into the history of her own specific religious community. The question of God's call to the person within Christian faith does not become an issue in the therapy. Rather, God's or Christ's call to commitment is seen as emanating from, determined by, and brought about as a striving of the in-dwelling personality to move toward religious unification. In every case, the striving for meaning, for deeper significance, for kinship with God, for fuller linkage with the world, is assimilated to the 'unfolding-of-the-collective-psyche.' The religious symbols are seen to emerge from the unconscious collective psyche and thus are seen as emanating from within, not from without. This is neither directly discussed nor brought up as one way of looking at religious development among others. Rather, the therapist lives out his faith in the unfolding of the collective psyche in the individual's life in such a way as to demonstrate convincingly the unfolding of the universal within.

The religious orientation taught by the Jungian therapist, then, is inward rather than outward; the god to be heard is the *collective psyche*. Throughout the therapy, obedience to the unfolding inner world has been concretized and lived as the ethical, proper, appropriate fullfillment of being human. Listening to and reading the dream as oracular utterance from the depths; developing an art form as a mode of listening to the inner depths; meditating and writing out thoughts on the meaning of dreams and painting—all of these have concretely embodied the lived-faith, now shared with the patient, of the appropriate, religious, reverential, binding nature of the world unfolding within as collectively given. Mary must listen to and obey these messages from her unconscious self, for they are the voice of God in her life.

The uncanny image of the king, priest, therapist is specifically tied to the actual characteristics of her therapist. The intense eyes, the magicianlike brooding quality, his evocative waiting for the emergence of the special magic (the symbolic transformation), his occasional oracular, inspired style of speaking—all have been important ingredients in the quality of the therapeutic relationship. This quality has led Mary to an uncanny sense of him when she is away and has participated in forming the picture of the Old Testament prophet she had had in her dream.

Although Dr. M.'s concrete presence has been importantly influential in the co-constitution of these images, ideas, and symbols, in specific Jungian style this area of co-constitution is disregarded as insignificant. The image of Dr. M. as priest, prophet, or king is interpreted as belonging primarily to Mary's collective unconscious, and she is referred to an Old Testament expression. In the conventional everyday sense it is obvious to Mary that this experience of Dr. M. is an exaggeration; thus, she is willing to locate the source of this estimate as a projection arising from her unconscious need for a king or prophet. However, beyond the actual characteristics of Dr. M. that are expressed in Mary's so-called projection, the very basic-collective form of it is also an important part of Dr. M.'s self-understanding. He sees himself as living out of a tradition of wise spiritual guides, priests, wise men, and wise kings. His participation in this order of being humanly spiritual is co-creative of the way in which his patient dreams of him. He lives out his life as therapist in a priestly way. The god he serves is the god within; for him the objective collective psyche is the real source of every religious faith.

He is, therefore, a disciple of the One True God and a servant of this God; to help others to conform to the will of his god is his work. Hence, Mary's experience of him as priest-king belongs to his own deepest experience of himself and is not only from within her. He has participated in the constitution of himself as wise guide, spiritual leader, and kingly prophet, and Mary has been receptive to this in her dream image of him—that is, she has imagined him as he symbolically and really is. This is obscured theoretically by the Jungian reduction of her fantasy to a projection arising out of the collective unconscious.

## THE HUMANE PRESENCE OF THE THERAPIST

The actual relationship between therapist and patient is the fundamental ground for the efficacy of orthodox psychoanalysis. The phenomenon of transference is therapeutically fruitful specifically because of the actual understanding, liking, warmth, and respect given between them. Analytic insights become helpful, therapeutic, and liberating only to the degree to which they open to the patient an affirmable world in which to live. Analytic truth in itself is seen to be neither constructive nor destructive for personal life.

Only when these analytic truths are intertwined with the personal qualities of a specific analyst as he lives them humanely with his patient can the analysis open a new world for the patient. The explicit truth taught in the formal orientation of the therapy does not alone make a valuable opening for the patient; nor does the neglected truth, or the truth overlooked, alone make the therapy destructive or life-limiting for the patient. In order to understand the therapeutic process, it is necessary to attend to its actual existential order. A therapist lives his orientation as a therapist within a larger horizon of cultural and human values of which he may not speak and may not even explicitly know. It is his personal qualities—of patience, understanding, reasonableness, intuitive facility, warmth—as he lives them out with his patient that are fundamental ground for the helpfulness of his truths.

The therapist's humane presence is also the fundamental ground for opening the patient into new or more ample life-modes. Explicitly and thematically, Jungian therapy develops toward articulating the mythic structures of the unconscious life, with particular emphasis on its collective or universal aspects. Thus, the patient's dream life, his developing artistic expressivity, the growth of his undeveloped functions, the emergence of images from the inner mythic powers of his personality—these are the explicit focis of the therapy. In Jungian therapy, there is a degree of participation between therapist and patient which can disclose thematically the crucial significance of the concrete existential situation between. The active, supportive presence, encouragement, and teaching, and the degree to which the reverential, religious attitude is directly inculcated makes it easier to bring descriptively to life the concrete presence of the therapist as transformative person in the patient's life.

The Jungian therapist does not move in pseudo anonymity. He faces the patient, encourages, exhorts, teaches, leads, guides, and explicitly fosters an in-dwelling, brooding self-presence. All of these modes of sharing his world with his patient and encouraging him to enter into that world are, as it were, *grounded* on a life-world basis. Each encouragement or speaking of the therapist means much more than it explicitly says.

For example, when in the early interviews the therapist spoke rather casually and yet intensely about Mary's one-sided self-development, there was contained an implicit horizon of meanings that were not directly stated. Dr. M. was affirming that Mary could grow and develop in the ways that she had not yet done. He was stating that he liked her, that he looked forward to spending more time with her in an interesting and fruitful enterprise, and he was also affirming her dissatisfaction as appropriate to her life (not reducing it to a craziness or to a mere lack of sexual fulfillment). He was affirming himself as warmly, intelligently, optimistically anticipating Mary's valuable self-growth, and he was confirming Mary as attractive, fun to be with, and worthwhile.

These horizons of meaning were not unconscious in the usual sense of that term, but they were primarily lived-meanings given in the interaction between Mary and Dr. M. As lived-meanings, they provided the life-ground of the speaking between them. But this life-ground, which made it possible for Mary not to feel insulted, denigrated, or put down by an explicit noting of her inferiorities, is not characteristically thematic. It is *ground* in the double sense of unnoticed, not focalized, and also in the sense of providing moving space for both therapist and patient.

These actual lived horizons of meaning which ground and give living space for both Dr. M. and Mary are not their personal inventions, nor are they to be found in the archetypes of the collective unconscious. Rather the possibility of speaking fruitfully to each other in a Jungian style finds its *value* ground in the fact that Dr. M. and Mary participate in a cultural situation which they had shared in common even before they had met. Already access is guaranteed as possible by virtue of their common Christian heritage. There is an already given-ground for their speaking to each other in their common language, their common beliefs, their common sense of the value of the individual, in the fact that both assume a behind-the-scenes unconscious, in their common implicit rationalism and scientism (their twentieth-century heritage which makes belief in angels and demons difficult but belief in an unconscious easy).

When in an uncondemning, warm, intense, interested way Dr. M. looks Mary in the face and speaks directly to her of her undevelopedness, they both understand the situation perfectly in a life-sense. The personal qualities of noncondemnation, warmth, intensity, and interest are already given culturally as positively valuable. They are *good* qualities that invite and attract the other person. Undevelopedness, as an idea, a word, a culturally given self-understood phrase, also refers to a horizon of pregiven, preestablished values. It is better to develop than not to develop one's talents; it is better to be richly endowed than poorly endowed; it is very important that each individual have the opportunity to develop his whole self. None of these values need explicit discussion, proof, or defense.

In a democratic society and culture based on Christian values, none of these value affirmations is questionable. The only attack that is *culturally allowable* is one made on the basis of other equally obvious values that may be threatened by such affirmations of the mere individual. It must be understood that this shared, culturally given, common basis or ground is not questionable, not thematic, not arguable precisely because it is *given* between Mary and Dr. M. They have concrete presence to each other within these values, embraced by these values. As sharers of the same culture, *we* can admire the graceful, full, ample way in which they live out many of these values, although this appreciation is likely to be implicit for us as well.

As onlookers, we may fail to see what it is that we are admiring. Dr. M.'s graceful, convincing, kindly, humane, encouraging presence is, after all, thematically focused around the emergence of the collective unconscious. Our attention can also be too much focused by this clear thematic presence. The unfolding of the inner world of the individual grounded on the collective-universal-objective psyche is fascinating. We too may find outselves entranced believers, and to some degree this is inevitable. To allow ourselves to participate understandingly in the world of humane values lived out within the Jungian perspective is to deliver ourselves momentarily to the spell of that expressive language, that framework of thinking and theory, which can be lived attractively, beautifully, gracefully.

## THE USE OF ACTIVE IMAGINATION

It is evident in both the interpretation of the dream and in the use of painting that Mary and Dr. M. have taken with utmost seriousness the interpreted hints, suggestions, and intuitions that have emerged as guides to life. The conscious attitude of respect and hopeful expectation toward these emerging works of the unconscious are a necessary part of this project. At times, however, in addition to these methods, it is useful to engage in active imagining. Sometimes this is done as an additional method of amplifying or enriching the emerging meanings of the unconscious. Sometimes it is done as a way of bringing the patient through a difficulty with the immediate and active support of the therapist.

Mary has been entering such a difficult area as she moves toward a fuller religious development. Because of her past experience of religion, she fears the possibility of its insanity; further, her own reasonable adaptation to life has always involved a fair degree of ego control, of self-control. The idea of subjecting herself radically to a numinous spiritual power is terrifying.

Thus far in her Jungian therapy, Mary has been willing to moderate the claims of her ego-self in the interests of life enrichment. However, this has not yet involved a radical disruption or recentering of her life. Her life has become richer, more emotional, more grounded in the

typical myths of mankind and therefore more universal and meaningful, but her ego control has not been transformed radically. She still
lives primarily the value of reason. Even the Jungian principle of com-
plementation has been taken up as a principle of moderation and
reasonableness.

As she now moves to a more explicit religious sense of her own
life, she resists. She does not like it, cannot stomach it; she is frightened.
Dr. M. has encouraged her to continue painting and to allow religious
themes to develop in her painting. Mary's response to this is to resist
painting altogether; her work becomes desultory, and her dream life
dries up somewhat. The next natural stage to which her dreams and
painting point, the development of a more ample religious sense, is
blocked in her.

Dr. M. considers this situation carefully. On the one hand, there are
clear indications from the world of both dreams and paintings that
Mary ought ideally to move toward a new synthesis in her psychic
development. At the same time, however, she has resisted this new
development for more than a month. Several times she has said to Dr.
M.: "Look, this is enough. I know I could go further with self-development, but I don't want to. Even when I try to want to, I just get tight,
anxious, and afraid."

Dr. M. knows that the depths of the unconscious life of archetypes
can be genuinely overwhelming to a person. It is not always wise to
dive into the collective unconscious, as a person may develop very
severe temporary or even permanent disturbance. As a result of these
considerations, as well as of his developing tender concern for Mary,
he does not wish to push her. At this point he decides to move toward
the method of active imagination; for in allowing the person to imagine
actively in the actual presence of the therapist, it is possible to know
accurately just what the patient can and cannot take.

Explaining to Mary that he wants to be more immediately present
to her fears, difficulties, and explorations of her unconscious life, he
tells her to lie down on a couch and to place herself imaginatively in
the first religious picture she has painted—the one with the small cross
in it. He reassures her that the will help her, join her in her explorations, and prevent anything from getting out of hand: "We're in no

great hurry. We don't have to dive in and be scared to death. Let's just begin our explorations with this first painting, which you already understand pretty well from our previous discussions and your own meditations on it."

Mary is tense, reminded of her first time on the couch with her former analyst, and she is not sure how to begin. Her therapist says, "Just start where you are in the painting. Tell me how you are with the painting now." Mary describes the painting, stating succinctly that there is a cross in the upper left-hand corner; she warms more to the description of the orange and red glowing mass overlaid by a dark brownish black layer. As she continues, the therapist encourages: "Go into that more! Let yourself down into that. How does that feel to you? What do you see? Are you alone?" His serious attentiveness to the emerging images, feelings, thoughts, and doubts underlines and helps substantialize this world of the imagination.

Together, Dr. M. and Mary are giving credence to this developing imaginative fantasy. She now goes deep into the earth, entranced by the brilliant efflorescence of her own imagination. Her thematizing consciousness has forgotten that she is on an imaginative religious quest. Hence, she is startled to find two splendidly carved oak doors (like great church doors) in her fantasy, with strange hieroglyphs on them. She is standing before them, uncertain what to do. There is a muttering noise inside as of a group of persons chanting some strange, unintelligible gibberish.

She stands transfixed before the doors, which seem to become darker and heavier; she is moving toward stark terror and paralysis; her breathing becomes shallower. Just before she is about to open her eyes to break out of the imaginative trance, Dr. M. speaks reassuringly to her of the different possibilities in this situation. "Perhaps we might join the worshippers; or perhaps we could enter to watch their rites as onlookers. Let's go through the doors and see what happens. We can always leave again if we have to."

Continuing in the active imagining, Mary enters the doorway and finds darkness inside. What had sounded like chanting through the doors now sounds like the gibbering of rodents. Ahead in the half-light she can dimly see an altar upon which a large rat is eating something;

Mary has an awful feeling that he is eating human flesh. Although this horrifies her, she somehow feels safer than when she stood before the church doors. Dr. M. is a reassuring presence beside her in this darkly ominous room. Rousing her courage, she approaches the altar. As she comes nearer, the rat takes on somewhat human features—half-rodent and half-old man, like a wizened, hunched, priestly dwarf. The look he directs at Mary is an invitation to join him in a sacrificial feast. When Mary demurs, he raises his hands first to heaven, then over the sacrifice on the altar, and finally over Mary's head. Feeling a sense of peace and quiet, Mary opens her eyes. Dr. M. terminates the interview a moment later saying: "Write it all out; meditate on this experience, and see if you aren't more relaxed, more able to paint again. Next time we'll talk about it."

## THE TRANSFORMATION OF MARY'S LIFE-WORLD

Mary and Dr. M. continue to employ active imagination, the use of which had come for Mary at a crucial moment in her development. She had already moderated her rationality and tight grip on the world and come to a richer inner horizon of meanings beyond mere technique or reason. But all of this had been done under the guise of moderation and reasonableness and the development of a superior adaptation in life. The deepest archetypes of the collective unconscious, those having to do with the fundamental unification of the personality on an irrational basis, are not moderate, pragmatic, or reasonable, however, but live out their lives in images of sacrifice, crucifixion, dark gods of the earth, and bright gods of the sky. They are obviously useless, unreasonable, even crazy and dangerous to the enlightened consciousness of rational Western man.

This enlightened consciousness was at the root of Mary's deficiency and is also at the root of the general deficiency of Western man. Mary's belief in the powers of rational technique had led her to leave in darkness and unrealization the most fundamental, universal meanings of being human. Now she comes to them for the first time through the progressively enriching mythic imagery of dreams and painting, grounded now in the great religious traditions. She now knows herself to be a servant of the 'god-within,' beyond any mere evanescent whim or mood, thought or project of the moment; there is for her an abiding sense of underlying unity with the whole of mankind and with the 'god-within-us-all.' She has found a deep peacefulness, which allows her to relax and savor the religious imagery evolving in her.

Others, too, notice the change in Mary. She speaks more slowly, moves somewhat more slowly, and is in a fairly obvious way more peaceful and relaxed. As she herself would insist, she has not attained nirvana; there remain moments of anxiety and tension. Sometimes the old machinelike, busy, rushing, pragmatic ego-self returns with its essential disquiet and unease. As she expresses it, borrowing from the spiritual writers:

"It is true that there are anxious moments in my life, but they are like waves or the churning of water on the surface of the ocean. In my deepest self there is a sense of peace and harmony, the quietude of the depths. I have a basic sense of at-oneness or harmony with all that is, including even pain, strife, difficulty, anxiety. I am like a bubble in the flow of bubbles that come out of the pitcher of the Great One, like a ray of light from the candle, like a traveler on a great wide way. And it is fitting that it should be so. I am aware, in a background way, all the time of this being at one with Being, this sense of being a part of a much larger, wider consciousness, and yet it is also mine and irreplaceable."

After her breakthrough to a religious consciousness, Mary's therapy sessions lessen in frequency. First she is meeting twice a month, then once a month. At this point she and her therapist are likely to be discussing Mary's patients or religion. It is hardly therapy at all, and so they terminate the formal arrangement.

## BIBLIOGRAPHY

Jung, C. G. *Memories, Dreams, Reflections.* New York: Random House, Vintage Books, 1961.

A fascinating autobiographical account of Jung's own religious search and its relation to the work of psychotherapy.

_____. *The Practice of Psychotherapy.* Bollingen Series 20. New York: Pantheon Books, 1954.

In "The Practical Use of Dream-Analysis," Jung describes the peculiar clarity and significance of the initial dream in therapy, a description used by the author of the present text in articulating Mary's first dream.

Van den Berg, J. H. *Different Existence.* Pittsburgh: Duquesne University Press, 1972.

According to Van den Berg, the patient enters into his therapist's world because their coming closer is relief from alienation and loneliness. By entering into discourse with another, the patient is saved from his fundamental isolationism—i.e., his neurosis.

# 8

# Client-centered view of the client

## BACKGROUND

Within the orientation of client-centered theory, as expressed by its founder and chief exponent, Carl Rogers, the client is a client because of tension or anxiety. This tension exists because he has been denying important aspects or areas of his experience to focal awareness. In agreement with Freud and Jung, the client-centered approach sees the patient as fundamentally split by the denial of significant realms of experience to conscious awareness.

The client's self-image is contradicted by his life experience; thus, he has constantly to minimize, overlook, deny, or distort this experience. Two levels of self-being are thereby constituted: one involving the conceptualized, allowable, or somewhat idealized self; the other touching on, and flowing from, the actual experience of self-in-process. Because he is determined to defend his self-concept, to maintain self-consistency, and to actualize himself as he understands himself, the client is unable to admit into clear awareness those experiences that would interfere with his sense of self-worth.

This is in clear accord with both Jung's and Freud's view of their patients. Jung states that the neurotic tends to stress the well-adapted, developed aspects of his personality and to repress the darker, inferior side. Freud sees the neurotic as inclined to maintain ego pride against the primitive, impulsive side of his personality, leading to a denial of the animal side. All three theorists fundamentally agree that the neurotic person posits a truncated, partial, fragmentary version of himself while denying the larger truth of his personality.

## FUNDAMENTAL CONCEPTION OF NEUROTIC DEVELOPMENT

In order to understand how a man can deny his own experience, it is necessary to view the fundamental structure of human motivation as Rogers understood it. Every person strives to maintain and enhance his total self, to satisfy partial needs (such as hunger and sex), and also to actualize his potentialities for fruitful contact with reality. This fundamental striving for self-fulfillment, which is seen as the most basic level of striving of all living creatures, is given an absolute, metaphysical, or religious quality within client-centered formulations of reality. The *really real* is seen to be this underlying striving, which is sometimes called "organismic striving."

In the case of human beings, however, an interesting and difficult complication arises in the unfolding of the self—namely, the fact that people are needed for the fulfillment and enhancement of the organism's self-fulfillment project. Other people enter most powerfully in the form of the person's inherent need for love, tenderness, and positive self-regard and in the possibilities they have for withholding love. Parents, among others, do not experience a child as equally lovable at all times. Therefore, the deep striving for love and regard on the part of the individual contains a basic weakness, a ready possibility for him to learn to distort, deny, overlook, and falsify his experience. For example, some things that a child does gladly and enjoys doing encounter strong disapproval and a withdrawal of love—indeed, even hostility and dislike. A young child who fulfills himself by knocking his baby brother on the head is unlikely to win his parents' approval. Consequently, his need to be liked and approved collides with his self-expressive need.

Here, then, is the groundwork for a transformation of the personality, the creation of a possible split in the person. Certain aspects of his person, experience, motivations, and environment may begin to be experienced as bad or unworthy. The young child is not able to distinguish sharply that it is his mother's anger that he wishes to avoid; rather, the feeling, thought, or action becomes bad and unworthy. To be the kind of person who would have such an impulse or idea becomes inconsistent with being cared for or likable. "Only when I am polite, kind, gentle, warm, loving, affectionate, well-behaved, neat, and clean am I a worthwhile, tolerable person"; or, "Only when I am weak, submissive, stupid, and agreeable." These "conditions of worth" participate in the construction of a highly pruned, truncated concept of self, which the person now maintains as consistently as he can. After the intervention of those parental taboos, certain significant areas of his personality and situation are neither perceivable nor accurately symbolizable in his consciousness. Thus, an inner contradiction exists within the personality.

The inability to symbolize, become aware, or experience accurately are used synonymously in the client-centered conception. The client is unable to focus on, see clearly, speak out, express in clear language, fully imagine, or otherwise incarnate the now taboo regions of his existence. It may be that very intense experiences must be denied to awareness—hot rage, a tender need to get close to others, sexual strivings, and so on. The tension or contradiction between the worthwhile 'self-I-must-be' and the 'self-I-experience' often becomes very intense and anxious and may lead to heightened vulnerability, unease, and a vigilant carefulness in relationships with the world. The split in the person is maintained only with great effort, as the self-image is more or less constantly threatened by ongoing experiential life. At any moment a flash of anger, a strong reaction to frustration, a dream, or an idea of a violent act may threaten to undo the version of myself that I allow myself. Built into the structure of the neurotic's split existence is a continuing lived-contradiction between the flow of experience and the self that must be maintained.

## THE THEORY OF NEUROSIS

Client-centered theory gives only an abstract, highly schematic description of development and personality. Unlike Freudian and Jungian theory, it does not specify with great detail the characteristics of the intrapsychic life or the stages of development; it does not relate the person's development to the prehistory of the human race, to his genetics, his constitutional type, the vicissitudes of his early life experience, or the experiences within specific organ modes of mouth, ear, anus, or phallus.

Rogerian theory is firmly rooted in a clear, simple, democratic sense of what is usefully therapeutic, liberating, warming, helping behavior in psychotherapy. The theory surrounding "conditions of worth" is minimal; there is no theoretical development of an intrapsychic agency called "superego" as in Freud's thought, nor is there an imaginative sketch of man's early tribal life as explanation and account of man's moral conscience. Rogers remains descriptively with the client, and his theory is closely tied to the events that occur when a kindly, understanding, tolerant, not very theoretically or speculatively inclined therapist meets with a client.

Rogers' theory of neurosis begins and ends with the client as he presents himself. The typical client entering therapy begins the interviews with comments relating to his "conditions of worth." He says things like: "I haven't been able to study recently, and I ought to be able to"; or, "I don't get along too well with people of the opposite sex"; or, "I am terribly shy." Any therapist who is not swept away into the client's problems can sense from the client's urgency that these conditions that he finds true of himself are terrible, intolerable, or otherwise indications of dreadful failure or inadequacy.

One might begin by asking, for example: "What's this all about? Lots of people are shy or have difficulty studying." The client will usually tell you without delay how absolutely essential it is for him to be better than he is if he is to be any good at all. If he does not study superlatively well, in discouragement he ceases to study; if he is not intensely attractive to the opposite sex, he retires from the fray. From the average client you hear early in the first interview a series of injunctions, prohibitions, commands, and musts which, if not obeyed, lead to self-deprecation and a loss of sense of worth. The typical client is clearly enmeshed in, discouraged and defeated, and ultimately prevented from attending to his own actual wants and inclinations by, a set of rules that detail how he *must* and *ought* to be.

Client-centered theory remains in a fairly commonsense way quite close to the phenomenon which the client presents. But this descriptive closeness is highly general and schematic and does not detail the ways in which the body posture blocks the clear experiencing and symbolizing of experience. Descriptions of the way in which grinding molars and a stiff neck serve the project of withholding the clear experiencing of anger, or elaborations on the way in which holding still, "playing possum," or freezing the body into a disdainful posture as ways of maintaining neurotic defensiveness, are not parts of client-centered theory. Client-centered theory is simply a theory of therapy events in which elaborate descriptions of defensive modes, speculative descriptions of mankind's prehistory, discussions of intra-psychic life, and elaborate descriptions of interpersonal communication have little place.

## THE THEORY OF VALUES AND VALUATIONAL PROCESSES

Implicit in the description of neurotic development as seen from the client-centered perspective is a theory of values that posits two principles of valuation, of determining the goodness or badness of things. The first principle is inherent in the organismic structure of the human being, and the second one is artificial, the result of interference from the culture on the unfolding of the child-man. This theory is rooted in the observable way in which clients arbitrarily and self-destructively impose value demands on themselves which are not in accord with their real possibilities.

The client typically demands of himself performances, characteristics, virtues, strengths, talents, and attributes that are totally out of keeping with his actual self and possibilities. The down-to-earth pragmatist is striving to be a speculative intellectual. The quiet meditative client insists on being a happy-go-lucky social extrovert. The sour, dry type wants to be sweetness and light. Hence, the client is obviously valuing in an "unnatural," "artificial," "false," or "introjected" way. He has adopted these values from others, seeking their approval, regard, and love. But in taking on these values as if they belong to himself, he is basically mistaken because they are not outgrowths of his own experience. In fact, in pursuit of these false values the client typically tightens and falsifies himself, dulls his contact with reality, becomes defensive, anxious, and is generally crippled.

He pursues an ideal image of himself which at the same time he cannot genuinely like or affirm as belonging to him, because it really does *not* belong to him. The more natural level of valuing—the feeling-sensing level given organismically—continues to operate in spite of all his distortions. He continues to respond positively to what he really likes and values and negatively to what he really dislikes and does not. But the natural response is blurred, obscured, even unconscious to him to the degree to which it is forbidden by the conditions of worth to which he holds himself.

The neurotic human being who comes into therapy has two processes going on that fundamentally contradict each other. There is the real valuing process, a fluid process of evaluation given to the person sensorially and feelingly as the ground of his fundamental organismic valuing. This is given in such simple expressions as: "This tastes good," "This feels good," "I like to do this," "I feel better when I do this," "I enjoy this very much," "I don't like to do that," "That feels unpleasant to me," "I don't enjoy that," and so on. When this process of natural-feeling valuation is not interfered with by elaborate conditions of worth, negative injunctions, and taboos, a complex feeling-sensing experience serves as the fundamental guide to values in the person's life.

However, this natural flow is confused by the valuing processes taken over from other people. "I like to be loud and boisterous," given naturally in the young active child, is replaced by the false value, "I only like quiet, calm, and order." "I like to walk in the rain, squish my feet in the mud, run wild and free" is replaced by, "Decorum, polite talk, and solemnity appeal to me as really adult virtues." The skilled client-centered therapist will help the client to get in touch with and develop that *feeling-sense* of life. The therapy must be directed toward fostering that natural, organismic, valuing sense postulated by the theory.

## BIBLIOGRAPHY

Rogers, C. R. *Client-centered Therapy: Its Current Practice, Implications, and Theory.* Boston: Houghton Mifflin, 1951.

The basic text of client-centered theory and practice and one of the primary sources for the Rogerian view of neurosis. Chapter 11 develops a theory of personality, of neurosis, and of therapy.

————. "A Theory of Therapy, Personality, and Interpersonal Relations as Developed in a Client-centered Framework." In *Psychology: A Study of a Science. Formulations of the Personal and the Social Context*, vol. 3. Edited by S. Koch. New York: McGraw-Hill, 1959.

A somewhat more scientifically formulated statement of client-centered theory, with some additions to the view of neurosis.

# 9

# Client-centered therapy

## BACKGROUND

The basic problem with the neurotic client who comes to therapy is that he has departed from his own values by taking on the values of others. Therefore, the client-centered therapist, especially, does not wish to impose his own values on the person. Rogers first introduced his view of therapy as "nondirective" out of a tradition of democratic humanism and Protestant individualism. He wanted to move away from any notion of therapist authority or priority of vision. It is not the therapist's theories, values, opinions, or feelings that count; rather, the center of the therapeutic process must reside in the client. Those approaches to psychotherapy which assign the priority of interpretation, understanding, value, and wisdom to the therapist fail to appreciate the individual's powers to shape his own destiny or to think his own thoughts. From the client-centered viewpoint, these traditional approaches are coercive, manipulative, authoritarian, and inefficient.

177

Client-centered thought arose within the context of two major traditions of therapeutic-counseling help but has distinguished itself from both. Within the traditions of both guidance counseling and the psychoanalytic therapies there is an extensive gathering of information from the patient and an assumption that the therapist is superior to the patient in knowledge, understanding, and wisdom. In these traditional therapies, in Rogers' view, the counselor-therapist tries to replace the client's will, thought, and feeling with his own superior will, thought, and feeling. From the beginning, however, Rogers had been greatly impressed by the exquisite rationality of what individuals do. Everyone, in his view, responds to "the world as he perceives it." The client is therefore seen as fundamentally making sense. It is only from an external point of view that his behavior is seen as irrational, stupid, or neurotic. From his own viewpoint, his behavior is finely attuned to his way of experiencing the world, and it is toward this internal experiential world that the client-centered therapist wishes to move in understanding his client.

It is true that the disturbed person does not allow himself to experience fully because he is afraid of appearing worthless to himself and others; but this is a perfectly reasonable, understandable response in the light of his training. His parents, teachers, peers, and other authorities all *told* him (from his point of view) that to feel his feelings was bad. He was instructed to hide his real feelings from others or to incur loss of respect and approval. It is therefore appropriate and fundamentally rational that he should feel and think that many of his experiences should be avoided and disowned.

The client has not arbitrarily and unreasonably developed his inhibitions, blocks, amnesias, or his inability to symbolize important areas of his experience clearly. He has disowned and blotted out those experiences which in his view would have led to the greatest disgrace, hatred, and trouble from others. Hence, the client who comes to a therapist because of intense social shyness, who complains that he can't raise his hand in class, can't initiate a conversation, who is always hanging back, afraid of censure, is not behaving irrationally. Only if one fails to understand his internal frame of reference will his behavior appear stupid or senseless.

This shy client was *called* stupid by his parents because he was not telling coherent stories when he was five years old (as almost no child can). The youngest child in the family, he was overawed by the fact that he was the youngest, dumbest, least articulate, and least socially skilled. His brothers and sisters called him "silly-baby." He was taught, and really believed, that children should be seen and not heard. Thus, when he hangs back from participating in class he has genuine reason to believe in his ineptitude: the fear he feels, which he himself may label foolish, is understandable in the light of his internal frame of reference. His idea that others will mock or attack him if he attempts to be competent and successful is firmly rooted in his experience. He therefore tries not to stand out, and he remains shy, backward, and awkward because that is the only permissible mode of being he has available.

It is noteworthy in this description that the client himself has been the source of understanding; he, *from his own point of view,* can gradually articulate the sense and meaning of his difficulties. Hence, there is no need for an elaborate developmental theory or complex theory of neurosis for an effective understanding of the client. The client can be helped to explain himself, to give an account of his own world, and it is *his* account, *his* description, *his* developing consciousness, and *his* expression of feeling that will make most ample sense of his life.

## NONDIRECTIVENESS

If the client's problems are rooted in the adoption of values from others and if he makes the best sense from his own internal frame of reference, many activities that are found in the Freudian, Jungian, and other approaches to therapy are unnecessary. Essentially, all forms of guidance and expert interpretation are grounded in the belief that knowledge, understanding, and wisdom reside in a frame of reference and experience *external* to the client's experiential world. It is a basic contention of the client-centered view, however, that the client makes sense within his own experiential world. Factually, this *is* the world in which he lives, and whatever development that world needs can most reasonably be provided from within that world rather than from judgments provided from outside.

The argument against expert interpretation and guidance is strengthened by the fact that the client's basic problems arose in the first place from his taking in the ideas, values, and feelings of others as if they were his own. To replace these with a new set of authoritative dictates, however justified, is only to continue the client in the fundamental self-alienation which is the core of his difficulty. Thus, every authoritatively based approach to therapy is seen to constitute a new self-alienation and, in that sense, a new neurosis. After such an authoritative therapy, the client will live out the values of his therapist as if they were his own. This cures the disease with a new disease.

The client-centered therapist therefore refrains from advising, directing, manipulating, or theoretically interpreting the client. The teaching of any characteristic set of interpretations is seen as distracting the client from his own internal frame of reference. At best, this is beside the point; at worst, it can prevent him from developing and clarifying his interior sense of himself. That the client should grow toward *himself*, not toward Freud, Jung, or Rogers, is the fundamental understanding of nondirectiveness. To advise him how to behave, what to do, what to think, or how to act is a violation of the priority of his own phenomenal world. It is the client, on the basis of his own self-understanding and a growing sense of his own values, who must decide. He must be brought back to himself and his own feelings.

The term "nondirective" is no longer used by Rogers and his co-workers because it conveys the false impression that the therapist is in some way passive or out of play in the therapeutic relationship. The therapist is not out of play but is totally given over to the task of under-standing the client by reaching to grasp his internal frame of reference, his interiority, the way the world appears and feels to him. The therapist places himself at the service of this understanding and lays aside his self of ordinary everyday interaction. He formally, officially, and purposefully lives out a purified consciousness and activity in which every thought, feeling, and perception is focused on the task of em-pathically understanding the client.

## Recent modifications

The literature of client-centered psychotherapy has always reflected a certain tension between understanding and self-expression on the part of the therapist. The therapist's specialized task to make himself an understanding, empathic presence to the client is a full-time occupation that leaves little space for free response. He is advised not to interpret, advise, press judgments, or allow his own feelings into play but to attune himself exclusively to expressing the client's feelings. His ordinary social self is to be left outside the therapy room. To be sensitively attuned to the client's feeling-life can only be achieved if other responses are "bracketed" or put out of play.

At the same time, however, Rogers has been sensitive to the vital importance of honest, full, congruent self-expression from the therapist. It is not the semblance of understanding and positive regard that cures but their vividly lived-reality as expressed by the therapist to the client. If the therapist is only willing to give understanding, empathic responses, he is living out an ideal rather than his own full-blooded reality. The client himself suffers from such ideal values, which forbid him to express himself directly and honestly; it is clearly bad therapy if the therapist lives out his own version of a narrowed ideal responsiveness.

Imagine, for example, a client who is afraid to be aggressive because "nice boys don't act like that" (a false value adopted from his parents). His therapist might get fed up with all that "butter-wouldn't-melt-in-his-mouth" business but is afraid to express his irritation and impatience because this would not be an understanding response. By suppressing his own aggressive response because he regards it as unworthy, he is living out the same neurotic dilemma as his client. That is, both live out of inhibiting conditions of worth and reinforce each other's inability to be directly and congruently expressive.

In the days when client-centered therapy was still called "nondirective," both the technique and spirit of the enterprise forbade the insertion of the person of the therapist. The technique was powerfully tied to the client's exact words; the therapist was to keep himself out and just become the understander of the other. Later, however, the mode and style of the therapist's attunement became of interest. He was encouraged to allow his intuition, sensitivity, and rich metaphorical expressivity to flow into his responses and hence to bring an enlivening richness to the therapy. The question of how richly expressive the therapist was, was seen as important to the client's "level of experiencing." During this same period, there was a sharp shift away from stressing the technique of "reflection of feeling" and an increasing emphasis on the attitude and fundamental philosophy of the therapist. Whole sections of Rogers' *Client-centered Therapy* are devoted to the therapist's attitude, an emphasis much less in evidence in his earlier work, *Counseling and Psychotherapy*.

During the 1960s and 1970s, the therapist's ability to express his own feelings has assumed increasing importance. In this respect, client-centered therapy has moved somewhat closer to Gestalt and encounter modes of therapy, coinciding with an increased emphasis on group therapy.

## THE VALUE STANCE OF THE THERAPIST

For the therapist, living out of the naturally given organismic-self is the basic goal of therapy and of the good life as well. He sees this organismic-self as the actual underlying reality of every human being. In his eyes, the client is always primarily expressing a level of experiencing which refers to his real strivings to actualize his real self. The therapist has faith in the person's capacity to grow given the proper noninterfering conditions, and he lives out this faith in his peculiarly refined attunement to the life of feelings, which he sees as the quintessence of the real self.

The *really natural self*, the organismic-self, is a fluid-like ground for a firmly realistic valuing process based on a naturally given life of feeling-valuing. This valuing process is understood to move toward goodwill, positive regard, understanding, love, and fellow-feeling, and these organic values (written, as it were, on the person's heart) emerge naturally out of the person. They do not have to be taught or explicitly fostered; they emerge of themselves out of the natural pregiven matrix of the personality.

These powerful presuppositions about man's fundamental nature and their implications for treatment comprise the basic groundwork for the practice of client-centered therapy. A therapist with such a vision and faith is, if he knows how to live out that conviction convincingly for others, potentially a power to transform lives. It is precisely the convincingness of these particular beliefs and their concrete application in the client's life that constitute the unique client-centered approach, which is the living out of a belief in the organismic, real feeling-self of the other.

This way of thinking about man is not a speculative theory to be understood or evaluated on its intellectual or scientific credentials. From the analysis of the Freudian and Jungian modes, it is clear that those modes of therapy incarnate specific human values. Client-centered therapy has less theoretical pretensions than these; primarily it should be understood as a specific way of respecting the other while understanding him at the same time. Client-centered therapy, then, is a stance grounded in certain fundamental convictions. Just as Freudian and Jungian therapists make their understandings and values convincing in the lives of their patients, so the client-centered therapist has developed a way to make his views convincing and transforming of his client's lives.

## The therapist's "objectivity"
Each psychotherapy orientation claims a certain objectivity for its approach. The psychoanalytic orientation claims that the patient's life can be understood as a repetition of early patterns of gratification and blockages. The Jungian approach grapples primarily with the patient's universal symbolic themes and archetypal motifs and strives to balance his one-sided development. In psychoanalysis, the analyst himself undergoes considerable analysis in the hope of purifying the neurotic and merely subjectivistic factors in his interpretations and interventions in therapy. He strives to remove his own blocks and to become an accurate attunement to the patient's underlying unconscious dynamisms, hoping in this way to become an objective, accurate interpreter.

Jungian therapy emphasizes that the particular therapist and patient catalyze the patient's unconscious processes in specific ways; as guide to the underworld, however, the therapist can only guide in ways that he knows and has tracked himself. It therefore behooves him to know well the great symbolic and transformation literature of the world to guide his patient aright. Within the Jungian schema, accuracy or objectivity is a twofold project. To intervene rightly means to aim carefully at the particular person present before the therapist and also to aim rightly at his particular stage of development with its problems and difficulties. In this sense, objectivity means aiming exactly at the patient who is there with the therapist as well as relating the particularities of that presence to the universal archetypes and collective unconscious—the objective mind, as it were—from which this particular patient is understood to be emerging.

Client-centered therapy, however, assumes the 'underlying-natural-giveness' of the organismic-self in such a way that the therapist's presence as transformative power is understood neutrally as "providing an atmosphere" and "not interfering with the natural unfolding." A phenomenological understanding of interaction is grounded on the insight that we 'make-each-other-be' and is, in this respect, at odds with a client-centered understanding of psychotherapy. In fact, phenomenological psychology varies from all traditional orientations insofar as these imagine that the patient's real being is untouched by the therapist's being. The therapist imagines that he discovers what is *actually there in the patient* in the same way as a physicist discovers the hardness of rocks and a chemist the $H_2O$ quality of water.

As phenomenological description suspends belief in "organismic-selves" or "natural unfolding," it notes that the therapist's belief in such a complex ideology is an important factor in making a certain kind of relationship possible. It is a rather extraordinary possibility for 'being-with-others' that emerges when one consistently treats the other as having a real, underlying organismic-self. For a genuine analysis of client-centered therapy, the power of this way of treating the other in reference to his organismic-self must be clarified.

The classic client-centered response is "you really feel," which is not mere technique but the counselor's fundamental stance, attitude, and orientation. The task of client-centered therapy as a whole is to bring the client more in touch with that sensing-feeling self, the organismic-self, in order that he will come to his true, underlying, fundamental valuational and self-process. The therapist's formal project is to understand the client's sensed-feelings empathically and to communicate this understanding to him. He must grasp the client's world in such a way that the client experiences himself as being understood. To understand the feeling-world of the other accurately and without distortion is the fundamental objectivity of the client-centered therapist.

## THE GENERAL PROCESS OF THERAPY

Thus far in the analysis of client-centered therapy, the primary focus has been on the therapist's project, theory, and attitudes. This is appropriate because client-centeredness is borne on the therapist's shoulders. At the same time, however, it is crucial to articulate the situation of the client-patient as he enters into therapy. The client is distressed and realizes that his distress has something to do with how he deals with the world. He knows that there is some deficiency in his ways of coping, of relating to himself and others, or in his conception of reality. This deficiency, however vaguely formulated, interferes with his living his life adequately. He therefore arrives at the therapist's as a cripple, in the special sense that he has lost or never attained the knack for living his life.

He hopes that through the intervention of a "special other," a "skilled helper," a "healer," "magician," or "wise man," he will regain or attain this knack, and this particular situation is an essential condition of formal psychotherapy. It is invented by neither the client-patient nor the therapist but is culturally-situationally constituted by the fact that a client-patient goes to see a therapist.

On the client's side, this hopeful turning to the therapist lends considerable power to the therapeutic relationship. The therapist is already seen as a "special other." Whatever other specific expectations the client may have, the hoped-for transformative power of the relationship is a given. Turning to a therapeutic relationship means that the readily available, everyday normal sources of learning are already exhausted or inadequate. In the face of this inadequacy, everything that occurs in therapy is experienced by the client within this horizon of hope for 'finding-the-way-which-has-been-blocked.' The therapist is seen as hopefully knowing the way, or in some way having the special gift, to make this transformation possible.

### Focus on the client

In client-centered therapy, both therapist and client typically sit upright in chairs of approximately the same size. While the therapist frequently sits at his desk, he arranges the chairs in such a way that there is no large desk or other obstacle between them; often the two speak over the corner of the desk. In this way a certain equality is respected from the beginning. That the client is invited to remain upright with his feet on the ground contrasts strikingly with orthodox psychoanalysis, in which the patient is instructed to lie down, lose his head, say everything that enters his mind without regard to rationality or sense, take his feet off the ground, and drift into unreality. In addition, there is no elaborate history-taking procedure in the client-centered situation, no psychological testing, and the client is told that whatever is discussed is up to him. Both attention and initiative seemingly belong totally to the client. Questions from the therapist are kept to a minimum and, when asked, are requests for elaboration and clarification rather than an initiation of new directions.

Both client and therapist are implicitly directed to fix their attention on the client. This means that the therapist characteristically looks, listens, and otherwise attends to the client; the client characteristically looks into space or at some object in the room so as to focus on himself. The client, then, is in the spotlight, directed by the total situation and the power of the therapist's steady attentiveness to be conscious of himself. This kind of attention to the client and waiting for his initiative in a steady, planful way (the client-centered strategy) energizes the situation, is an enormously powerful living out of the belief in the organismic-self, and casts the client steadily back upon himself.

This can be seen more clearly if the client-centered strategy is contrasted with a more rationalistic, problem-solving approach to counseling in which the total attention of therapist and client is directed toward the specification and grasping of "problems." Attention to the client would clarify the logic of the problems, but the intensity of focus would be devoted to pinning down the exact nature of the problems and what actions or strategies might help to solve them. In such a situation, client and therapist would equally direct their attention to the problem and notice each other only peripherally. The structure of the client-centered situation is quite the contrary. There is a powerfully induced attentiveness to the client and relatively little direct focus on problems.

This intense degree of focused attention is not just a generalized attention, however. The therapist is to make himself into a highly

refined attunement to the client's "feelings"—not to be neutrally attentive to each and every manifestation of the client's life but to focus
on the life of "sensed-feelings." Cognitions, cogitations, complex
theories or ideas receive little attention from the therapist except insofar as they imply or express the client's feelings. The therapist is explicitly instructed to put aside his ordinary social self in order to
become totally attuned to the other's feelings. Ideally, then, he becomes a "mirror of feeling."

This mirroring of feeling may require considerable effort, discipline,
and talent on the part of the therapist, but he must nonetheless be suf-
ficiently objective that his own individuality is of little importance.
As long as he tunes into and expresses back the client's feeling-life,
this therapist is presumably replaceable by any other therapist who
would do the same. This ideal of objectivity is characteristic of all traditional therapeutic orientations. The therapist is expected to reduce
himself as much as possible to a pure instrumentality for understanding,
empathizing, and expressing the feelings of the other.

## The therapist accepts the client

Client-centered therapy holds that if the client is to come to his own
organismic valuing self, the conditions of worth that he learned when
he adopted the values of others must be unlearned. Hence, the therapist
must not enforce conditions of worth himself. Stated negatively, he
is instructed not to condemn, moralize, judge, or dislike the other on
the grounds of his behaviors, values, or beliefs because teaching conditions of worth to the client would simply institute or maintain the
client's difficulties. It would mean that he is not free to pursue his own
feelings. He already pretends to be less aggressive than he really feels
out of his sense of the terrible unworthiness of feeling really angry.
If the therapist should happen to like and affirm gentleness and to feel
negatively disposed toward anger, and if he directly expressed these
judgments, this would reinforce the patient's neurotic bind and make
the therapist but one more set of eyes before which he must pretend
to be worthy.

As the therapist is, first and foremost, just another member of the
culture, it is likely that directly expressing his preferences and values

to his client would result in his directly reinforcing the client's hesitations, self-doubts, and conditions of worth. Normally the therapist prefers smooth interactions, cordiality, kindness, and liveliness, like everyone else. But these are precisely the conditions that many neurotic clients cannot live up to. The neurotic is angry, irritable, unpleasant, or bogusly pleasant; he finds himself full of unworthy traits and feelings, such as envy, laziness, discouragement, depression, and so on. For the therapist to like his patient better when he lives up to the "good ways" is to encourage precisely the problems from which the neurotic already suffers. To repeat, however, the therapist is also a normal member of his culture and cannot help preferring those positive social values within which he has himself been bred. To instruct him to like, love, or positively regard the client no matter what is to recommend an exercise in well-nigh impossible virtue.

There is a way for the therapist to maintain a positive regard or liking for the client even in the face of culturally distasteful or negative qualities, attributes, behaviors, and characteristics, and this involves being able to "bracket" or temporarily lay aside certain aspects of the world. In the middle of an operation, a surgeon does not concern himself with the quality of his staff relations. The shoemaker does not concern himself with the cultural significance of his work when he is making shoes. Similarly, the psychologist interviewing a patient does not keep in mind his own heritage of religious-ethical values.

Every occupation and specialization involves the development of a focus and a placing on the fringes of realities declared or lived as "unimportant" or "not requiring attention now." Thus, the therapist "puts out of play" his normal social expectations and judgments in order to be genuinely understanding. At certain moments a strong negative or positive valuation of something the client has brought up may call him out of his work, but this is only a temporary interruption of his therapeutic effort.

Like every other specialized intention in the world, however, there are always values that are lived and communicated within the therapeutic intention and focus. The shoemaker works to make good shoes, and he enjoys, affirms, and fosters all the things that express and fulfill that intention. It is not that he brackets out values totally but rather that his specialization is also a concrete embodiment of some few values. That the client-centered therapist affirms the client's organismic-life as good is not a mere therapeutic stratagem but an expression of the client-centered ideology and value system. Within his orientation, the therapist positively values, hovers attentively and lovingly over, the client's feeling-self. This may often involve a reversal of his ordinary cultural values, in that he may, as a therapist, prefer hostile feelings to mild, relatively nonfeeling neutrality, or anger and hatred to nonfeeling. Any clear and forceful expression from the center of the client's feeling-self is affirmed and valued within the client-centered orientation.

The therapist's attitude and orientation is expressed in his responses to the client—in concrete verbal tonalities, warm approving glances, and articulations in specific expressive language. The fundamental response of the client-centered therapist is "you really feel." Before proceeding to an analysis of this response, it must be reemphasized that the specific persons who come together as client and therapist are crucial to the actual ways in which the therapy proceeds. A warm, emotionally expressive, poetic client-centered therapist with a rather matter-of-fact businessman-client constitute a specific therapy between them, which will differ considerably from the therapy that a more matter-of-fact, prosaic therapist will constitute with such a client. A phenomenologically-oriented study may temporarily put aside such specific variances in style, approach, and mood but must never lose sight of the fundamental phenomena which always occur concretely and include many such differences.

## THE THERAPIST SPEAKS

### "You really feel"

To enter into the concrete situation of therapy is to see a therapist transformed into a finely attuned, sensitive understander of feelings looking at and listening to his client. The therapist is devoting his total attention to the client, and the client is expressing himself as fully as he is able. At a certain moment the therapist speaks, and a fundamental entrance into the transformation of client-centered therapy can be achieved by a careful attention to what he says.

Understood phenomenologically, language or speech is a specifically human embodiment of intentions that shape a particular human world. Thus, the therapist's words are crucial. He says *you*. Very often he says this explicitly, but in light of the dedication to understanding the other's feelings within his internal frame of reference the "you" is always implied. The therapist does not say: "That reminds me of . . . ," or "It seems to me that the meaning of that is . . . ," or "The other fellow's viewpoint counts too." Rather, he directs his attention totally to the client and says *you*. The therapist's task is an attunement to, a reflection, amplification, and expression of "you." He wishes to express with purity, fullness, and accuracy the "you" of his client.

At this moment, and as it is repeated in virtually every response of the therapist, this *you* shapes the whole relationship on both sides. On the therapist's side, the *you* expresses his determination not to be side-tracked onto elements of lesser importance to his lived-theory; thus, he is insistent in his focus on the "you" and guards himself against distractions from within and without. "*You* are crucial, not I or my opinions; not your interesting mother of whom you were just speaking, your fascinating uncle with his insight into the complexity of the relationships within your family, the intricacies of the finances you were describing, the behaviors that give you such difficulty, the judgment you were just making, not even the feeling that you were just describing—but rather *you*."

On the client's side, this emphasis on *you* makes everything that he says be pointed back by the therapist to the invisible source from which these statements are seen as coming. The client typically begins the therapy speaking about all sorts of things. He does not start by saying *I* with the kind of underlined emphasis that the therapist gives to the *you*. Rather, he discusses his world as it surrounds him, the externals of his life, the people and things that he experiences as troublesome. He describes the difficulties of his work or his social problems and feelings as if they belonged out there in the world. He offers, in short, a complex panorama of statements which describe his situation, other people in it, behaviors, external objects, and so on, in response to which the therapist uniformly responds *you*.

The fact that a skillful therapist can do this smoothly and unobtrusively may obscure its impact on the client. The client may emphasize that others and the way they treat him cause his difficulties, or he may localize his problems in bad habits, others' attitudes, situations, or his mother's training. But the therapist's *you* transforms the client's experience by sharply and relentlessly redirecting him to the sphere of *self* attitudes and feelings.

## "You *really* feel"

The highly emphasized *you* of the therapist, which gradually becomes the highly emphasized *I* of the client, does not exist in isolation; it is inserted into the total ongoing relationship and dialogue and also into the larger statement, "You *really* . . . ." The therapist is not interested in everything equally. He is interested in that which is real, important, significant, or fundamental. By means of his implicit and explicit use of the word *really* as both adjective and adverb, he announces the "really real" as his primary focus. As adjective, *real* modifies *you*, so that the "really real" is seen to refer to some fundamental layer, aspect, or ground of the "you"—a precise expression of client-centered theory, which holds that the client is one in whom the real self has become distorted, disowned, or hidden through the interventions of false value processes adopted from others.

The therapist is always reaching for and trying to express the client's real self, or as close an approximation of this as he can. This "you" which is "real" is declared by the therapist to be fundamental in virtually his every response. In this way, together with his exquisitely concentrated attention, the therapist concretizes his theoretical lived-faith that the pathway out of the blocked or inadequate life lies in increased contact with the real self. It is obvious that this emphasis on the real adds weight, force, and power to the therapist's impact. The client, a somewhat lost, confused, not too well ordered person, has typically never met anyone with such a powerfully directed focus and lived-belief. As already indicated, the client's position as a failed person hoping to find his way also lends substance to the therapist's power. It is obvious to the client that he is in some way fragmented and at cross-purposes with himself.

The therapist's firm, convincing, and continuing reiteration that the real self is what has been lost and must be found therefore encounters receptive ears. The client can genuinely say, "I don't know myself really," and this is met with the omnipresent therapist's concern with helping him know his real self. It must also be kept in mind that the concentrated attentiveness to his person, concerns, and his feelings is an extraordinary event in the client's life, naturally increasing his sense of substantiality and reality and lending dignity to his self and his concerns.

### "You really *feel*"

In both the theory and practice of client-centered therapy, the "you *really* . . ." is not left as a vague, undefinable spiritual essence. The real self is a feeling-sensing self, and to emphasize this the therapist's every response is "you really *feel*." He reasserts literally thousands of times that the qualification for being a real self is first and foremost to be a feeling-self. The sharp therapeutic directedness and focus that was first noticed in the attention to the client's perceptual world, elaborated in the *you*, then reemphasized in the *really*, is now further articulated and differentiated in the *feel*.

Without the therapist's forceful focus on feeling, the client is as likely to engage in cognitions, thoughts, theories, explanations, and problem solving as he is to focus on situations, others, and externals. The *you* directs him away from externals toward himself; the *feel* directs him away from the cognitive, meditative, thinking, or coolly perceptual aspects of his experience. "You really feel," a constantly repeated thematization, is the one fundamentally approved mode of response within the client-centered orientation. If the client imagines that finding a rational answer to his problems is the right direction for him, in very short order he is redirected by the therapist back to himself and his feelings. Thus, if the therapist is skillfull at responding forcefully and accurately to the client's feeling-flow, the client is powerfully induced to remain focused on his feeling-self.

The therapist continues to assert his highly selective interest in the real and important through the fact that *really* also qualifies *feel*. He is not interested in every faint blush of feeling but wishes to tune in on the patient's most significant or most pervasively real feelings. It is the *real* feelings, those closest to the organismic-self, that constitute the true essence of a human being, and there is implicit here a whole hierarchy of reality to different feelings. Some feelings are mistaken because they are based on the borrowed evaluations of others. Some are responses to conditions of worth and, as such, are presented back to the client to be tested by the organismic experience and found inadequate expressions of the true feelings.

The response "you really feel" can be made in a genuinely skillful way. The therapist may speak the truth of the client's experience far better than he has ever heard it before. "You speak for me, for me really. You speak to me, and when you speak I recognize and come to myself, my real self, so well expressed in your words. You seem to capture the person that I really am in what you say." Thus, coming from a skilled, sensitive, intuitive therapist, the client-centered modes of response are enormously convincing. They express the reality of the feeling-self in a way far superior to what the client could come to unaided. The specialized skill of tuning in on the sense-feeling level is experienced by the client as a focusing on something crucially real. That it is the therapist's initiative that is represented by constituting the feeling-self as central is usually overlooked.

## "I" and "you"

The client's feeling-self, then, is affirmed in therapy as a small self-contained universe isolated from culture, from others, and from the world. Whenever the client-centered therapist says *you*, if he is properly attuned to the client's feeling-life, it is possible to ask "who is it that says *you*?" or "what is the client-centered therapist striving to be?" Because the therapist is formally attuned to the feelings of the other, he strives to obliterate himself except insofar as he is a reflection of the other's feeling-life. Also, the one to whom he is an attunement is in a reduced state. The therapist is regarding the other in a specialized way as feeling-life, organismic-life, as a bodily life of sense-feeling.

On both sides of the therapeutic dialogue, therefore, there is an enormous emphasis on a pathic, bodily, sensing-feeling life, and real communication is understood to exist at that level. Thus, the therapist, putting aside his judgments, opinions, and reactions (at least within his formal project), suffers pathically with the feelings that come from the client. "I suffer in, through, and for the other. By expressing this shared feeling-life as clearly as I can, he comes to experience his own feelings more clearly." This shared pathic involvement means that, sometimes to a lesser degree, the therapist participates at an organic bodily level in the pathos of the client's feeling-life, and to the degree that he has reduced himself to attunement to this organismic bodily life the distinction between his feelings and his client's feelings seemingly disappears.

The therapist may now begin to replace the ubiquitous client-centered *you* with the word *I*. Responding to a client's deeply felt description of his tyrannical, arbitrary, vindictive boss, the therapist may whisper, "I could kill him." Client and therapist alike may now speak in the first person, replacing with "*I* really feel" the "*you* really feel" that has heretofore represented the two sides of the dialogue. The client-centered *I* and *you* have been emphasized throughout the therapy as an organismic bodily-sensing process, and thus both client and therapist can bend themselves to expressing what appears to be a virtually anonymous prepersonal body. Both client and therapist deliver themselves over to the feeling-life surging up within the life of the body and strive to articulate it. Both now express hatred of the father, though in the background one or both of them may realize more or less clearly that this is on the way to some other feeling. They become pathic, resonating bodies striving to express themselves in language.

When, in moments of supreme empathic understanding and communion, the client-centered therapist says *I* for the client, he becomes to an enormous degree an affectively feeling, sensing, organic, bodily, resonative communion with the suffering and feeling flesh of the other. *I* may be expressed in dramatic utterance as well. The therapist may plead for the client: "Mother, mother, I need you," or "It's so damned lonely." In fact, whenever the therapist is powerfully moved by the client's affective life, he speaks the *I* or *you* ambiguously, as both he and the client are involved at the 'communion-of-bodies' level.

A situation was described earlier in which the client experienced his therapist as being more fully expressive of his experience than he was himself. This is a fairly natural state of affairs in client-centered therapy because the therapist is a specialist in this kind of empathic attunement. In the communion of bodies, the therapist feels the client's sense-feeling bodily life more clearly and intensely than the client does himself. Thus, the client may express but the barest hint of sadness to the therapist, who amplifies it back as, "Sounds as if you're feeling pretty forlorn, is that it?" Such amplification and underlining of a mood increases the client's experience of the mood so that he can insert himself more fully into it.

## The therapist speaks for himself

Early client-centered literature struggled to distinguish itself from the more authoritarian and activistic approaches of traditional counseling-therapy. During the period when client-centered therapy was still called "nondirective," the therapist was urged to speak strictly for the client, in the virtual words of the client, and to keep his own ideas, opinions, feelings, interpretations, and judgments out of it. Later, especially in the 1960s and 1970s when group work became more central, the idea gained ground that the therapist should speak his own feelings honestly. This has not meant an abdication but rather an enrichment of understanding-speaking and resonant attunement to the client's world of feeling.

The therapist who says *I* is therefore sometimes speaking for himself. He may say (though this is still not the average response of a client-centered therapist): "I feel very much annoyed by the way you're attacking that person"; "I feel deeply moved and saddened"; or "I really do care for you." In these moments he speaks for himself, out of his own feelings, and this slipping away from pure understanding toward sharing his feelings with the client is perfectly consistent with the basic thrust of client-centered thought and practice.

From the beginning, and with increasing emphasis as time has passed, Rogers has stressed the centrality of sincerity, honesty, and genuineness in the therapist's responses. It is only his genuinely felt understanding and honest positive regard that can be deeply helpful and curative; technique alone is not enough and may even be irrelevant or harmful at certain moments in psychotherapy. If, for instance, the therapist uses his nondirectiveness as a way of suppressing his own annoyance because the poor weak client couldn't possibly take it, an attitude of fundamental disrespect, annoyance, and lack of real regard for the client's powers will be communicated. Even with the best of intentions, such communication of lack of understanding and regard is damaging because the sneaky obscurity of it tends to poison the atmosphere and inhibit that flow of honest feeling that is at the heart of client-centered help.

Rogers has discovered empirically that the therapist who speaks honestly out of his strongly felt feelings tends to liberate the client to speak out of his own feelings. This can occur only if the therapist speaks his own feelings as his own, not as judgments, interpretations, or guides in the "right direction." The therapist is therefore urged to "own" his feelings as his own, not, as it were, to act them out on the client. If the therapist says, "I'm annoyed and angered by the way you're attacking that person," the client may quite naturally ask, "Do you mean that I shouldn't attack, or that it's wrong for me to attack that person, or wrong to attack people in general?" The therapist is encouraged to respond with something like: "I can't tell you what it means. I can only tell you my feeling as my own. Perhaps you should change that behavior, perhaps not; but I come back to telling you that it made me angry when you were attacking Joan." It is noteworthy that the therapist is encouraged to express his feeling when it seems appropriate but to discipline his expression and shape it so as to leave the client free to have his own feelings, thoughts, and reactions.

The effectiveness of such feelingful expression from the therapist is rooted in the fact that he has been attuning himself to understanding the client's feelings faithfully from the beginning. This is quite different from what would emerge if he expressed his feelings in a random, undisciplined way. The therapist's "*I* feel this or that" has previously been, and will continue to be, grounded in "*you* feel this or that." Hence, there is a resonating pool of shared feelings and understandings out of which the therapist speaks a feeling of his own. That feeling, clearly and honestly spoken, tends to enrich both the resonant pool of shared feelings and the flow of feeling-life issuing from the client. The feelings from both flow together into a unity of organismic, pathic feeling-life.

## THE GROWING ORGANISMIC-SELF

The obscuring of the normal I-you distinction is a significant part of the client-centered process. For the client, the reality of the pathic-self continues to have force and effect outside the therapy hour. He comes to have a sense of a highly energetic organismic-self, and he learns to refer to this vital, vibrant flow of experiencing within himself to find out how he "really" feels; it becomes for him the touchstone of the authentic in his life, of the fundamentally valuable and the "really real." To the degree that the therapy experience has been a lively illumination of this feeling aspect of human reality, that aspect of life takes on vital significance for the client. Feeling becomes a kind of absolute, a pure essence or soul, which has to be treated religiously, as transcending the individual involved.

This real self is not primarily a thinking self, a perceiving, seeing, judging, imagining, or an explaining self. The touchstone for reality is that pathic, suffering, feeling-self which has been constituted as fundamental reality through the therapy process. The real you is, in short, the you who feels.

A purification process is implied here, penetrating to the fundamental pathic level of feeling through the various falsifications that have obscured this genuine felt-self. As an example, consider the following dialogue.

CLIENT: I get so angry when somebody whines!

THERAPIST: Just feel like choking them.

CLIENT: Well, it isn't exactly only anger. It's partly an uncomfortable feeling of not knowing what to do with them.

THERAPIST: Not only being angry but also an uneasiness, a discomfort—what can I do?

CLIENT: My mother used to get so angry when we demanded anything from her. It's kind of the demand. I guess I've taken that over from her; she told me she couldn't stand whining.

THERAPIST: You're really feeling that this is more your mother speaking than you. She didn't like whining.

CLIENT: Yes, for me it's more just not knowing what to do with them.

THERAPIST: So for *you*, it's more of an uncomfortable feeling, a kind of helplessness when someone whines.

CLIENT: Yes, it's like a mixed thing. I want to shout "cut it out," but that's more of my mother. Another feeling comes and I just want to comfort them.

THERAPIST: So you really feel now your mother's voice speaking through you and shouting "cut it out!" and also a feeling of really wanting to comfort and be comforted?

CLIENT: Yes, I always wanted comfort. I really always wanted comfort for myself. Yes, I can really feel that.

THERAPIST: You always wanted comfort. The deepest thing is that wanting of comfort and being afraid to make demands, to ask for it.

In this example there is a constitution of a genuine-you, a pathic felt-sense of self which is purified or stripped of the mother's values and the accidents of the life of the particular child and particular mother. It is noticeable that the desire for comfort and acceptance exists at a much more universal, pathic, feeling, body level than the original annoyance with whining. Needing comfort and being afraid to make demands is, as many personality theorists stress, central to the development of neurosis. The pathic feeling-self that needs comfort and love is not to be understood as merely this or that particular person's needs. These needs of the organismic underlying self are, as it were, needs of the Self, a self that transcends any particular individual. It is the naked self, which, like the naked body, is a fairly general human body.

At a pathic, bodily, feeling level, then, the fundamental underlying "I" or "you" is much the same from one person to another; it is mine and everyone's alike. Thus, the fact that the well-cured client-centered client refers almost religiously to the 'real-flow-of-feeling' of his underlying self for life-guidance makes excellent sense. The 'self-flow-of-feeling' to which he refers has, for him, an absolute, transcendent, self-justifying quality. "I really deeply feel" becomes for him the strongest, most committed, most fundamental statement he can make. It shares the quality of the "this I believe" in the life of the ordinary religious person.

To challenge the person in his "deepest feelings" is to deny his most fundamental being, because in his most fundamental feeling-self he is in some felt way a universal, human pathic-self. Paradoxically, that which is most universally human at the pathic, feeling level is also experienced as the most individually personal. This is characteristic of body-feeling life, for man's body is always individually his and yet general at the same time, in the sense of being much like all human bodies.

In summary, client-centered therapy may be briefly characterized as follows. A client who is unclear about how to live his life meets with a therapist who believes fervently that contact with the pathic feeling-self is the touchstone for effective and authentic living. Between the therapist and the client a lively field is made in which first significance and reality is given to the 'life-of-feeling-of-the-body'. The client finds himself strongly affirmed, loved, and positively regarded insofar as he is lively, pathic, bodily life, and he experiences an extraordinary growth of this aspect of his existence. Gradually, through this life of cure, the therapist's faith in the underlying organismic-self as the best, most authentic human life becomes the client's faith. The client emerges from the therapy with a much more highly differentiated pathic feeling-life, which has undergone considerable symbolization and socialization through the process of therapy.

## An alternative vision

A slightly different therapeutic orientation derived from the client-centered approach has been developed by Charles Curran. Coming out of a rationalistic Catholic tradition, Curran wished to identify the 'real-self-toward-which-the-counselor-aims' as a prudent, reasoning, judging, perceiving self. Thus, he developed as the central response within his client-centered orientation the statement "you really per-ceive, see, judge, evaluate" as distinct from "you really feel." In ac-cord with the increased objectivity and coolness of this approach, there is a decreased emphasis on the "you" and a somewhat increased em-phasis on the way things seem or appear to the client.

Within this approach to counseling, the democratic noninterven-tionistic respect for the inviolability of the other's world is just as much respected as with orthodox client-centered therapy. The therapist does not judge, evaluate, condemn, moralize, advise, or opinionate. His task is to grasp the client's world from the client's internal frame of reference. The accuracy and objectivity of his penetration into that world of meanings is attested to by the degree to which his expression matches the client's sense of the world. Curran's approach thus preserves the center or heart of client-centered therapy, but the shift in the way of understanding the 'self-toward-which-the-counselor-aims' makes for a radical difference.

It is true that the person who comes for therapy is out of touch with his feelings and also suffering eruptions of feelings. It is equally true, and Curran has emphasized, that the client is not making proper sense of his life either. Curran therefore emphasizes the perceptual, judging, sense-making aspects of the client, directing the therapist's empathy not primarily to the feeling level but to the imaginative-perceptual grasp of the world the client sees.

To the enraged client, the Rogerian therapist would say with gritted teeth: "You really feel angry. You could just kill him! Boy, that made you mad!" Following the Curran formula would mean saying: "You really experience the person who made you so angry as totally unfair. It really appeared to you that he played a mean, unjustified trick. From your point of view, what he did was totally irrational. As you see it, he ought to be punished or beaten or in some way made to pay for that offense." The grasp of feeling-life and the grasp of perceptual-life are both modes of remaining faithful to the client's world, but they remain faithful in different ways and with rather different consequences.

The traditional client-centered response "you really feel" leads to a highly developed, differentiated, pathic feeling-life in which the client comes to treat the flow of feelings that he most basically is as the touchstone of reality. Curran's approach is based on the Thomist notion of counsel as the ability to make good sense. The client does not become rational in the cold, unfeeling sense of that term but can develop a certain quality of reasonableness and balance, a perceptual, thoughtful clarity. By emphasizing in every response the client's perceiving, judging, understanding, making-sense self, this aspect of the client is brought to its fullest flower.

## THERAPISTS AND CLIENTS VARY

So far in this developing description of client-centered therapy, the actual therapeutic response, as it is lived out by the therapist in response to the client, has hardly been touched. Therapists' ways of articulating their grasp of the client's inner feeling-world vary greatly in their range of selectivity and emphasis. Each therapist must come to a highly specific articulation of just what it is that the client feels, and the specifics will depend on the characteristic style and life history of the individual therapist. For one who is especially attuned to the need for self-assertion and intrusive, outgoing modes of feeling, and who is very sensitive to the tendency of most clients to have become excessively nice, supple, and self-effacing in their efforts to be acceptable, the disowning of angry feelings may appear to have great weight in the development of neurosis. Another client-centered therapist may be especially sensitive to how his clients react against a sense of incompetence or inferiority by becoming either self-effacing or falsely conceited.

Each therapist has his favorite themes, specific sensitivities, and degrees of high attunement. With each special attunement, there are characteristic areas of low emphasis in which each therapist is fairly opaque, insensitive, and even neglectful. It has already been indicated that the therapist does not respond to the assertion of every slight feeling in the client's life but selects those feelings which in some way are strikingly real-seeming, important, and close to the center of the person's real self. The centrality of a certain feeling does not merely lie out there in the client, however. Rather, it is constituted in the lively attunement and emphasis of the 'therapist-together-with-his-client.'

The areas of genuinely felt competence, free self-assertion, aggression, anger, tender feelings, sensual gratification, and strong self-determination are significant to every human being. Thus, the therapist has a certain leeway to emphasize those themes which are most individually and personally meaningful to him while still remaining true to the feelings of his client. This is not an infinite leeway, however, and the therapist's responses are not merely arbitrary. Within the ambience of any set of therapeutic leanings there is the possibility of accurate and inaccurate empathy.

For example, a patient may speak at length about the way in which his parents made him feel small and inadequate as a child by always treating him like a plaything. The range of possible therapeutic responses to this story is very great. One therapist may emphasize the client's rage; another, his profound sense of nonrecognition; another may focus on the sense of being nothing; another may emphasize the sense of inadequacy and futility; still another may focus on his sense of feeling toylike, of being a mere object to his parents. Each of these responses profoundly alters the therapist's developing understanding and response to the client's self.

If inadequacy and futility are themes characteristic of the therapist's sensitivity, their alternatives are likely to be seen as adequacy, competence, and a sense of "directed-able" action. Thus, this therapist, together with his client, is likely to help to constitute a person who moves from felt-inferiority toward feelings of competence and confidence. The therapist who tends to emphasize self-assertion and rage may, through the selectivity of his response, help the client to move from a timid, bashful, inhibited mode to one of more direct expression of anger and self. The therapist who emphasizes the client's experience of himself as toylike or objectlike may well help the client to a sharply articulated sense of self-value and independence from others.

All of these changes, while differing in emphasis, are therapeutic or positive changes. There are differences between those who tend to value their individuality, those who tend to value their competence, and those who tend to value their direct honesty as primary virtues or values. Each is a somewhat different style of personal-cultural life which is fostered by some client-centered therapists and not fostered by others. The idea that one therapist can be replaced by any other equally competent client-centered therapist is therefore false. Each therapist selects and emphasizes those aspects of human life which are most individually meaningful to him. His part in constituting the client's way toward self-actualization depends on his own personal development, his own values, and what he personally considers important.

In addition to emphasis in terms of content areas, the client-centered therapist also lives out certain values which he may not formally emphasize but which have been given to him out of his own personal, individual, and cultural heritage. Thus the therapist who comes from a family that values meditative thought and quiet self-inwardness may in every response to his client embody the value of thoughtful, meditative, self-reflection, whatever other specific emphasis he carries out as therapist. Another therapist may come from a cultural background of easy, spontaneous, quick emotional expressivity, so that this spontaneous ease of being moved emotionally will be lived out as a model of good human life in every response. The effect of all these aspects of the therapist's personal style will inevitably constitute a different therapy for his clients.

Each client also brings a specific range of attunements, sensitivities, and proclivities to the therapy and elicits specific aspects of the therapist's repertoire. The client is not a tabula rasa upon which the therapist writes; he is moved by the therapist differentially and thereby evokes the therapist differentially. One client may elicit from a therapist a much greater than average (even for him) degree of sympathy, tenderness, and warm attentiveness; another client may bring out much more of the same therapist's cool, objective, factual mode of responding. The therapist, too, is encouraged to respond in ways that move the client, so that if his usual warm style is met with indifference by certain clients, he may find himself moving to a more objective mode of response.

Variability, then, belongs to the client as well as to the therapist, and the interaction between the two makes for a very wide range of therapies practiced under the general style of client-centered. The final outcome for change of client-centered therapy may vary from moving clients toward highly individualistic, even eccentric, life styles or toward highly social, political, adaptive styles; toward intuitive softness or sharp self-assertive aggression; toward prosaic matter-of-factness or intense dramatic styles. The range will depend on the complex interaction between client and therapist, within the larger structure of the fact that this is a therapy practiced within a client-centered framework.

## RESULTS OF CLIENT-CENTERED THERAPY

The client-centered therapist sees the client as an organismic feeling-self that has been contaminated by the intervention of the cultural values of others. The quintessential real self of the person exists in a kind of 'isolated-bodily-flow-of-feeling-experience'. In this context, the therapist understands himself to be a kind of objective attunement to the client's real self, who does not influence the client except in the sense of providing the atmosphere or support for the unfolding of the client's pregiven, real organismic-self.

The highly focused, specialized attentiveness and valuing of the person's feeling-life is an extraordinary transformation of the field of personal interaction. Under the special conditions of the therapist-client relationship, it therefore participates in constituting a therapeutic change of a specific kind. By constantly emphasizing the person's feeling-life in an accurate, skilled and creative way, the therapist convinces the client of the fundamental reality and priority of the underlying feeling-self. Thus, the ideology of client-centered therapy is transmitted and made into a faith to be lived. The feeling-self is not blindly affirmed but is developed, fostered, articulated, differentiated, spoken of, and spoken to. Therapist and client together enliven and illuminate that flow of feeling that the client concretely finds within himself.

Neither the client nor the therapist can clearly see the co-constituting of this organismic feeling-self. Both teach, and are taught, that the underlying 'self-feeling-flow-of-organismic-life' exists in a kind of objective truth independent of others, outside of culture, and, like the Jungian Self, outside of history and time. The therapist fosters an individualism in the other, an idea of the nondependence of self, which is false even to the way in which the organismic-self has actually developed in therapy. Both therapist and client overlook, minimize, and formally ignore the profound teaching effect of the therapy as well as the extraordinary degree to which the values transmitted belong to the therapist. By virtue of the specialized attentiveness to feeling-life, both therapist and client refer themselves to that flow of feeling as the real.

"Feelings are all" is the client-centered myth, and its living out is at the heart of the therapeutic transformation. The birth of an organismic real self fostered by an atmosphere of attentive, concerned understanding and positive regard is a powerfully convincing teaching of the client-centered theory in the light of concrete life-experience. Convinced that his feeling-self is the center of his life, the client becomes skillfully attuned to that aspect of his existence and refers to it as the touchstone of reality, the guide for his life, the source of his initiative and power. "I used to wonder who I was and never felt anything as belonging to me. Now I *feel* myself, my substantiality in my feelings, and they are *mine* and not to be treated lightly. I really know now how much I really am my feelings."

## BIBLIOGRAPHY

Curran, Charles Arthur. *Counseling in Catholic Life and Education*. New York: Macmillan, 1952.

An alternative view of the basic self as a perceptual, judging, thinking self, a variant of the client-centered mode of therapy. This view is employed in the present text to sharpen and amplify the importance of the 'feeling-organismic-self-is-all' feature of Rogerian client-centered therapy.

Merleau-Ponty, Maurice. *The Phenomenology of Perception*. New York: Humanities Press, 1962.

A seminal text for the psychologist interested in genuine phenomenological psychology but too rigorous and complex for the general reader. The analysis of lived-body and language as "singing-a-world" is the background for the analysis of the client-centered therapist's 'speech-ideology-lived-faith' in the present text.

Rogers, Carl R. *Client-centered Therapy: Its Current Practice, Implications, and Theory*. Boston: Houghton Mifflin, 1951.

A readable basic text of client-centered theory and practice and a primary source for basic conceptions of neurosis, the therapy process, and the orienting attitudes of the therapist.

_____. *Counseling and Psychotherapy*. New York: New York: Houghton Mifflin, 1942.

An early statement by Rogers on his growing idea of nondirective counseling and therapy, with a clear expression of the break with traditional modes of guidance and authoritative interpretation. The movement toward giving virtually absolute priority to the client's perceptual field, and the therapist's bending to understand that field, on its own terms is already present. Although feeling is greatly emphasized, it does not yet have the absolute priority that it will have in Rogers' later work.

_____. *On Becoming a Person: A Therapist's View of Psychotherapy*. Boston: Houghton Mifflin, 1961.

A series of well-written articles describing Rogers' position in relation to psychotherapy, life, education, the nature of man, etc., in which the philosophic-religious underpinnings of his thought and practice are clearly visible.

_____. *The Therapeutic Relationship and Its Impact: A Study of Psychotherapy with Schizophrenics*. Madison: University of Wisconsin Press, 1967.

A text describing client-centered therapy as both theoretically and concretely involving the honest self-expression of the therapist, thus indicating an important shift in which the absolute priority of empathic understanding has been replaced by a priority of honest, congruent self-expression. The tension between honesty and understanding has been expressed before in Rogers' work but never more clearly articulated than here. Reaching for the underlying organismic-self still remains a basic theoretical and practical theme.

Rogers, Carl R., and Stevens, Barry. *Person to Person: The Problem of Being Human*. New York: Pocket Books, 1971.

The articles by Rogers written in the 1960s are expansions and elaborations of earlier writings. The book as a whole makes lively reading and sharpens the already enormously individualistic and feeling-centeredness of the client-centered style. Barry Stevens' commentary brings this individualistic, antistructure, anticulture facet vividly to life.

# 10

# Mary's case renewed

○────────────────────○────────────────────○

## BACKGROUND

Mary is thirty-two years old, a physician who has been considering psychotherapy for herself for several years. She does not feel that much is the matter with her compared with some of the patients she meets in her work as a pediatric resident. Her approach to life is calm, competent, and matter-of-fact; by herself and by others as well she is regarded as tough, businesslike, orderly, and sensible. But Mary experiences herself as stiff and inhibited and is concerned about her close relations with others. In all of her relationships she serves as the big mother and strong helper. At the same time, she has no boyfriends, and no man ever treats her as a woman.

As part of her pediatric work at the university hospital, Mary is encouraged to attend lectures on psychiatry and is given the privilege of observing the work of a child therapist and some adult psychotherapy interactions through a one-way mirror. The style to which she is exposed is mostly a modified form of psychoanalysis, which impresses her, for the most part, negatively.

"The fellow whose therapy I've been observing is incredibly precise," she tells a friend. "He has a kind of icy clarity. He's almost terrifyingly correct. You can see how he catches the irrational edges of the patient's behavior exactly and brings them into the light. But it's too much like watching a dissection; it's too cold. Somehow the patient is always the dummy."

She wonders whether she is oversentimental about relationships, but she is also dimly aware that this cool precision of manner is precisely her own self-complaint. It is hard for her to imagine herself being liberated as a result of this reasonable clarity of vision, and this discourages her because she wants to find a way out from the narrowness of her life.

Hearing of an Adlerian institute in town, Mary considers taking a course there to determine whether it might appeal to her as a style of help for herself. In the hospital cafeteria one day she meets Jack, a young man who is doing a clinical psychology internship in the hospital's psychiatric section, and asks him what he thinks of the psychiatric staff and its approach. He surprises her by saying, "They're all so busy being correct and playing God that they don't listen to what the person is really saying."

"Yes," she exclaims excitedly, "that's it. It isn't just the coolness and accuracy that's been bothering me; it's that the patient never gets heard on *his* terms."

"Hey," cries Jack, "you might be interested in the psych center on campus. They're mostly Rogerians."

Briefly he describes the approach and ideology of client-centered therapy, and Mary likes the idea of it but is doubtful at the same time. What about diagnosis? What about the problem of transference? The client-centered therapist seems not to be responsible for the patient. Jack offers to lend her his copy of *Client-centered Therapy*, in which Rogers deals with these issues at length. Mary reads the book and likes its simplicity, directness, and dissimilarity to a dissection. A physician notwithstanding, she has a horror of being physically or psychologically invaded, and she pictures psychoanalytic therapy as being massively intrusive. "Nondirective" therapy seems less invasive to her on the whole, and while this may mean that it is more superficial, she nevertheless prefers it for herself. Basically, though, it seems to her almost too simple.

"The idea," she says to Jack later, "is that I just talk and the counselor understands me and helps me to get in touch with the feelings I've already expressed. It sounds as if I'll keep spinning around in my own circle of thoughts and feelings."

"It doesn't work that way," replies Jack, who has had some Rogerian therapy himself.

## MARY ENTERS THERAPY

Learning that the head of the psychology center has a private practice, Mary phones for an appointment. Dr. G. agrees to see her, and they meet in his office at the center, an old building on campus, not too well maintained. The receptionist is dressed casually in slacks and sweater, and the few others whom Mary sees on the way to Dr. G.'s third-floor office are similarly dressed. Without being especially reflective about it, Mary feels that she is overdressed and senses that her style of dress and professional manner are going to be out of place here. As she puts it later to her roommate, "It was a shock to find the place so 'unprofessional,' so unlike any medical clinic I've ever seen. The whole thing struck me as a bit shabby."

She finds Dr. G.'s office—"third floor, first on the left," the receptionist had said cheerily, not checking to see whether Mary is expected or whether Dr. G. is busy. The door is open, and he is standing at his desk doing some calculations on an enormous sheet of paper covered with numbers. Mary hesitates at the door, Dr. G. sees her, and they introduce themselves. He removes some technical books from the wooden chair next to his desk and invites her to sit.

Mary begins to talk first, introducing herself, describing her position, age, and place in life, then describing at some length the general background of her life, her being an overprotected, even stifled only child; and finally talking about her dissatisfaction with her relationships, which are never relationships of real equality. She is always the strong helper, never the equal friend or the lover. Finally she talks about her search for a therapist, her reading of Rogers' *Client-centered Therapy*, and how she was referred to Dr. G.

During the first forty-five minutes of their interview Dr. G.'s main contribution has been a frequent, "Uh huh, yes, I see." Only twice during the course of the interview does he speak more fully. When Mary has finished describing the intrusive, overbearing, prodding presence of her mother, Dr. G. responds, "Sounds like you felt invaded, disgusted, repelled." And after Mary has described having wanted to please and be close to her father, Dr. G. says, "You liked him, wanted him, but it seems as if you felt pretty forlorn and hopeless about having him stand with you against your mother."

Near the end of the interview, Mary's semiprepared story line runs dry, and she feels stymied and helpless. When she indicates this, her therapist responds, "You really don't know what to say, and I guess it's making you feel nervous and unsure of yourself." They briefly explore the theme of her liking to know what is going to happen, of wanting a map for life, her horror of uncertainty, her basic sense of feeling, "Well, tell me what to do. I want you to tell me and relieve the strain of the uncertainty." The fifty-minute interview is over, and they agree to meet again later the same week.

Leaving the first interview, Mary's most immediate response has to do with how little the therapist *did* and how totally unspectacular it was. She does not have the feeling that he knows much about her, that she has been penetrated to the depths. The experience had been ordinary, devoid of therapeutic mystique, even banal. Yet she liked Dr. G. and had, in fact, felt understood. The one part of the interview that jolted her a bit was their discussion of her need for orderly life maps. As she left the interview she realized that Dr. G. had not met her expectation of what a therapist would be like. Somehow it was already clear to her that he would not initiate, order, or in any way guide the course of their meetings. She felt that he had been saying to her again and again, "*You* are going to do it."

She had immediately liked him as a person, however. Standing at his desk over those sheafs of numbers, he appeared to be an earnest, hardworking man, sincerely dedicated to his job. The slightly rumpled baggy tweed jacket that seemed not quite to fit his lanky frame had also appealed to her. His speech and tone of voice had been appealingly matter-of-fact, down-to-earth, masculine, and workmanlike and yet very relaxed. She had felt totally attended to; nothing had interrupted his unflinching, steady, but relaxed gaze. It was she herself who had mostly looked away. How unlike her father, who had never been able to face her or her mother. She liked that feeling of strength about him, but it seemed as if he, too, like her father, was not going to *do* anything but just leave her to do everything for herself. She did not like that feeling, but she did like Dr. G. and hoped that it would work out.

## INTRODUCTION TO DR. G.

Dr. G. has been involved in two different lines of work virtually all his life. As a child, he was fascinated by the order and coherence of mathematics and logic; he enjoyed intricate games, loved the world of science fiction, and working with chemistry sets. When he was ten, he tried to invent a perpetual motion machine. At the same time, he was always interested in people and enjoyed listening to conversations or watching people interact. At an early age he wondered how people differed from one another. This was partly brought on by the fact that while adults found him special, his age mates were often amazed and annoyed by his "peculiar" interests. But people generally liked him, and he found ways to be acceptable to adults and peers alike. His liking and being interested in people added a dimension of warmth and tolerability to what they would otherwise have experienced as an arrogant precocity.

Both the mathematical style of thought and the interest in people had continued throughout high school and college. For enjoyment he pursued algebra, geometry, solid geometry, trigonometry, calculus, set theory, and topology, which he regarded as games and enjoyed sharing with the few others who were interested. Studying physics, biology, and chemistry, he became impressed by the genuine impact that these mathematical games have on life. Especially struck by the philosophic idea that the universe is written in the language of mathematics, it seemed increasingly clear to him that mathematics revealed the intricate latticework of reality in a particularly beautiful and delightful way.

In college, he began by majoring in mathematics and physics, but two factors gradually weaned him away from these disciplines. First, it dawned on him that his enjoyment of chess and his enjoyment of science were virtually identical, and he began to question whether he really wanted to play "science games" all of his life. The second and perhaps more important factor was that friends and acquaintances gravitated toward him to talk about their lives and problems. Some combination of qualities in him made him a natural counselor—at the simplest level, probably the fact that he liked people and was interested in what they felt and saw, how life made sense to them, invited this response. He often appeared to others to be steady, calm, disciplined, and orderly but in a relaxed, relatively effortless way.

In his studies, he moved naturally toward the social sciences, discovering that many persons in the fields of sociology, anthropology, and psychology were convinced that the quantification of these areas was crucial to making them proper sciences. This appealed to him, and he delved into experimental psychology with gusto. In his second year of graduate studies in experimental psychology, he found himself once again involved in the game-playing aspect of life, which was still fun for him but now seemed somewhat empty. At one point he remarked to a friend, "At the end of my life I'd like to be able to say something other than that I'd played a lot of intricate games rather well."

Taking courses in counseling-therapy, he discovered client-centered therapy, which immediately appealed to his practical side. The client-centered description of understanding closely resembled what he was already doing with people. The further discovery that client-centered therapists were interested in developing scientific research methods to study the process of therapy clinched his interest. Within the field of psychotherapy and counseling he could blend and live out the dual interest in science and people that had characterized his life from the beginning.

At forty-five, Dr. G. has been a practitioner and researcher for eighteen years. He practices client-centered therapy, supervises and participates in the training of therapists, and is constantly involved in elaborate mathematical research projects in the process of psychotherapy. It is a good life for him and his family. He feels that he is genuinely useful to others in his counseling work; in addition, he has the chance to work closely with students, is free to pursue his research interests, and, as professor and director of the counseling institute, has the prestige and power to foster this good work with others.

When Mary leaves the interview, Dr. G. immediately returns to his research project calculations. He feels good about his first interview with her. At a certain moment in his calculations he smiles because he realizes that his approach to research is very like Mary's approach to her life; he is mapping, calculating, trying to analyze, make precise, make clarity. But unlike Mary, he knows that however useful this may be at certain moments, the scientific research game is not life. Life is more to be found in feelings than in thoughts.

As he works at his calculations, it also occurs to him that Mary's a hard worker who genuinely wants to make sense of things. Dr. G. likes this in people and later tells his wife, "I think Mary and I will be able to work together well." This strikes him as an unusual phrasing on his part; usually he would say, "I'll be able to help her" or "We'll get along well." Something about Mary makes him think of "working well together." She is earnest, dedicated, sincere, hard-working, and striving to understand with the eagerness of a child trying to figure things out. For a moment Dr. G. imagines himself telling Mary about his research and knows that she would enjoy hearing about it.

## FIVE INTERVIEWS

When they meet again, Mary does not know where to start because she does not know what is appropriate. She knows from her reading that the purpose of client-centered therapy is to get her more in touch with her feelings. Just before the interview, she has a fantasy of becoming totally speechless and helpless, of her therapist saying, "You feel totally speechless and helpless," and of herself nodding speechlessly and helplessly yes.

Mary actually does say, "I don't know where to start," and Dr. G. does reply, "You're feeling uncertain where to start," but the real situation is quite different from what she had imagined. Dr. G. is attentive but is not pressuring her to produce; he is not impatient but is trying to understand the exact nature of the uncertainty and insecurity she is feeling.

"I'm just not used to not having things well in hand," Mary says. "I'm used to being on top of things."

"You're just not used to not being master of the situation," responds Dr. G., "and that makes this pretty frightening."

She describes again how greatly she controls her relationships with others and how she is certain that she learned this in relation to her suffocating mother. Dr. G. says, "So you feel pretty sure—it really feels that way—that you had to keep her away or you would have been engulfed, taken over, swallowed up." The interview ends here.

In the next interview Mary still does not know where to begin, but now she and Dr. G. smile at the familiarity of this. "Maybe it's all right not to know where to start," she says. "Our last session was hard work and I felt scared a couple of times, but I really feel that this is going in the right direction." Again she picks up on the question of self-control, of mastering others and dominating her situation. Dr. G. reflects and expresses as exactly as he can her feeling of needing to be on top of each situation, of not allowing anything unexpected to happen. At one point in the interview Mary says softly, "I'm so tired of that. It's so hard to have to take care of everything like that." Dr. G. responds, "I guess you've only done that out of necessity. You don't really want to run the universe, it's such a sad and lonely way to be." The weariness in Mary's tone evokes Dr. G.'s sense of loneliness. In response, she weeps a little, admitting that she does get awfully lonely. The interview soon ends.

During the next several interviews Mary expresses her feelings of sadness and forlorn loneliness more amply. She describes her childhood as an almost unrelieved solitude. Friends could not come to her home, her family had no friends; the house was like a great dark castle in which no one talked to anyone. In addition, she had had to protect herself against her mother's intrusive presence. But, she adds: "I was always competent, and people outside the family always found me useful. I could do things; I could organize. Even my parents liked that I was doing well in school, getting jobs on committees and such. I could be with people some, if I was serviceable to them."

During these few interviews the therapist says very little beyond, "Uh huh, yes, I see." Although he frequently expresses his understanding of Mary's feelings, such are his delicacy and skill that this is for the most part hardly noticeable to Mary. It is as if he is only participating in her self-expression as an adjunctive amplifier, clarifier, and intuitor of feelings. The only times his participation stands out for Mary is when he captures a feeling and leads her to experience it more intensely. Certain of his responses sharply intensify her feelings. His response to her need for control somehow dramatizes and intensifies for her how desperately she clutches at the world. His response to her insecurity and uncertainty in the face of less control emphasizes how intensely fearful she is. His response to her fatigue, weariness, and sadness leads her to experience sharply the depth of forlorn loneliness and hopelessness that she has often felt in relation to others.

## Dr. G.'s style of participation

Considering the degree to which Dr. G.'s presence is mostly one of background and support, investigating the particularities of his style and its effect on the psychotherapy process may appear gratuitous. The actual therapeutic process is not merely general, however. It is not a universal patient speaking to a universal therapist; it is Mary speaking with Dr. G., whose particular client-centered style can hide from Mary, from himself, and from us the centrality of just who he is in the unfolding of the particular relationship.

Dr. G. is very attentive to Mary, but the style of his attentiveness is guided by his wanting to understand precisely what she is saying. It occurs neither to him nor to her to question this concern with precision of expression; both take it for granted as an appropriate mode of being therapeutically and helpfully present. Without noticing it explicitly, Mary finds this precision very reassuring, experiencing it much as she would experience carefulness in a physical examination, as a mark of professional competence.

The fact that he is hard at work in a relaxed way is deeply reassuring to her. His style of careful and exact articulation gives her a sense of orderly process and helps to bind the anxious, chaotic feelings that threaten to overwhelm her. His relaxed, self-confident, assured way of systematically pursuing her feelings and their meanings helps her to feel that she is in good hands. Further, the way in which he systematically pursues meanings, feelings, and themes gives her clear guidelines to follow in the moment-by-moment interaction of the therapy. He normally does not leave her hanging, uncertain of what to say next. The very way he pursues themes implicitly instructs her to pursue further whatever theme they happen to be on.

In the first few interviews Mary will already be saying things like, "It was more a question of being all alone to do it on my own rather than of just feeling helpless"; or, "It wasn't just being frightened but more of being frightened by an overwhelmingly uncanny, bizarre presence." These responses indicate that she is learning to differentiate and articulate feelings with precision as part of the task of the therapy. Mary has brought to her therapy a penchant for orderliness, clarity, and hard work, and this facilitates their ability to proceed in the mode of hard-working, systematically making precise what Mary means and feels. In fact, this hard-working systematic quality is something that they share and like about each other, and that, too, makes the therapeutic work flow easily.

Still another aspect of Dr. G.'s style participates in shaping his interaction with Mary—namely, the mode of his being interested in persons. The quality of his interest in persons resembles the quality of his interest in puzzles and scientific problems. This is not an absence of warmth and involvement so much as it is the presence of a certain style of *interested detachment*. While approaching an understanding of Mary's relationship with her mother and of how painfully difficult this was for her, he is also interested in understanding how Mary's physical rigidity prevented her from feeling. He is thus coming to understand something general—the relation of bodily posture to modes of experience—at the same time that he is understanding Mary's particular feelings toward her mother.

He is fascinated by the way human beings are as well as sympathetically attuned to where Mary is; that is, he is partly interested in Mary as a human being. Although he restrains himself, at any moment he could articulate the general structures of life that he is coming to understand by understanding Mary. This comes through explicitly at times, as when he says, for example: "It's very *interesting* how you could block off things just by being rigid like that. Isn't it *amazing* how you instinctively knew to stay away from your mother and seek relations outside the home."

It is an interest in how things work that informs his presence to Mary. He wants to *see* the whole style that Mary lives in all of its articulations. He tends to summarize and interrelate what she said this week with what she said last week, to unify her apparently disparate expressions of feeling. He wants to come to a thematic, feeling-filled unification of Mary as a person in all her interrelated aspects. Hence, he is seldom merely sympathetic with her; he is usually trying to grasp the inner unity of her world and experiences. Since Mary also responds readily to experiences as "interesting," fun to examine and figure out, Dr. G.'s lively, warm, and yet detached interest in how she is resonates with her own style.

## A different style

The characteristic effect of Dr. G.'s style can be made clearer by comparing him with another therapist at the same psychology center. Dr. S., who has a much more passionate, aesthetically intense, hypnotic style, prepares himself for his interviews by being alone for fifteen minutes and, as he puts it, "getting into a receptive mood." His language is vividly dramatic, charged with poetic imagery, and he broods over what his client tells him, waiting for an intuition that will help him to articulate a depth of feeling.

Dr. S. came to psychology late, having worked as an artist during most of his youth. His background is not rigorously scientific or calculative but, on the contrary, vigorously poetic and intuitive. From the moment he meets with a client, Dr. S. strives more or less explicitly to be a resonant, sensitive, intuitive speaker for the client; indeed, he is often given to speaking as if he were the client. Mary's interviews with such a client-centered therapist would differ considerably from her relaxed, matter-of-fact, hard-working, and systematic interviews with Dr. G.

She would find Dr. S. sitting at his desk looking very serious, almost Buddahlike, an image Mary brushes away from her consciousness, although something about his brooding, serious, rather intense presence makes it difficult for her to go into her more or less prepared story line. She gives the general details of her life very weakly and then describes how she was referred to him—a matter of about fifteen minutes, during which Dr. S.'s main contribution is silence interrupted by an occasional, 'Uh huh, yes." Mary is feeling tight and scared by the way this interview is going. Dr. S. is paying very close attention to her, but she feels that what she is saying is beside the point. He is so intense and serious that he seems to be reaching toward some mysterious interiority, some dark core of something within her, so that her words seem frivolous, unimportant, and irrelevant.

"I don't know what you want me to say," she stammers. "I feel so foolish, like I've been rattling on without sense. This is pretty frightening to me."

"Are you feeling like someone who puts on her party clothes and party manners only to discover that she is at a funeral?" As Dr. S. asks this, he acts it slightly, giving a lilt and swing to the "party" idea and a somber tonality to the "funeral" image.

Mary is suddenly depressed, imaging herself in a clown's costume pretending a joviality she does not feel. She says nothing, struck dumb by the intensity of this feeling. Normally she would immediately cover such a feeling with some well-organized talking, but somehow this has no place in the brooding presence of Dr. S. The interview proceeds with a halting, stumbling, painful intensity of feeling, Mary experiencing a sharply focused series of dark feelings and images of lonely, isolated, trackless wastelands. As she leaves the first interview, she is both exhausted and tremendously impressed by the surprising depth and intensity of her heretofore buried feelings.

The contrast between the two processes with the same client is striking. With Dr. G., there is the matter-of-fact, careful, systematic unfolding of Mary's feeling-world; with Dr. S., there is a highly dramatic intensity of style and an evocation of images designed to express her inner life aesthetically and yet feelingly.

## The self-effacement of the therapist

There is a curious duality in the description thus far given of the client-centered process. On the one hand, it is clear that the therapist's specific style of presence is crucial to the ongoing process of the client's self-unfolding. At the same time, there is a sense in which Dr. G.'s presence is manifested primarily in a mode of invisibility, of putting himself at the service of the self-expressive project of the other. In a very real sense, Mary often does not notice Dr. G. except as a kind of supportive, facilitative background; Dr. G., likewise, does not notice himself except as tuning into and expressing Mary's feelings.

It should be recalled here that Freudian and Jungian psychotherapy are also qualitatively shaped by the concrete modes of personal presence which the therapist lives out with his client. Therapies as concretely practiced and lived can never be reduced to the abstraction of being merely Freudian, Jungian, or Rogerian; therapy as lived is always a relationship between actual persons with actual preferences, tastes, styles, and modes that are not fully explainable on the basis of therapeutic orientation or school alone.

In Freudian therapy, the therapist is deliberately *invisible* in order to foster the complex processes of transference, reenactment, reliving, and clear lively insight. This invisibility is also a mode of self-effacement insofar as the therapist's peculiarities, specific value commitments, and life style are relatively hidden from the patient. The Freudian does this in the interests of fostering a project transcending the particularities of his individual style. He does not want to impose his traits, values, or preferences arbitrarily on the other; he effaces himself in the service of the interpretive-therapeutic project.

Although the Jungian therapist is much freer in self-expression and in manifesting himself, he is also disciplined by the task of evoking and articulating the collective unconscious in the patient's life. Seeking a higher level of integration of the patient's personality remains the task at hand. Thus, the Jungian therapist, too, does not randomly express arbitrary personal preferences, tastes, and values but bends his preferences, styles, and individual experiences to the purpose of articulating the underlying universals in the patient's life. The therapist says ultimately, "It is not important what I, individually, feel and think about what you say but only how that helps you unfold the dynamic archaic levels of your life where your true self resides."

In each of these therapies the objective goal is to unfold that which is already given in the patient. The therapist adapts himself to this project and succeeds to the degree to which he becomes a self-effaced presence. In her Freudian therapy, Mary moved into the dialectics of the transference, her past relationship with her parents, and the way in which those past relationships continued to live themselves out in her life. She and her intrapsychic life were the focus of the therapy. In the Jungian therapy, too, the formal focus was the interiority of her life as collectivity and as moving toward a more integrated self-expression. Who and how the therapist is served as a background for this process; experientially, the therapist was relatively invisible as his particular self. In Rogerian therapy, this process of self-effacement is visible. Both Mary and her therapist experience him as background to the explicit focus on the unfolding of Mary as feeling-self.

## DEVELOPMENT OF THE SENSING-FEELING SELF

At the end of her first interview, Mary had the general impression that Dr. G. had been saying to her, "*You* are going to do it." The steady and planful waiting for her to come to her feelings and to speak her piece had already given her a slight sense of self-focus. Even at that point she had experienced the fullness of attention to her feeling-self as an increase in the weight of her words and a preliminary shifting toward the centrality of her bodily feeling-self.

As the therapy continues this shift toward bodily feelings and expression has increased. She now experiences her body's stiffness against invasion, its readiness to be competent against a background of fear, and its softness as forlorn, sad, and alone. The concentration on these feelings and their contexts during the first six interviews has increased her felt presence to herself as feeling-sensing. During the seventh interview, she remarks that her body feels more substantial and more attached to herself than it had at first. "A lot more of me is here now," she says, indicating her stomach and heart.

*The next ten interviews.* As the therapy unfolds, Mary continues frequently to describe her early life and its continuing effect on her, the theme of competence and her need for it, and her sense of isolation and loneliness. It is a rather undramatic therapy for the most part.

Mary is feeling better about herself and her life. She has discovered in the awkward moments of therapy that she does not have always to be on top of things. She is much more in tune with her feeling-life than she has ever been before and has even wept a few times in the therapy. As she becomes more relaxed with Dr. G. and with herself certain themes begin to emerge which she is not sure she wants to pursue. At this point, however, she is accustomed to speaking in detail about her feelings, knowing that this is expected and appropriate in her relationship with Dr. G.

*The seventeenth meeting.* Dr. G. leaves for two weeks to attend a convention, and during his absence Mary thinks about how the therapy is going. She likes meeting with Dr. G. and knows that it is doing her some real good, but she wonders whether it isn't too comfortable and easy for her. "He's never picked up in any special way on sexual themes. I guess it's up to me to go into what I want to with him." Although the idea scares her and she would like to avoid it, she nevertheless decides that at their next meeting she will bring up her growing interest in, confusion about, and feelings of sexuality.

She begins the next interview saying, "I don't know where to start," and they both chuckle because this has become almost a formula for her. She explains that she has been thinking of talking with him about sex but is not clear how to approach it.

"You feel that you want to bring this up with me, but you're also feeling uncomfortable about how to proceed."

After a brief silence, Mary asks, "Can't you help me with this somehow?"

"You really are feeling a bit helpless, unable to go ahead, and you're wishing I would break the impasse for you. Is that how you're feeling?"

"Yes."

Mary grows increasingly tense during the next few minutes, repeating that she does not know what to do or how to do it. For a moment she feels angry toward Dr. G. and turns to him, looking him in the face, almost begging for his help. Calmly he says, "You're just feeling stuck and helpless."

"Can't you help?" Mary pleads angrily.

"You're even mad at me, feeling that I'm deliberately holding out."

Mary hears this as, "You can do it alone, by yourself. You are competent," and she responds angrily.

"You're always leaving it up to me, telling me that I can do it. Why do I always have to do everything by myself?"

"It's like everything is always your lonely, solitary burden, all your life long."

Mary cries a bit, saying softly and tensely, "Oh, damn it, damn it, damn it!" She says that she wants something more from him; it's not enough for him just to sit there understanding. Glancing at Dr. G., she finds him fully attentive, responding with empathy to everything she expresses. Relaxing, she sighs and remarks: "You don't go away just because I'm hard to get along with. You are good to me."

"You're always afraid that if you aren't nice, the other person will go away," he responds. "It's nice to be able to be a pain and a burden without having to be afraid of desertion."

Mary spends the last twenty minutes talking disjointedly about her sexual anxieties. She mentions her mother's peculiar eroticism, touches briefly on some intense relations she has had with girlfriends, and says that she is attracted to older men, especially if they are safely married and out of reach. Finally she blurts, "I'm afraid that I'm queer."

"In the background now for some time," says Dr. G., "you've been living with this fear that you are sexually abnormal, homosexual, lesbian. Just the way you say it, I can feel how very much of a haunting, spooky fear is connected with that for you."

Although their time is up, they speak for another fifteen minutes, which is unusual for Dr. G. He wants to give her a chance to speak out a bit more, to allow the weight and power of this uncanny fear to dissipate a bit before she leaves. He is spontaneously responding to her special plea for help, saying, "Yes, I will support you more vigorously, firmly, and fully when you especially need it." Mary leaves this session tired, relieved, obscurely happy, although still nervous about the sexual theme, which she knows she is going to pursue in the next interviews.

*Seven more meetings.* Mary now talks about her sexual life and feelings, at first primarily in terms of their absence. She had not experienced childhood crushes or the everyday flirtations and sexual innuendos that accompany adolescence. She had dated neither in high school nor in college. Her "good" relations with young men were of the brother-sister type, with herself usually being the older sister. Together, Dr. G. and Mary verbalize this world of inhibited activity, thought, and feeling. She had not let herself feel very bodily, warmly, sexually, or even close affection. Each time they speak of this, the question of fear, tension, and disgust, of not being allowed to feel, comes up as well.

Mary identifies bodily feeling with her crazed, bizarre mother, whose feelings were spilling out all over the place. Not to feel was Mary's way of maintaining a part of herself away from her mother. "It was so bad, the way she was. She would get this crazy, hungry look in her eyes and want to hug you, pat you, touch you. I was scared and disgusted. I hated that. I wasn't going to have anything to do with that." As they discuss this feeling structure further, it becomes evident that Mary had closed off those body feelings defensively, identifying them as bad and crazy, as not allowed, as dangerous; not to feel these things was to be sane, reasonable and decent. Her mother had wanted to bathe her, give her enemas, be in the bathroom with her, inspect her stools, and invade her body in almost every way, always justifying these invasions with expressions of care and concern.

"To be close and warm was to be a disgusting cripple. *She* was, and she wanted me to be that way too."

"It almost came to mean that to be a human body, a needful human body at all, was forbidden. You couldn't be yourself in your body. You had to be cautious, careful, and vigilant not to slip up and be *you*."

## "TO BE A HUMAN BODY AND TO BE YOU"

Faithful to the general client-centered ideology, Dr. G. has focused on the client's feeling-self, has liked and positively regarded Mary, especially when her feeling-self has been suffering, and has referred her and himself to the level of body-feeling and body-sensing as the fundamental mode of meaning of her life. Both directly and indirectly, he has consistently expressed that all feelings, all experiences of the sensing organism, are allowable. Nasty aggression, perverse sexual feelings, hatred of and disgust with one's mother, rigid fearfulness, tender affection, loneliness, and despair—all are part of a basically acceptable human condition. The positive rule has been that it is necessary, allowable, and good to "be a human body and to be you." They specifically discuss the fact that she has prevented herself from being her body and how this has prevented her from being herself.

But "to be a human body and to be you," which is affirmed as valuable and good in client-centered therapy, does not mean the human body in *all* of its possibilities. It is not the brutally insensitive human body of the rapist or murderer who lives out gross, one-sided impulses. It is the 'human-feeling-body-to-be-understood-and-differentiated' that is valued as the "true self." It is a basically civilized human body which strives to articulate and understand itself in expressive verbal formulations, to live out this or that impulse in a way that is balanced with other feelings or impulses. The true self is the body in its sensitive attunement to reality, to others, and to its own inner life. It is the feeling-body in its harmonic interplay of movements and feelings in a balanced, expressive unity.

In a variety of ways Dr. G. has lived out with Mary this belief in, and articulation of, a highly refined, socialized, differentiated view of the body. His basic interest, in understanding the precise nuances that she is feeling, participates in the constitution of a highly refined body that can feel not only rage, fear, and lust but also anxious expectancy, shy tenderness, timorous disgust, invasion by uncanny, ghostly fingers, or excited interest. Although each response is directed toward "you really feel," there are a great variety of feelings.

The inclusion of these feelings in intricate social contexts militates against a primitive or undifferentiated sense of the body. Further, because both Dr. G. and Mary direct themselves to an empathic attunement to Mary's feelings, the 'body-feeling-self' which they develop and articulate is a highly empathic, attuned body. Dr. G. stands firmly in his task and so does Mary; they both place themselves seriously and resolutely in therapy. Hence, the body that develops is not one that floats or drifts aimlessly but is a substantial, standing, firm body filled with firm directionality and competent set.

Not all body-selves that develop in client-centered therapy are differentiated and articulated in the same style as Mary's, however. Some patients are less solid, substantial, and competent than Mary, and their development (unless they have therapists totally given over to being solid, substantial, competant, and workmanlike) as bodily feeling-selves would be quite different. Many therapists are very different in style from Dr. G. and encourage the development of an intense, ever-changing, dramatic, more fluid and kaleidoscopic sense of feeling-self.

Another alternative could occur if Mary had worked with a therapist whose style and emphasis were directed toward delicacy, aesthetic distance, a finely nuanced sense of touch with, but seldom firm commitment to, the world. For such a therapist, Mary's whole style of matter-of-fact ego functioning could arouse a certain doubt. For him, *all* hardness or toughness might be regarded as simply defensive. Further, he would live out in his own style a constant "perhaps" or "maybe." His responses would all tend toward, "You might be feeling this or that or, on the other hand, perhaps some mixture."

His very delicacy, the nuanced and probing questioning and doubting, tasting and testing, not easily coming to a decisive stand, would be taken up by Mary in her natural cooperative eagerness to learn, into her developing sense of feeling-self. In this way, her organismic-self would be experientially more fluid, changeable, delicate, more full of maybes. Instead of developing, as she has with Dr. G., the sense of, "I really feel this, and that's the way it is," she would be directed toward a questioning, probing stand toward herself: "Let me see just how I do feel in that mixed, fluid sense of myself as bodily feeling."

*The twenty-fifth interview.* At this point, Dr. G. and Mary have been working together for a little more than four months. Mary is much more in tune with her feeling-self and with the feelings of others as well. Dr. G.'s style and tonality are reflected in the interviews she holds with her own patients at the hospital. She continually directs herself to how they feel; in conversations, she is now likely to speak about how she feels. This is a manner of speaking ("Well, the way I feel about that . . . but what do you feel about that?"), and it is also a way of attuning herself to the world, to herself, and to others. The first question that arises for her, quite spontaneously now, is in reference to the feeling-tones of things. When she sees something beautiful, she is immediately struck by the resonating chords of affective bodily life which the sight stirs in her. For her, this is a significant shift from a cooler, more perceptual focused style of engagement with the world.

Mary feels better about her life, less like a rational machine, and much more substantially in her body. She is dieting and losing weight, partly because she is growing more interested in being attractive to men. She can allow herself to feel sexual now, and she enjoys it, sometimes going to bed naked just to get in touch with her body. Her romantic or sexual experiences with men are still almost nonexistent, but dating is something she is beginning to fantasize about and want. Without noticing it clearly, Dr. G.'s approval of her and her feelings, his desire for her to feel more and more, has been very encouraging to Mary. His consistent speaking to her feelings, even the frightening ones, has meant for her that, in principle, none of her feelings is taboo, and this is liberating for her in ways far beyond what they actually talk about.

Because her whole life has been structured around the premise that to have feelings is crazy, illegitimate, perverse, and terrible, this shift toward a socialized feeling-life of permissible and encourageable emotions is a revelation to the very heart of her existence. During her childhood, her cool father had been the sane, proper one, slightly helpless against the insane behaviors of her mother but still basically on the side of right. Now, as she grows more in touch with her own feelings, she is beginning to question her attitude toward her father. She had always felt disappointed that he had not protected her against her mother; she now sees that his passivity and unresponsiveness had been a terrible thing for her and for her mother as well.

During the twenty-fifth interview, they begin to explore in detail her feelings toward her father in particular and toward men in general. She has always fared better with men than women and has always felt more trust in them. Exploring this feeling, however, she discovers that what she has called trust is partly based on a mistaken image of male passivity. Men don't invade or attack you; they don't peer and poke and pry as her mother had. They wait for you to approach them, and that makes them safe. Even as she verbalizes this, Mary knows that it is not entirely accurate, but she is free to express herself to Dr. G. now without concern about rightness or wrongness.

Thus, she follows her feelings and describes men as passive, inactive, and attractive, to be wooed rather than wooing, not dangerously after you, always at a safe distance. But the more she feelingly pursues this image of men—especially of her father but also of the "safe" older men toward whom she has always gravitated—the more she feels it to be wrong and not what she really wants. "I guess all I hoped for was that no one would invade me as my mother had. If they just vaguely kind of liked me at a distance, that was nice and safe." Later in the same interview she says: "I really do like men. I mean, I get a kind of glow, a happy, buoyant, joyous feeling inside me when I work with a man I like. I get that here sometimes, but here it's scary because you know me so well."

"It's scary here because it's so intimate, so close, not so distant and safe?"

"Yes," Mary breathes softly. "Yes, I guess so."

## Client-centered questioning

Dr. G., and client-centered therapists generally, often responds to his sense of what Mary is feeling with a slight interrogative lift at the end of an otherwise straight empathic statement. Sometimes his questioning is more explicit. "Is that right?" he may ask. "Does that catch it for you?" or, "That's not quite it. How would you say it?" In Dr. G.'s case, this questioning is usually in the interests of exactitude and precision. For another therapist, the same interrogative mode would be directed primarily toward dramatic intensification. For still another, it might be directed toward the unfolding of an infinite variety of feeling nuances.

Within the client-centered orientation, the interrogative mode has, first, a general social function: it places each of the client's statements back into the client's own hands and formally asks him to judge their accuracy. It is an explicit, formal, virtually contractual way of reminding client and therapist alike that here, the client is judge; here, the client evaluates; here, rightness and wrongness, truth and value, feelings and thoughts belong radically to the client and to his inner sense of himself. Client-centered questioning places the client firmly and repeatedly in the position of locus of evaluation, center of his own world, center of the meanings that belong to him.

The interrogative mode is not, however, addressed to just any un-differentiated "you." It is addressed to the expressively full tasting, testing, feeling, and sensing of the client. The client is not asked for a snap judgment or flippant reply but is asked to test carefully for fit, to explore in a deepening inward spiral of feeling just precisely what he feels-senses to be so. Through this probing, the client is invited into the inward sense of himself as an amplitude of meaningful, feelingful being. The therapist asks "Is it only this lonely feeling that you are feeling?" The client is invited to ask himself, "Is it only this lonely feeling, or is it perhaps mixed with anger? Is there something in the loneliness like fixed despair, or is the lonely feeling a grand imperial loneliness announcing my special destiny, or what?"

The spiral is toward the inner feeling-sense. Sometimes it may seem as if the client were feeling with ghostly hands into his own stomach, bowels, and heart for the answer to "what do I feel?" For other client-therapist pairs, the client directs himself into a world of evocative, poetic, aesthetic imagery where he searches to find his true feelings. In each of these cases, the client-centered questioning directs the client toward a fuller, truer sense of his feeling organismic-self.

This differentiated feeling-self is firmly located *within* the client. When questioned, the client inspects his inside self which is center of his world, a self which is ultimately arbiter of the private world. It is the self of client-centered theory which is individualist, solitary, solipsist, final judge. Thus, for client-centered practice, it is appropriate that it be called into its rightful kingship of the world through the questioning, probing, empathic responsiveness of the therapist. "You who are the *sole true knower*, how does it stand inside yourself with your feelings?"

## ELEVEN MORE INTERVIEWS

During the next set of interviews Mary pursues her feelings toward men, discovering in herself a jumble of contradictory thoughts and feelings: men never really *do* for you; men leave you alone and lonely; you have to be careful not to make demands on men; men desert you; men are sane and reasonable; men are unfeeling; men are helpless against feelings. Her image of men is primarily one of Olympian, immovable, silent beings with sanity and truth on their side.

But alongside and intermixed with these images is a terrible fear of men, which Mary has difficulty expressing. In the background she still hears her mother's secret message that in intimate relations men are savage beasts who rip, tear, destroy, and invade. She still remembers her mother's descriptions of childbirth as a ripping, tearing, pain-racked horror of blood and destruction. After her birth, Mary's mother had moved into Mary's room, and the parents had never slept together again. All of this, together with the excessive gentleness of her father and Mary's fear of bodily feeling and invasion, combines to evoke images of terror. Mary's father had been so gentle and soft that his disapproval and occasional anger seemed like the most terrifying wrath. The question she had never asked herself was, "What is he holding back? I have to be so careful to be just what he wants or he will destroy me."

Even though Mary knew that her mother was crazy, her mother had convinced her that "they" are dangerous. "Be careful of men, you never know," her mother had said, adding a bizarre, uncanny quality to the spooky outside world of strangers who can do you in, of men who will take advantage of you.

As Mary begins to experience the fear, awe, and terror, and most especially her fear of intimacy, as primarily coming from her mother, this relaxes it somehow. "I've been living out my mother's fears and taboos. I myself like men and want to be close to one. Actually I've always liked men." She finds that she can enjoy looking at attractive men now. Before this she had not allowed herself to look at a man's face or body, to admire or feel attracted to a man, or even to dwell on this. Although she had immediately responded to Dr. G.'s attractiveness, she had quickly bypassed this feeling in the brother-sister working-type relationship toward which she had moved. A man as attractive potential mate or partner had never been allowed to surface in her consciousness for more than an instant.

Looking at men is something she now practices a bit with Dr. G. "I like the way you're put together," she says at one point. She carries this practice outside the therapy hour as well. She begins to notice men and to engage in some flirtatious joking with fellow doctors at work. She is better able to relate to men as she experiences them as more accessible, less remote, and less terrifying. The comfortable quality of her relationship with Dr. G. has been very important, as he has neither invaded her, moved in on her too fast, nor left her alone. He has lived out with her the strength of sanity, reasonableness, and solidarity without the terrible cost of unfeelingness, desertion, and the need for great carefulness on her part to retain his goodwill. In short, he has been a good man for her, has liked and enjoyed her, given her freedom, empathized with her, and opened her to new worlds of feeling and sensing.

## Termination of therapy

When Mary and Dr. G. have been meeting regularly for about seven months, she raises the possibility of ending therapy. Her goals are already fairly well realized. She is more comfortable in her body, less rigid, less anxious, and beginning to move toward men sexually. Although still a novice, she no longer feels that she has to be just buddies with men, nor is she as caught up in being the big sister or mother figure with women that she once was. Dieting and a new, more feminine wardrobe make her feel like a transformed woman; indeed, the way she is now received socially tells her that many changes have occurred in her self-presentation. More importantly, she feels more fluid, more in her body, happier with her life, more full of life and fun and feeling.

It is difficult to move toward quitting therapy because she likes Dr. G. and enjoys being with him. Although she knows she may return, her own sense of workmanship tells her that the work of therapy is finished, at least for now. They agree to meet a few more times, "just in case," as Mary says. She feels as if she is being orphaned because in this therapy she has had undivided attention, careful understanding, and a chance to explore her feelings freely.

"You know," she says, "you don't get this chance in everyday life. It feels so warm, so receptive; you offer this space and time and yourself to be mine and only mine. I've been able to do exactly what I wanted to; it's all been up to me. You opened up this space for me and

6 Mary's case renewed

just stood there providing a kind of atmosphere in which I could learn to feel myself in myself. You haven't interfered, except by being understanding and by letting me know somehow that I was O.K. Thanks so much for that."

At the end of the session she kisses Dr. G. goodbye. They embrace awkwardly and agree to meet again in a few weeks, "just in case."

## BIBLIOGRAPHY

Rogers, Carl R. *Carl Rogers on Encounter Groups.* New York: Harper & Row, 1970.

As in most of Rogers' later works, the personal element predominates here, so that one can gain a concrete sense of the things that Rogers does and the flavor of his style as well. Chapter 3, "Can I Be a Facilitative Person in a Group?" is an especially striking informal schematization of what Rogers finds himself doing and not doing as a therapist.

———. *Freedom to Learn.* Columbus, Ohio: Charles E. Merrill, 1969.

A personal statement of the underlying ideology of client-centeredness as applied especially to educational practices.

# 11

# The dialectics of psychotherapy

○ ———————————————— ○ ———————————————— ○

## THE CONVINCINGNESS OF THERAPY

The preceding chapters have constituted a descriptive voyage through three therapeutic transformations. This chapter will survey the therapies in a more comprehensive, existential, and phenomenological way in order to bring this book to its point, which is the need for a deeper understanding of the nature of therapy and therapeutic transformation. Because the purpose of this text is not primarily critical, its focus has so far been on successful therapy. Nevertheless, description and understanding have consistently revealed certain characteristic blind spots in these traditional therapeutic orientations.

Even the most cursory examination of the therapies so far explored will demonstrate to the reader that each of these visions of psychotherapy and therapeutic cure is powerfully convincing. Even for us as onlookers, the language of each orientation weaves a powerful spell of conviction. Insofar as we allow ourselves to enter sympathetically into the processes described, there is a deep sense of plausibility, be-

235

lievability, and convincingness to each approach. In empathically and descriptively participating in orthodox psychoanalysis it became progressively obvious how the patient came to experience his past as continuing to live itself. We ourselves were also convinced by the fascination of the therapy itself, even though our onlooking of the process was designed precisely to help us escape total enrapture. To the degree that our descriptive reading has been an authentic participation in them, we have been convinced (if only temporarily) by each approach.

This plausibility which we as onlooking readers experience in each therapeutic approach is not an accident but is a central structure of the therapeutic transformation itself. The empathic onlooker is the last person to be convinced and is, of all participants, therefore the most immune to total belief. The therapist, for his part, is totally convinced. Freudian, Jungian, or Rogerian, his orientation and approach to therapy are ways of perceiving and relating to his patient on the basis of a lived-conviction informed and shaped by the fundamental theoretical ideas. As a Freudian, he *is* attuned to the past reliving itself in the present. As a Jungian, he *is* attuned to the collective unconscious, or mythic, symbolic universals, of his patient. As a Rogerian, he *is* attuned to the patient's underlying feeling-life.

For the therapist, then, theory is not mere hypothesis or one interesting notion among others. The therapist lives the basic structure of the theory as a way of looking, of asking questions, of interpreting—indeed, as a way of arranging his office furniture. Theory is his way of being oriented toward that unique space-time in which he and his patient "live together." In this sense, the therapist's orientation is a small subculture that provides the unquestioned ground for their 'being-together', formally defines their work together, and gives answers to the questions "what are we doing here together?" and "what are our duties in relation to each other?"

The patient's moving toward conviction must likewise be understood not as mere theoretical ideation but in the life-sense. The patient comes to the therapist because he does not know how to live his life without undue anxiety or mysterious, frustrating, apparently senseless difficulties blocking his way; because he has either lost or never attained the knack for living his life; and because the more everyday ways of seeking help are either not useful or are unavailable to him. The fact that the therapist has a way to help—an orientation or approach that is more or less convincing to, and livable by, both therapist and patient—is therefore essential to the therapy process. The pathway of help or cure, which belongs at first to the therapist by virtue of his training, knowledge, and position in the relationship, must also become the pathway for the patient.

Orthodox psychoanalysis clearly articulates the ways in which the analyst's convictions are lived out, because every detail of psychoanalysis is related precisely to the Freudian theoretical overview and to the living out of that overview. The theoretical belief in the patient's irrationality is expressed in a number of ways, among them: in the patient's being instructed to lie down and free associate, laid out, as it were, before the analyst's gaze; in the characteristic interpretation of the patient as trapped in irrational repetitions from the past; in the cool inaccessibility of the analyst to the patient; in the relatively few words spoken by the analyst to the patient.

All of these arrangements, which leave the patient unmoored from normal everyday realities, encourage repetition from the past. The patient is virtually told to be irrational and infantile and to repeat his past affectively. Thus, the reality of the theory is not just a matter of point of view or of perspective on reality; the theory comes to life as a result of the total analyst-patient dialogue. The patient is not only told verbally about the past repeating itself in him, about his irrationality and drivenness; he is inserted into a context in which these aspects of his being come into forceful expression and manifest themselves as concrete truth.

The analyst's every gesture, his tone of voice, his way of listening and of being silent, his invisibility, tolerance, and calm, his general receptivity, his reasonableness—all open up a certain style of lived-space for the patient in which a certain style of emotional expressivity is fitting and a certain other style is not. All of the feelings, thoughts, and experiences that belong to the patient's young, impotent, helplessly driven past, for example, belong in a special way to the situation of lying on the analyst's couch. Other experiences—of dignity, reasonable self-control, order, and appropriate self-assertion—do not fit the situation of babbling associatively on the couch. The analyst's embodiment of a certain style of open receptivity invites the patient into a space which is already shaped and formed in a particular way and within which only a certain style of life can be lived—namely, that style of life which is already partially precomprehended by analytic thought.

When the patient responds well to this opening, the analyst also responds well. The patient responds well when he places himself amply and relatively fully present within that space. The analyst responds to the patient's opening up with attention, interpretive remarks, and encouragement, all directed toward expressively reasserting the analytic faith in the past repeating itself irrationally in the patient.

This rhythmic and harmonic interplay between patient and therapist concretely articulates that prestructured space for both of them. The patient moves into the space of irrational repetition in such a way that both can experience it convincingly. The therapist reasserts and concretizes his conviction in his every gesture. The patient once again cooperatively (with whatever difficulties, hesitations, or blockages) reinserts himself in such a way as to provide more data for the development of the therapist's convictions. The patient, then, who wants to be convinced, receptively awaits the fullness of the revelation. It is precisely in this harmonic dialectic that the therapeutic process becomes convincing and takes effect in the patient's life.

In successful psychotherapy, the patient generally comes to live out various aspects of the therapist's theory to a remarkable degree, not as a scientific or intellectual activity but as an active moving into and shaping of his life in the light of the therapist-patient dialectic. Just which aspects of the theory will come to have such existential significance for the patient and therapist is seldom given within the structure of the theory, rather, it is given in the concrete manner in which the therapist's theory preshapes and organizes the 'space-of-receptivity' and affirmable life in the therapy session.

The therapist is the way he is partly on account of his theory, partly on account of his life history, and partly on account of the particular patient he has. But the theory, as objectively transcendent of his particularities, remains for him the fundamental touchstone of reality and truth.

These truths which become genuinely inscribed in the life of the patient can be thought of as the fundament of the therapy-as-therapy, assisting the patient in the life transformation process in the hope of which he came to therapy in the first place. Most especially they are the attitudes, habitual gestures, and fundamental stances of the therapist, which are virtually omnipresent in his life with his patient.

In orthodox psychoanalysis, the constant presence of a receptive, interpretive attitude on the part of the therapist is such a factor. The therapist's presence as interpretive-mind to the efflorescent data provided by the patient gradually becomes a powerful factor in the patient's life. The patient develops a doubled or twinned consciousness, one-half of which is a developing analytic consciousness which looks upon his life very much as the analyst looks upon the free associations. In short, the analyst's habitual attitude becomes an attitude of the patient. It becomes, in fact, his reasonable, understanding, knowing, intelligent side.

The analyst, then, deliberately models himself, in the interests of objectivity and truth, after a definite theoretical-scientific model. The consciousness which he lives is therefore the consciousness of the other as 'complex-dynamic-object-to-be-explained-in-terms-of-its-past'. This, in turn, is the consciousness which the patient learns. He learns to view himself as an objective 'unwinding-of-an-objective-past-history', while at the same time learning to live that history (within the theory to repeat the past again).

## THE APPEAL OF THE THEORY

### Coherence, clarity, control, objectivity

In all of the therapies a patient-client who is more or less lost, confused, and unable to live as he wishes turns hopefully to a skilled, professional, knowing other. The patient's expectation, hope, and urgent need for expert principled treatment is already given culturally in the situation. That is, the fact that he seeks a professional therapist already points to his felt-need for objective help. He does not need merely friendship or a shoulder to cry on, though these may be part of what is called for therapeutically. He wants his therapist to be genuinely knowledgeable about what is helpful and unhelpful in life. Hence, for the therapist to respond with a specific, coherent, consistent orientation and style of treatment already accords with his needs.

For his part, the therapist also needs a guide for dealing with the complex problematics of people who are difficult to help. He cannot proceed on the basis of whim, guess, or hunch, and he does not wish simply to repeat cultural clichés to his patients. In order to help as many patients as he possibly can, with their variety of difficulties, modes of expression, and cultural backgrounds, he needs some mode of simplifying, ordering, and managing the complex field of interaction. All therapeutic orientations are responses to this need.

Both therapist and patient, then, need a mutually guiding frame of reference, and this knowledgeable guiding is rationally grounded in the therapist's theory, which he lives in his every response—in his questions and silences, in his mode of empathy, in his way of noticing or not noticing, in the index of meanings that the patient's utterances have for him. This is not to suggest that the therapist lives in a world of pure clarity but only to suggest that he is oriented and knows his way. Further, it is precisely this way of the therapist that the patient hopes will become a useful way for himself. To the patient's "How shall I get better, learn to live more amply, become less inhibited?" the therapist answers with his oriented, expert, more or less consistent ordering of the world that is constituted between them.

In Jungian therapy, for example, the constant turning of the therapist to the patient's inward sense of the symbolic—to his dreams and fantasies and their symbolic meanings—provides a coherent emphasis, language, and way of approach for therapist and patient alike. The way in which the therapist constantly looks for the "other side" encourages and helps to articulate a consistently expanding world of symbolic meanings. By means of this emphasis and style of interaction fundamentally given within Jungian thought, both the therapist and patient find a coherent, clear, controlled, and objective way of proceeding. They are thus engaged in a clearly structured process of interaction which has rules for uncovering truth about the patient.

Transcendent tru

All three theorists describe the patient as a split, nonintegrated being. Different aspects of his life are at war with, in some way isolated from, one another, which makes his commerce with the world tenuous and difficult. In the Freudian view, he is seen as living his particular idiosyncratic past history. In the Jungian view, he is seen as living his one-sided face and striving desperately to keep the other sides at bay. In the Rogerian view, he is seen as trying to maintain the self he ought to be according to false values he has adopted from others, instead of finding his true feeling-self and authentic inner values. Thus, the patient lives a doubled life. 'Being-more-than-he-lets-himself-be', means that he strives 'to-be-what-he-cannot-be', disowning what he could be and most fundamentally is. This disordered, false, neurotic mode of being has its counterpart in a too narrow, incoherent vision of the world and of truth.

The three theorists also agree, though in very different ways, that the patient must come to know, and to feel a wider, truer, fuller, more ample world. This coming to the truth is not only ideational but must involve lived-conviction, affective substantiality, and thereby a transformed life. The therapist's theory hammered out in a community of experts, grounded on the work of scholars, thinkers, and empirical researchers, lived in a fairly consistent language, and embodied in consensual communal gestures and techniques, opens up a space of inter-subjective truth.

When the Rogerian therapist refuses simply to answer his client's question but resolutely attends and responds to the client's feeling-life, he is expressing more than just his client and himself in an individual way. They stand together in a tradition of truth and value, a way of living, a language, a culture with its own standards. The therapist, especially stands for a truth that transcends his whim, impulse, momentary thought or feeling, and his personal appeal as a likable, admirable human being. This stand in something beyond and greater than himself is absolutely necessary for the therapeutic process because it is just this vision of the world within which the client's disorder can find principled integration and order. It is the therapist's world as opening on the truth and as able to comprehend the client's disunity in a living way that is necessary to the help of therapy.

The patient must be more than causally influenced; he must be introduced into a world of truth that is not subject to whim, not evanescent, and not caught in the grip of his own split self. For an effective therapy, this lived-vision of the world must be able to unite and integrate the 'self-in-the-world' into a vision of truth and reality. Each theory provides a more or less adequate vision within which the patient can find a greater unity or harmony, a greater openness and receptivity, a greater amplitude of life and of truth than he has been able to live before, because each theory is more unified and principled than the world view the usual patient brings into therapy.

The patient, having lost himself in disunity and the conflict of his split life, turns to the therapist, after all, for a principled, unified, expert pathway of help. It is already presupposed by the patient and the therapist that this will not be arbitrary help but will be grounded in the search for the true and the good. Further, it is expected that the therapist will be somewhat a specialist in getting people better in touch with what is really real and really important.

## SPECIAL PATHS OF LIFE

For the student of psychotherapy, it is obvious that each orientation and approach has a grip on *some* reality and that persons in each orientation can and do shape helpful relationships, even though each therapy is unique, special, and strange. In the pursuit of their special visions and special experience, each engages the patient in out-of-the-ordinary pursuits, leads him to experience the world at peculiar angles, and brings him to twists and turns of consciousness which take him out of the everyday world.

The Jungian will typically get the nonartist patient to paint, to make up imaginative stories, to daydream and talk about his daydreams as they are occurring, to pay close attention to his dreams and write them out, to develop an interest in the symbolic-imaginative collective realism of human existence, and so on. While this can be, and often is, helpful to individuals, it is also a highly specialized group of activities aimed at a highly specialized style of consciousness. In some way, each therapy orientation tends to introduce the patient to a specialized view of reality by employing special, unusual mode of 'living-in-relation' to the patient.

It is not immediately obvious, however, why each orientation sustains itself as separate from the other orientations to psychotherapy.

As each plausibly expresses some truth about man, it would seem that they could be fruitfully combined in some way. To this end, many therapists and therapeutic thinkers have sought increasingly more comprehensive and adequate ways of dealing with patients and comprehending their varieties. Jung, especially, understands that each school of therapy constitutes a certain way of being a person. Within Jung's thought, this means that Freudian theory is appropriate to certain persons at certain stages of their development, whereas Adlerian theory is more appropriate to others.

There is certainly some truth in this idea; the reader may have noticed that he himself found one or another of the different theories in this text most convincing. Careful examination reveals, however, that logical coherence or objective evidence are not the only grounds for this preference. These special views are not just abstractive or purely scientific theories. They are ways of experiencing and living in the world; styles of interacting with people; modes of understanding, comprehending, and making sense of the world; they are even affectively toned colorations of certain modes of life. As such, they attract or repel.

The world that we bring to these specialized worlds is already a special world shaped by our own particular histories, specific sensitivities, cultural backgrounds, habits of thought, and social ways. Before we ever read Freud, Jung, or Rogers, our way of life is already in hidden harmony or disharmony with the ways of living which they open up. Thus, our ease of understanding or not understanding the theories, our liking or disliking of them, our response to the specialized worlds they open up, is not based on a neutral objectivity or logic. As specialized worlds with special emphases and specific values, they appeal to us as ways to live, and we respond intuitively, and quite properly, in terms of our sense of whether they would be helpful in describing, unifying, or making sense of our own lives.

Some of the divergencies in therapeutic orientation can be understood in this way. Each offers not only a scientific theory, an expert approach to working helpfully with people, but also a whole world view of goals, values, and meanings. Each offers a specification of thought within a specific style or group of styles of life. Hence, the Freudian theory offers more than certain ideas about the inner psychic life, a certain view of development from infancy to adulthood, and a certain empiric-scientific idea about the distribution of energy in the body-mind of persons. The Freudian way of thinking offers itself as a mode of seeking to be reasonable and rational in a world that can be chaotic and irrational; as a skepticism about values, traditional truths, and religious views; as a mode of suspicion, doubtfulness, and an attempt to penetrate the deceptive surfaces of things. Hence, liking or not liking the Freudian approach, finding it inwardly and importantly convincing to one's life, is primarily a question of the consonance of that life with these value-laden attitudes. In this sense, a person is predisposed toward or away from Freudian, Jungian, or Rogerian thought and practice before his formal exposure to them as theorists, therapists, or thinkers.

## The manner of specialization

It is a fundamental structure of psychotherapy that a successful therapeutic relationship provides a specific pathway of help, opening up new truth and experience for the patient; that the therapist has to offer this specific pathway (to put it more properly, the therapist-patient pair has to find a specific pathway); and that the particular pathway of help will focus on such things as the past reliving itself, the collective symbolic universals, the organismic feeling-life, or some other specification of thought-conviction-practice.

More generally, the patient-therapist in effective treatment operates in a principled way to open up certain specific areas for thought, contact, feeling, choice, or perception. That is, in therapy one moves toward speaking about some things (not everything), focusing in certain ways (not every way), speaking a certain language (not every language), and living out a very specific mode, style, and actuality of relationship between. Further, each of the three orientations described here does in fact succeed in providing this principled, focused, useful, and healing structure for some patients.

However, none of the orientations is able to penetrate to the significance of having an orientation or a theory of therapy. None of the languages developed within each special group is able to speak to the fact that the development of a special language *is* the cure, or at least a fundamental structure of the help. Each theorist enters into his specialization more or less blindly, living out his conviction unaware of the power of the convinced living-out. The theorist-therapist is radically unaware of the principle of co-constitution; hence, for him, the patient *is as he is*. This patient's independent being, this 'being-in-itself', is understood as merely revealed, not transformed, by the theorist-therapist.

In client-centered therapy, this blindness to the therapist and his power—most especially the blindness to the power of his theoretical specialization—is carried to its ultimate point. The therapist's ideology is lived out totally in the natural attitude, so that he imagines that he is bringing out only what is actually *there* in the client, never noticing the very special mode and manner of perceiving, responding, and shaping of feelings in his very attitude toward feelings. In fact, however, his attitude that feelings are pure gold, the most valued part of the communication process, and the really real, focuses him in such an attentive, hovering emphasis on those feelings he considers most real that the whole situation between him and his client is enormously, powerfully transformed.

But the client-centered theorist-therapist is totally enraptured within the natural attitude by the purity, depth, and intensity of the feelings emerging from within the client-over-there. He is *in principle*, by virtue of his theory, its biases, and the very enrapture of client-centeredness, unable to notice the fundamental structure of what he is doing. He can only understand himself as understanding, empathizing, or expressing the feelings that belong to the client. He cannot understand himself *in principle* as transformer, selector, emphasizer, indoctrinator of ideology, teacher of theory, convinced expressive articulator of a view of reality, life, and values or understand the actual centering of the process in that space-between shaped by client and therapist together. In short, he is not able to made focal, thematic, and theoretical what is actually going on in the 'lived-world-space' between his client and himself.

Rather, his specialized language and conviction, lived out in a totalized systematic understanding of the situation, positively prevent him from seeing what is happening, except in that angle given in the rapture of 'seeking-the-feelings-of-my-client-over-there, 'responding-empathically-to-the-feelings-of-my-client-over-there'. The peculiarity of the specialization, then, is that on the one hand it provides a way to go, a focus to maintain, a pathway of openness between client and therapist, while at the same time it creates a fundamental structural blindness to reality for the therapist and ultimately for the client as well. That is, reality is present to both under the rubrics and style of an ideoligized, narrowed, and specialized vision of such a nature that most of it must be systematically ignored. Since the reality which must be overlooked is precisely that which is lived between them, this is a serious matter.

### The source of blindness

The Freudian, Jungian, and Rogerian theories, while fostering an openness to a specific sphere of reality, tend at the same time to close the therapist to other important areas of reality because of their narrowness of style and angularity of vision. This narrowness and angularity is built into the therapist's work and is therefore in addition to whatever specificity and narrowness belong to him in a personal way.

Phenomenological description reveals that the closed narrowness of these theories is partly grounded on a natural fascination given to both therapist and patient. The patient appears to the therapist in the mode of 'being-as-he-is', and the articulation of the 'patient-being-as-he-is' is given, in principle, in the therapist's already established theory. As readers of the theories and their application, we ourselves have participated in that systematic blindness. It became obvious to us that the patient really is reliving his past; later, the transparency of the patient's being was given to us as the resonance of archaic and universal archetypal symbols; finally, the pure feeling-self in hiding became the fundamental truth. In each case, to the degree that we participated in that blindness and sharpened focus, it was as if the patient's being were being uncovered in its untouched, untransformed, really real condition.

The blindness of the theories, and of ourselves when we participate in them, is given in their ignorance of the transformative power-of-having-a-theory and in their inability to grasp the principle of co-constitution. The therapist-theorist, in the attitude fostered by his natural science training, forgets himself too much. First, he is so fascinated by the spectacle unfolding before his eyes that he forgets that it is his way of looking and his language that opens it up for him to look at. He forgets his vision and the special skills, training, talent, theoretical learning, years of practice, seminars, and transformation of vocabulary that were involved for him. He may, of course, admit that his skilled sensitivity tunes him more sharply into reality, but he will insist that it is objectively given reality itself to which he responds.

We, as readers, are not so sure, however, that the therapist is responding simply to what is there given. It is not that he invents it out of whole cloth; rather, it is that we now are as fascinated and intrigued by the fact that three such different transformations of reality are possible as we are by the fact that each is individually convincing.

All of these theories are quite totally caught in the "natural attitude." To everyday man living in the ordinary world, the world simply is as it is. Some objects are hard, others are soft; some men are cruel, others are kind. Within this world, the patient who comes to the therapist has something wrong with him to some degree or in some manner, just as a car brought to a mechanic has something wrong with it. Further, within this world the mechanic or therapist has to know how to fix what is wrong. Virtually all science and specialization are lived out as refinements of this attitude.

The attitude that everything is fixable, changeable, manipulable, calculable, and handleable and that it is necessary to reduce "nature" to the size of the grasping consciousness and technology has led in modern times to an enormous variety of specializations between and within fields. This reduction of a complex life-field to the technical grasping consciousness always means a reduction and focusing of consciousness on only a few aspects of reality. Such reductions are manifest within psychotherapy, in which each traditional orientation focuses on a special aspect of reality, constitutes a specialized consciousness, overlooks much of the life-world, and does so in principle.

The specialized consciousness of technology in its many forms is paradoxical. On the one hand, it seeks to change, shape, order, and transform the world by making it more efficient. On the other hand, it forgets that its own pragmatic technical attitude is a powerful transformer of the world. The technical economist, for example, to whom the economic system is a given one, may easily develop an ideology which states that *this* given is the most basic given, forgetting that as an economist he (and/or society, which is becoming fascinated with technological economics) views the world in specialized, developed, narrowed ways. On the basis of his specialization, the psychoanalyst will, in turn, explain the economist's interest as basically an expression of early problems in giving and receiving within the family. Both experience themselves as attuned to reality as it is given, but neither sees clearly that reality gives itself to his highly attuned, specialized, narrowed consciousness. Reality always speaks the language one knows best, at least when it follows one's systematic, theoretical biases. To be fascinated only by that which presents itself as an 'in-itself' is to forget the perceiving conscousness as a co-participant in the shaping of reality.

In this very general sense, the power of theory or of language to co-constitute things to be as they are to us is significantly overlooked as part of the therapy situation. Although the therapist's theory typically gives some account, and even a specialized explanation of, the biases or narrowness of the patient, his theory does not adequately describe, understand, or explain his theory. While this section has dealt so far only with a general critique of technical, specialized, narrowed consciousness, the principle of co-constitution in psychotherapy has been demonstrated to be a much more powerfully concrete factor in therapy. For psychotherapy is not a situation in which a scientist approaches a more or less inert object to reveal some highly specialized side or other. It is a relationship between two persons, in which the systematic approach transforms meanings on both sides of the relationship.

## Effect of therapeutic one-sidedness

The power of the principle of co-constitution as lived in the psychotherapeutic interaction far exceeds being a question of angle on reality or theoretical way of looking. The basic ways of looking, thinking, living, and feeling that therapist and patient work out between them *are* the help which the therapy provides and, when lived convincingly with a cooperative and willing patient, come to be *lived-truth* between them. But to exactly the degree to which it is specialized, technicalized lived-truth, the world opened up is narrowed, specialized, technicalized. Everything is strained through the sieve of the specialized consciousness; life itself undergoes a kind of angular distortion; therefore, it is a life-movement that fails radically to comprehend itself rightly.

As way of life, value stance, and point of view, each theory selects rather arbitrarily from the richness of the life-world this or that truth to be affirmed, this or that value to be lived; it provides a set of spectacles, a template for viewing reality, and also a set of values for affirming and disaffirming what is given. Thus within Freudian theory, there is skepticism, methodical doubt of what is given to experience, and emphasis on the value of reasonably balanced free self-assertion and proper uninhibited pleasure experience. Within Jungian theory, there is a priority on inward symbolic unfolding, self-actualization as the goal of life, and a strong emphasis on balance and wholeness, which leads to searching for more and more varied inner experiences. Within Rogerian theory, there is an emphasis on a democratic sense of individuality, care and respect for persons, the life of feeling as the real life, and social harmony.

While each set of values and truths is good, especially when it is lived well by its adherents, each can easily move to a kind of exclusivity and ideologizing which buries, or tries to bury, the richness and complexity of reality and values given in the lived-world. When the analyst striving to be objective neutral interpreter finds it difficult to be warmly supportive, or labels such an impulse in himself as countertransference and therefore *bad*, this difficulty becomes a lived-difficulty in the therapy. Warmth, kindness, supportiveness, and loyalty are values which live in the world along with truthfulness, objectivity, carefulness, and accuracy.

A theory that hopes to sustain and foster life-values should not select one set of values over another, thereby neglecting to affirm values and truths necessary to good living. But to the degree to which the analyst places first and foremost his theoretical bias for interpretive clarity, his skeptical, suspicious style of examining every gift horse carefully for its underlying aggressive or sexual underpinnings—to exactly that degree, spontaneity, childlike trust, warmth, kindness, and goodwill are undermined or at least attenuated as values.

In Jungian therapy, the pursuit of inward, symbolic, self-actualization motifs is clearly an attentuation or neglect of social values. It is a constant self-preoccupation, a reduction of every situation to its *symbolic import for me*; even my relations to others are fundamentally reduced to a shadow play of projections, meanings, and archetypes that belong to my consciousness and unconsciousness. While this leads in gifted people to a certain kind of poetic, imaginative efflorescence of consciousness and an enormous sensitivity to the nuances of symbolic meanings, it also leads away from good, commonsense relations with, and direct concern for, others.

In Rogerian therapy, which is genuinely concerned with the non-imposition of theory and values built into its operative method of understanding-reflection, there is a genuine gain in remaining faithful to the life-world. The client's self-interpretation is radically affirmed and respected, so that, in this sense, the client is left in the pretheoretical life-world and asked to express it with a minimum of theoretical bias (except insofar as that bias is in the life-world already). However, the one-sided emphasis on *feeling* as the real, and the total emphasis on the client's person as a kind of isolated, solipsist feeling-flow, removes that therapy from a full appreciation of thinking or judging; the slight theory is also unable to understand genuine 'being-together-with-others', which cannot be encompassed by modes of understanding harmonic presence.

## Common values

In retrospect then, the narrowness and bias of each theorist-therapist is evident. It is also evident that their helpfulness as therapists involves transcending theoretic biases. Dr. R., in spite of living out a skeptical, suspicious mode of consciousness and fostering in himself and his patient primarily the values of coolness, clarity, and rationality, was warm and, in many specific instances, trusting. In order for him to provide support, reassurance, and direct approval at appropriate times, it was necessary for him to convey much of his caring presence, approving stance, and supportive being through modest variations of interpretation. Although he could not announce himself directly, his respect for his patient, his care, support, and warmth nevertheless communicated and were clearly integral to the development of an affirmable, livable world for his patient. Without these common life values being expressed and lived between Mary and Dr. R., no therapy help would have been possible.

Likewise, in spite of the formal emphasis of client-centered theory on feelings and the flow of feeling-filled experience, Dr. G. lived out with Mary a style of interested, often nearly intellectual detachment. Thus, thought, intellectual clarity, and precision, which are common values lived in the everyday world along with the values of flexibility, feeling, warmth, and good rapport, were all lived in the therapy. In the Jungian therapy, along with the strong emphasis on the inward self, there was lived out between Mary and Dr. M. a hard-working cooperativeness on common tasks, friendliness and mutual support, social consideration, tact, and courtesy.

In each therapy and therapy orientation, it can therefore be seen that much more is lived out than the theory can describe, especially the way in which therapist and patient together live out of and from a far wider ground of values than is articulated, emphasized, and lived in the specialized theoretic consciousness. As an ordinary man steeped in the value traditions of the culture, the therapist cannot fail to live out of that broad horizon of values which are given by his culture to him and his client alike. Clarity is valued more than vagueness, and the client-centered therapist implicitly lives out this value by continuing to pursue vague feelings, to work them through, whereas when he arrives at the rock bottom of a clear, concise, unified expression of feeling he has reached a goal. Thus, the therapist's presence is never reducible to merely providing an atmosphere of understanding but includes a stand in a variety of mixed, even somewhat contradictory, and yet lived-out values as taught within the context of his culture. Hence, thoughtfulness, kindness, love, care, clarity of vision, honesty, precision, and accuracy are lived, embodied, and expressed by the therapist and client together, either in harmony with, or in spite of, the theoretic therapeutic bias.

## A MORE ADEQUATE DESCRIPTIVE THEORY

If it is to be helpful to life, each therapy as lived concretely between patient and therapist must help to shape an affirmable world of living for the patient to carry into his everyday cultural life. It is clear that helpful relations are carried out within the traditional orientations to psychotherapy. It has been indicated as well that personal historical and temperamental factors cause therapists to prefer and be able to live better within certain theoretic biases than others. Certain life styles are already predisposed to a Freudian, Jungian, or Rogerian therapy and theory of life.

Hence, the constant concern with theoretic adequacy to life, and with the ability of a therapeutic theory to comprehend itself and its own operations in a relationship, may seem impractical and unnecessary. From the vantage point of actual therapeutic work, the inspiration of this text to find a more adequate, encompassing, more comprehensive, and more life-realistic understanding of the therapeutic process is perhaps unnecessary. But theory is not all that harmless or beside the point. Each therapy involves different transformations, introduces the patient-client into different worlds of consciousness, life, and values. Each traditional therapy delimits itself formally and through deliberate emphasis to a rather arbitrarily narrow set of concepts, procedures, language, and selected values. To exactly the degree to which it effectively constitutes a specialized world of understanding, each therapeutic orientation places itself at variance with, or is fragmented from, the common world of values which serves implicitly as its ground.

Freudian-cured patients and Freudian therapists thus constitute a special cultural subgroup with very special ways of looking at reality and characteristic blindnesses. Their twinned consciousness, their onlooking self with its formal theory about the past repeating itself and its emphasis on pleasure seeking and aggression expression, leads to a whole range of difficulties in their social life. As a group, they lack spontaneity and are hyperrational; but even the hyperrationality is not that of a normally intellectual cultural subgroup but is more exactly specified by the theory they learn. They are prepared to be skeptical about almost anything held with great conviction, because it is assumed that irrationality and drivenness inform emotions that show too clearly. Certain political, social, and religious issues will be seen by them as projections of personal problems and thus automatically invalidated as genuine human issues. Hence, their world tends to recede to the size and scope of their understandings of the intrapsychic life; their long trained, onlooking watching of themselves is given to them in their life as a cautious, nonadventurous, self-preoccupied style of approach. Viewed from the outside, they seem to share many characteristics of ideologically brainwashed persons.

While a more adequate, comprehensive, and life-descriptive theory cannot prevent all forms of narrowness in therapy, it may reduce in a practical way the extraordinary specialization of consciousness and ideologizing so characteristic of traditional orientations to psychotherapy. From the point of view of the development of a human science, an encompassing, descriptive sense of psychotherapy which is cognizant, and takes descriptive account, of lived-theory as a factor in therapy is obviously superior to a merely parochial view of therapy that is unable to describe its own localization.

## Personal factors

That personal, individual temperamental factors also play a significant part in the therapy process has already been seen. The therapist's individual style, temperament, background of lived-values, and specific cultural modes of expression all participate in, and shape the space of, the therapeutic interaction, and this individuality is a crucial aspect of the transformation possibilities of the therapy. A personal emphasis on coolness or calm thoughtfulness, on aesthetic sensitivity or inspired affectivity made therapies within the same orientation strikingly and significantly different in their effect.

The therapist's personal value predilections, likes and dislikes were also seen to shape the relationship and transform the interpretations. Therapeutic communities are very aware of this—e.g., "Dr. B. is very good with compulsives but can't stand hysterics." It is understood that each therapist has his special talents and special blindnesses. In this way, theorist-practitioners admit a kind of personal equation in psychotherapy, which is, in practice, irreducible.

At the level of practice, therapists know that some basic kind of "hitting if off well with," "having a clear feel for," or "having an accurate intuition into" is essential for the best and most helpful therapy. As technical specializations, however, the theories can only vaguely describe this aspect of therapeutic life. They handle the problem, fundamentally, by bending their specialized views back upon the therapist and including him in their interpretations. Because none of the theories seriously tries to take into account the life-world in its fullness, their interpretation of the individual problematics of the therapist-patient relationship is plagued by a continuing narrowness. Getting along well with someone is a life-world phenomenon which encompasses and gives ground to the possibilities, in the more specialized worlds, of such things as "good timing of analytic interpretations," "good reflection of feeling," or "good therapeutic grasp of the archetypal symbols."

In other words, if people don't get along, they don't get along. In the life-world, this means that they don't work well together, don't like one another, are disinclined to believe or trust one another, and so on. But any specialized therapeutic practice requires that the persons involved get along well, grow to trust and believe each other. In turn, this possibility of getting along well, trusting, and understanding is grounded not only on common values but also on the individual matching of temperament, style, and values. The patient, who is a concrete being and much more of a person than the neurotic described by the theory, meets with a therapist who is himself much more than the therapeutic agent described by the theory. Both concretely embody their personal styles in every moment of their interaction.

The cool, cerebral, ironically humorous, tolerant, godlike analyst is a very different therapist from the passionate, aesthetic, impetuous, warm, antiintellectual therapist trained in the same institute by the same teachers. Their therapies with the same patient would not appear as therapies with the same patient. The patient, if helped, would be invited into very different worlds; indeed, his very strengths and weaknesses would appear as different. With the more cerebral analyst, the weak ego, the lack of clear, orderly integrative powers, might stand out as the crucial pathologic factor. With the more passionate, affectively "tuned-up" analyst, the problem of strangulated affect, blocked and inhibited expressivity, would be the central pathology.

Depending on the therapist's individuality, the patient appears differently not only to the therapist but to an onlooker as well. The passionate therapist shapes the space between them in such a way that emotion and its blocking constitute the life of the patient lived in the session. The cerebral therapist shapes a space between them in which the inability to integrate, to maintain order, to contain and control, are strikingly lived by the patient in the hour.

## Traditional theories

The narrowness and specialization of these traditional theories make them radically unable to comprehend the dialectics of psychotherapy. They can adequately describe neither the common values lived in the therapy nor, indeed, the concrete particularities of the therapist and patient. Nevertheless, our attention should be directed toward them as something more than simply misunderstandings or mistakes. This text has been directed toward them primarily as examples of psychotherapeutic help. They are readily available modern methods about which there is considerable literature; they also are popular methods, at least in their overall influence on the culture. As examples, therefore, they lend themselves to descriptive and theoretical commentary. Unlike mesmerism or the work of African witch doctors, however, they are already ordered within a developing science of man and can be seen, in spite of fragmentation, as related in a line of growing understanding of therapy and therapeutic intervention.

Freud initiated a work in which conversation of a special kind was understood as leading to a systematic scientific understanding of human beings. He developed a systematic theory bound on the one side by a natural scientific conception of man and on the other by the wish to understand and interpret the sufferings of neurotic patients. Jung built upon this work, correcting, criticizing, and enlarging its scope, in places refuting Freud's work but still working clearly within a framework of interpretation in terms of unconscious dynamics. Above all, Jung attempted to overcome the natural scientific style of theorizing of his age. In certain areas he succeeded in doing so, though in terms of his overall theories it must be admitted that natural science as entrance to reality won the day. Since for both Freud and Jung the temptation to a wild occultism was so strong, it is perhaps just as well that they remained more or less bound to the systematic rigors of natural scientific thinking. In this way they could build systematically upon each other's work and make it possible for us to learn from them.

Rogers continued this work, reinterpreting within the understandings of a democratic, more egalitarian society, challenging in a different way the absolute priority of technical expertise and natural science. The movement away from reading the client's speech as the hiding place of complex unconscious dynamics, the movement toward taking the client's words at face value, the trend toward giving first priority to the client's self-interpretation—all moved Rogers away from a technical natural science view of therapy.

In the Freudian view (though not always in practice), meanings were veiled and required the expert scientist to penetrate their behind-the-scene causes. In the Jungian view, meanings were richly amplified from within the patient's view as informed and elaborated by the collectively known. But to Jung, the meanings were seen in some radical sense as there to be read, to be seen, given in the patient's expression. In the Rogerian view, this trend toward granting sense, meaning, and status to the patient's expression reaches its fullness, in that the therapist actively reflects what the client says or means and constantly uses the client as the touchstone of accuracy and validity.

Freud, Jung, and Rogers represent a line of thinkers and theorists who have each understood something important about reality and expressed it systematically. Each has built upon the others, and each is a rich mine of insights and understandings in himself. The work of the social sciences richly benefits from the work of such men. Our own understanding of therapy and of man is enriched by attending seriously to what they say as a teaching, a learning for life. Their thought is even more crucial for understanding the possibilities of psychotherapy and its actualities, as each has developed a "way of help" unique in history and yet each interrelated to the other "ways of help."

They each show us man, especially neurotic man, struggling to find a better life. It is true that each shows us a specialized view of man and that their pathways to the better life therefore suffer a peculiar systematic distortion. Nonetheless, when they show us 'man-in-therapy', the 'patient-and-therapist-together', the neurotic personality, the striving to be whole and well, each reveals some aspect of what man is, and what they show is necessary to the work of those who would understand and carry on the work of therapy.

An existential-phenomenological approach seeks to describe, comprehend, and ultimately to encompass the work of these theories, carrying further what is positive in the theories while rejecting their obscure, narrow, merely aberrant aspects. For such a goal to be realized, it is necessary to attend to these theories seriously and systematically so as to express their truth in a new and greater fullness by going beyond their narrowness.

## VALUES AND TRUTHS

### Orthodox psychoanalysis

The theme of the past repeating itself in the present is among the most important and enduring contributions that orthodox psychoanalysis has made to the field of psychotherapy. As modern men, we find this insight so in harmony with the even more basic presupposition of natural science that any event may be reduced to its causes that we may overlook the enormously fruitful horizon which such an interpretation opens. Whether or not the therapist uses it often as an explicit interpretation with his patients, it nevertheless gives meaning to the fixity, repetition, and difficulty in learning that characterize his patients, and it remains an underlying insight informing his work.

In Jungian therapy, the repetition theme is expressed in terms of the patient's one-sidedness, an imbalance learned in the course of an individual history in which certain specific talents, attributes, or aspects of his personality were encouraged and others discouraged. The patient continues to live as if this early pattern of encouragement-discouragement were valid and fails to develop the other, less approved sides of his person. In client-centered therapy, the repetition theme is clearly stated in the theoretical idea of "conditions of worth." The client has learned values, allowed and nonallowed conditions, which if he continues to live them even when his situation permits him more latitude, is the heart of his neurosis.

No post-Freudian therapist can neglect this pervasive insight of the past repeating itself. Even those who believe, like Rank and Adler, that overattention to the past is part and parcel of the neurotic condition and to be discouraged, attest the truth of the repetition theme by implying that neurosis is grounded in the past repeating itself. Since Freud, therapy has been designed to assist the patient to stop this dreadful repetition.

Another insight which has grounded all modern psychotherapy since Freud is the realization of the split, disfunction, or radical alienation of the person within himself and from others. In Freud, this split into neurosis-inducing conscious and unconscious is grounded on the favoring of a certain ideal self and fear of being the bad self. Anxiety, fear of condemnation, annihilation, or loss of value, or profound discomfort prevent the person from allowing himself or reality to exist in certain ways.

Jung and Rogers echo this insight in their theories, although their way of understanding it accords with their own value preferences and characteristic interpretive styles. Even the behavior therapists, who are interpretively far afield from the therapies studied in this text, shape their therapies in such a way as to help the patient to enter into fields of action, behavior, and thought which had heretofore been unavailable to him. They help him to relax the anxiety and develop the actional competencies that open up the previously forbidden, dangerous areas of the world.

Freud's reduction of behavior to the underlying motivations of sexuality-sensuality and aggression-assertion is still another enduring contribution to psychotherapeutic theory and practice. The first aspect of this twofold interpretive work is rooted in methodic doubt or suspicion and involves a recognition that the surfaces of behavior may obscure deeper, less obvious levels of motivation. All therapists deal with man in the light of this insight; their theories of neurosis and psychosis are precise articulations of the structure of these implicit realms of meaning.

In Jungian theory, this unconscious level is panoplied with rich heritages from both the patient's individual history and the collective history of mankind. In Rogerian therapy, this level of unawareness carries the conditions of worth and conditions of condemnation that the client learned socially as he grew up; just beneath that level is an organismic striving for actualization which surges from the mysterious depths of the personality. In the "body armor" theories of Reich and Lowen, this implicit level of meanings is to be found in the habitual postures, poses, and rigidities of the body, which has shaped itself in accord with a certain fear-filled vision of the world and its attacks.

Hence, Freud's concern with penetrating the conventional, deceptive surfaces of behaviors to the fantastical, powerfully affective, implicit structures behind them, or only obscurely expressed in them, is a permanent contribution to psychotherapeutic theory and practice. Although the modes of theoretical understanding and of treatment-practice in relation to that rich background of meanings may vary, the fundamental insight into a behind-the-scenes life of meanings is a perduring and fruitful insight.

Freud's view of the unconscious fantasy life as grounded on sexuality and aggression—the second aspect of this interpretive work—is also a permanent contribution, though perhaps at a lesser level of generality than the other insights mentioned. Jung, Rogers, Adler, Rank, and other theorists tell us that this level of motivational analysis is inappropriate in a variety of ways—as an arbitrary reduction, a reduction corrosive to life values, a reduction that properly fits certain behaviors only at certain times and distorts the meanings of other behaviors. However limited in range and value, this interpretation is nevertheless very much a part of the contemporary therapist's understanding. His ability to see aggression behind apparent niceness, stubborn refusal behind smiling compliance, or sexual seductiveness behind coy purity—all are grounded in that peculiarly skeptical, reductive stance given in Freud's sex-aggression interpretations. How this narrowly specialized, angulated interpretation can become part of a speaking grounded more broadly in the life-world of common values is a problem for the theorist-practitioner.

The practice of orthodox psychoanalysis also expresses some important enduring truths about the process of human helpfulness. The analyst's emphasis on resistance to change reminds us that habituation and repetition are a deep truth in human life. This emphasis on unchangingness, if it does not become a doctrine of helpless pessimism, is a genuinely helpful inducement toward relaxed patience and modesty of goals on the therapist's part. Much that is given in early life is permanent, but the cluster of life-values surrounding this insight into neurotic being do not necessarily contradict an attitude of hopeful optimism and belief in the future.

Rather, genuine human helpfulness and hope for new learning must be rooted in an appreciation of that which is unchangeable and must be accepted; otherwise the hope for change becomes an idealization, yet another source of unrest, agitation, and anxious self-disapproval. Seeking to change comes to mean that I constantly condemn the 'self-I-am' in favor of the 'hoped-for-self' I can become. While Freudian theory and practice have overspecialized in the themes of unchanging, invariance, and repetition compulsion, it is nonetheless true that each therapy must come to terms with the fact of sedimented habituation and resistance to change among its patients.

Another permanent contribution of orthodox psychoanalysis to the theory and practice of psychotherapy is the recognition that intellectual apprehension and clarity of understanding are not enough. Freud said that you cannot kill a person in effigy, meaning that the concrete, emotional, experiential factors in the neurosis have first to be brought back to life and understood in their vivid actuality if therapeutic help is to be given.

Jung constantly affirms this necessity for vivid apprehension and committed involvement on the part of both patient and therapist. The dream must be taken seriously as a guide for life. Commitment, moral earnestness, and dedication are necessary if aesthetic or intellectual notions are to take root and transform a person's life. Rogers' vital emphasis on feeling addresses the same issue. Feelings must be understood, amplified, contacted, expressed, vivified, and brought to life. In this way there is expansion of contact and feeling together with speaking and other expression. Action and change of behavior are the focus in the behavior therapies, which also affirm that, more than understanding, movement in actual life is the change needed. Thus, recognizing the limitations of mere thought, the relative uselessness of abstract or merely notional understanding, and the necessity of finding ways to make therapy more concretely effective were already among Freud's permanent contributions to therapeutic theory-practice.

## Jungian psychotherapy

Because Jung was already seeking an overarching comprehension of psychotherapy, his work is in direct line with the comprehensive intention of the present work. Jung's first movement toward comprehensiveness lay in the profound yet obvious recognition that as human beings differ in significant ways, their ways of being different involve different psychologies, different ways of theorizing, different ways of apprehending reality—indeed, different therapeutic needs. Corresponding to these differences in type, temperament, and modes of life there would naturally be different distortions of life and different pathways of help. The excessively outwardly-directed patient would need to develop inwardness; the overly introverted patient would need to learn to attend to the external world; the overskeptical patient would need to develop trust and faith. This individualizing attentiveness to the specificity of the person—his age, type, personal deficiencies, strengths and weaknesses—and the recognition of the need for a corresponding individualized responsiveness on the therapist's part in accord with just exactly who the patient is, is among Jung's contributions to therapeutic understanding and theorizing.

While all therapists do, at some practical level, make individual adjustments in their ongoing relationships with patients, this is lived out primarily at a commonsense, socially intuitive level. The theories allow little space for differences, presupposing a fundamental sameness to the patients. Thus, in the Freudian theory, all patients are basically suffering a repression of sexuality and aggression; in the Rogerian theory, all clients suffer a loss of contact with their feelings. Jung's understanding that one man's meat is another man's poison points even more radically to his apprehension of man as multileveled or many-sided. By positing as valuable and appropriate a balanced multifaceted development of personality, he foreshadows the existential understanding of the "life-world."

Freudian theory posits methodic skepticism and self-assertion, good ego control, and appropriate sexual expression as veritable absolutes, so that this very narrow range of values, characteristics, and life-themes is made to stand for the whole life. In Jung, this style of interpretation and self-control is seen as one value appropriate in bringing people down from self-inflation or overidealization. Thus, what is absolutized in Freud is relativized in Jung; that is, it is seen as useful and true but of limited value. Jung knew that many truths must be affirmed if there is to be room for the whole man: feelings count, thought, images, and fantasy count, the unconscious counts, the conscious purposes count. This highly practical concern with what the particular patient actually needs to balance himself, and the insight into the concrete differences between patients as necessitating a genuine variety of pathways of help, are permanent contributions of Jung to psychotherapeutic practice and theory. However, both these insights are so close to the good commonsense level that they do not belong in a special way to Jung, although he deepens them through the context of a special vision and understanding.

Two other aspects of Jung's thought belong more particularly to him and are almost certainly permanent contributions as well. The first is his recognition that symbols transform personality. Although Freud had also recognized the power of the symbolic, he only dimly understood or appreciated the power of man as signifier, symbolizer, and creator of worlds of meaning. Freud constantly emphasized the unchanging invariance given in a body-self conceived as a purely material, almost electrical-hydraulic body. The energy system as an 'in-itself' was conceived as difficult to change. He saw talk, imagination, fantasy, and symbolizing as relatively powerless to effect change—hence, the pessimism and doubt about therapy which appeared in his later writings.

While Jung retained some of the language of energy systems, he conceived the body-self as a symbolic system. Complexes were organizations of meaning-units—patterns of signification, responses, gestalts of symbolic systems. This deep appreciation of man's inherently symbolic nature coupled with an appreciation of the power of the symbolic enabled Jung to believe more radically in the power of speaking to people and in the possibility of personal transformation and change.

To imagine a thing differently, with genuine effort, is to change it; to think it differently, with seriousness and commitment, is to have it differently; to dare in one's mind—in imagery, symbols, fantasy, and thought—if done properly, is to become courageous in fact. Thus, Jung taught us that the power of the symbol, of thought, and of imagination can under certain circumstances transform life. The development of those circumstances is the challenge of therapy.

Every therapy must contend with, and live itself out in, the light of this insight. In existential thought and practice, this insight into the power of the imagination as actual lived-possibility is raised to an even higher level of understanding. But each therapy, no matter what its special emphasis, must seek to find ways to open up new worlds of possibility for its patients. Jung's insight is that the world of possibility is profoundly tied to the imaginative, symbolic realms. The patient must sense as actually possible that which has heretofore been unimaginable.

Imagining as possible new realms of action and behavior is built into the structure of behaviorist therapy, which says in effect, "We will get you gradually, through our techniques, to do what you previously have been unable to do." The patient, at first only timorously imagining and hoping, is inserted into that new symbolic, meaningful possible through the assured, expert, convincing structure of the training processes. But this works only if the imagined-real (as in Wolpe's deconditioning therapy method) is taken as meaning the really-actual. It is lived skepticism on the patient's part that makes the cure impossible. In lived skepticism, that which is imagined in the therapist's office is not related to what is really feared in the world; hence, no cure is effected. The power of the symbolic—that which is signified in the therapist's office—to become real, actual, and transformative in the patient-client's actual life is at the heart of the therapy transformation.

Jung has also offered a mode of interpreting the patient's behaviors, dreams, and symbolic products. This mode looks for, and is especially attuned to, the ways in which the patient lives out collective or universal symbolic processes in his life. In principle, this opens up a broad horizon of valuable interpretations of the patient's life. Everything he says or does is interpretable as an expression of universal, collective strivings shared in common with all mankind. Every dream can be seen in its archetypal or universal-collective aspects. Each man at each moment is in some way or manner all men, or at least a typification of all men.

This mode of interpretation is therapeutically very valuable for overcoming the sense of individual isolation that characterizes so much of psychopathology. The patient is helped to see himself in the light of mankind, all men, the collectively valid and real. Just as, in principle, every behavior can be seen in terms of the past repeating itself in the present, so is it possible to view every behavior as an example of man in his strivings. Regardless of his orientation, the therapist's ability to make general, universal human sense of the 'patient-in-his-life' is genuinely sanity evoking. Even the Rogerian therapist, who makes no use of the Jungian theory of archetypes, helps his patient to arrive at certain basic and universal human feelings. The client's discovery of the sense, universality, and basic humanity of these feelings is necessary in order for him to express them, live them, and contact them. By understanding them, the therapist essentially asserts and teaches their general human sense.

Another of Jung's permanent contributions is the interpretation in terms of the future. This is not a uniquely Jungian contribution, as many other theorists and therapists have also stressed it. Nonetheless, Jung raised it to the level of principle, placing it alongside the past repeating itself and the collectively symbolic. His vision of each man as rising from the collective universal past, through the past of his own idiosyncratic life, through the present now given, toward a future which provides the pull, sense, or goal of life is an angulated, specialized expression of common sense and a significant feature of any comprehensive understanding of psychotherapeutic work. The patient's being in therapy makes sense only within this temporal structure. He comes in hope for the future, experiencing anxiety and concern about the present, and carrying his past with him as a burden rather than as a resource. An existential understanding raises this grasp of man's temporality to an even more refined and explicit level. But Jung's contribution within a therapeutic tradition beginning with Freud, and his showing us varieties of temporal imterpretation as therapeutically fruitful, gives him an important place in a comprehensive therapeutic understanding.

## Client-centered therapy

It is relatively easy to place the contributions of Jung and Freud in some comprehensive historical perspective, but Carl Rogers is a contemporary who continues to develop and change his thought and practice in slight but significant ways. As a contemporary American and as a kind of existentialist, humanist, and phenomenologist, his thought and practice are more closely related to existential-phenomonological theory, all of which makes the work of placing him within the context of this book more difficult.

Unlike Freud and Jung, Rogers is not an original theoretical genius with a complex system of ideas and interpretations. His basic genius arises at the level of working out a way of relating differently to his patients, transforming the role of patient-therapist and changing the relation of expert knowledge to therapeutic practice. Roger's theory of personality is, as empirical theory, only a slight variation on Freud's, but it changes practice and involves a radical transformation of the meaning of the therapy relationship. It is within this shift in attitude within the therapeutic relationship and its implications for therapeutic theory and practice that his permanent contribution lies.

In Freudian therapy, the therapist is the knower, armed with a knowledge of his own unconscious, a knowledge of the working of personality in general, and with years of developing skill and practice. Placed within a situation designed to foster his vision, knowledge, and understanding, he gradually inserts this knowledge concretely and effectively in the patient's life. In Jungian therapy, the therapist is the guide. Out of his past wrestling with his own individual and collective unconscious, out of a general knowledge of human beings with a special emphasis on the universally and collectively human, out of a trained attunement to the symbolic, and with years of developing skill and practice, he guides the patient toward new symbolic modes and experiences.

In client-centered therapy, the questions of wisdom, knowledge, expertise, and theoretical sophistication become fundamentally irrel-event. The client is the center, the knower, the feeler; the client is the basic expert, the basic interpreter, the one who makes sense. The therapist's task is to follow the client's sense, to remain faithful to the meanings given by the client, and to stay within the client's feeling-sensing life. Even the client's words are respected as the primary words. They are characteristically repeated by the therapist. Client and therapist dwell together in the words and meanings originating from the client. The therapist is led by the client, with only that slight but powerful bias given in the emphasis on the feelingful organismic-life as his particular theoretical therapeutic contribution. For the rest, everything is mirrored, reflected, given back to the client as originating in himself.

The therapist's task is to express as faithfully as possible only those meanings, feelings, sensings, and interpretations that are given by the client. A certain aspect of phenomenological thought and work is em-bodied in all of this. Husserl said, "Back to the things themselves," meaning to suspend the specialist visions, theoretical assumptions, and other blinders that prevent a dwelling descriptively in the 'world-as-it-presents-itself'. Within client-centered practice, this dwelling on the face-presentation, of not leaping to theoretical, explanatory, or high-level interpretive ideas, is lived out in a faithful, plodding dwelling within what the client says.

Thus, the client-centered therapist suspends his expertise in favor of understanding the client on his own terms. In Freudian therapy, the analyst carefully suspends the ordinary self of everyday interactions in favor of objective, analytical attunement to the dynamics of the unconscious. He suspends himself, as it were, in favor of his specialized vision, his theoretical mode of comprehending his patient's situation. In Jungian therapy, a more individualizing attentiveness to the patient shapes a more ample space. But still the theorist-therapist, the expert guide, has priority at the lived-level. In the actual interaction, he is teacher, interpreter, and learned one who shares that learning with his patient. In client-centered therapy and theory, the therapist relin-quishes being the specialist in favor of the client.

The therapist's relative success in giving up his specialist knowledge is visible in the very obviousness of his remarks in the therapeutic situation. He simply repeats the client's own words. He may well need experienced skill to capture the client's meanings, but he does not need theory to any great extent. In principle, a housewife or uneducated laborer could do client-centered therapy if their natural attunement and social skills were fairly good. A knowledge of personality theory, diagnostics, or the rich symbolic heritage of the past are unnecessary to the work of the client-centered therapist, who tries merely to understand how the client understands himself.

From the point of view of the specialist-expert, what the client-centered therapist does seems uninformed, stupid, and obvious. The patient says, "I get really angry," and the therapist responds, "That really makes you mad." While it is obvious that the therapist can be more or less skilled at expressing the client's feelings and views, it is apparent that no great specialized knowledge or scientific development is required for that. It is also obvious that the development of theory is slight in client-centered therapy. Rogers has done just that amount of low-level theorizing that American psychological science requires. From a theoretical-specialist point of view, his theory is hardly more than slightly elevated common sense. He affirms that understanding, accepting, caring about, and being attentive to another's feelings is good and productive in human relations, which sounds like good advice from a Portestant minister, the common sense of the Judaic-Christian tradition.

But it is precisely this deep movement toward common sense and away from specialization that is the heart of the client-centered contribution to the psychotherapeutic enterprise. The therapist's abdication of the expert role inserts him into the room together with his client in a commonsense, mundane obviousness. Here is no arcane universe or specialist consciousness; here is ordinary human understanding elevated to principle, made consistent, and angulated toward feeling, to be sure, but fundamentally common human understanding rooted in the common tradition of values shared by client and therapist.

Just precisely the slightness of specialist theory reinserts the therapist-client into the common world—precisely the fidelity to the client's expression in his own language, the priority given to self-interpretation rather than to expert objective interpretation, reroots the interaction in the world of commonsense. Attention is then focused on what is actually given over there in the client's self-expressive self-interpretation, which is to be refined, developed, and spoken. And all of this is to be done in the obviousness and clarity of the common language and common life already lived by the client and therapist.

Existential-phenomenological practice would carry this even further, moving even more radically into the sphere of the obvious and the given to bring it to speech. Such a practice would do away with the complex underlying ideological fixity of *feelings are all*. In the real world, feelings, values, judgments, and thoughts all have weight and deserve consideration. An ideological preference for feelings can move, unfortunately, toward constituting yet another eccentric world of specialization. A world awash in organismic feelings is not the lifeworld in its wholeness but an eccentric, arbitrary, ideologically specialized variant on the life-world. Insofar as client-centered thought remains rooted in that totalization of feeling, it, too, constitutes a specialist world.

## TOWARD A DESCRIPTIVE, COMPREHENSIVE SCIENCE OF THERAPY

The movement toward common sense and the life-world, already partially begun in client-centered practice, is at the heart of existential-phenomenological practice. While a full articulation of the meaning of that practice cannot be detailed here, some of its underlying structures have already been discussed in this text. The problem of narrowness and specialization lived out in traditional theories and, to a lesser degree, in their practice points clearly to the need for more adequate descriptive work and a more comprehensive style of theorizing for the proper development of therapeutic practice and, even more essentially, for the development of a science concerned with therapy.

A properly descriptive theory of psychotherapy must meet certain criteria not met by the current theories. A genuinely comprehensive theory must include: (1) a description of the theorist-therapist as meaning-transformer of the situation; (2) a description of the way in which this meaning transformation becomes convincing to both therapist and patient; (3) a viewing that is as thoroughly attentive to, and descriptive of, the therapist as it is of the patient; (4) a detailed concern and investigation of the life-world meanings of the actual activities of both therapist and patient as they work together. Such description must not be wedded totally to a specialized theory but must be grounded in analysis of the 'ordinary-world-of-life-meeting' of which therapeutic meeting is a variant; (5) all of these descriptions must be open to consensual validation, be recognizable by practitioners and patients as accurate, and be correctable and expandable by further descriptive studies which will illuminate areas not yet touched. Such a comprehensive human-scientific approach to theorizing and research must be able to become part of a growing science and developing insightful practice.

## BIBLIOGRAPHY

Boss, Medard. *Psychoanalysis and Dasein Analysis.* New York: Basic Books, 1963.

In this text, the existentializing of psychoanalytic thought and practice is carried out by laying aside the fundamental natural scientific assumptions of Freud in order to allow the patient's person to be seen as it is. A clear exposition of Heideggerian thought in relation to psychotherapy.

Fischer, W. *Theories of Anxiety.* New York: Harper & Row, 1970.

A well-done text with an approach similar to the present one, in which the author examines certain traditional theories in order to arrive at a more comprehensive existential understanding of a phenomenon.

Giorgi, A. *Psychology as a Human Science.* New York: Harper & Row, 1970.

A fine exposition of the historical necessity for a reconceptualization of psychology away from the natural scientific model toward a human scientific model. The carefully documented study of the inadequacies and distortions of the older psychology, and the articulation of standards for a new human psychology, both provide the ground for the present text.

Heidegger, Martin. *Poetry, Language, and Thought*. New York: Harper & Row, 1971.

Heidegger's view of the central power of language as the place where "truth comes to pass" is very much at the heart of the convincingness of therapeutic visions.

Husserl, Edmund. *Ideas: General Introduction to Pure Phenomenology*. London: Collier Books, 1962.

A complex, difficult text in which the fundamental idea of phenomenology as a movement toward bracketing the obscuring assumptions of the "natural attitude" in order to allow things themselves to speak is well developed.

Lowen, Alexander. *The Betrayal of the Body*. New York: Macmillan, 1967.

A well-written case-related account of the structures of the unconscious life as lived in the pattern of movements, rigidities, and withholdings of the body as expressive psychic life. Reich's insights into character as lived in bodily armor and bodily style are here further differentiated and clarified.

Merleau-Ponty, Maurice. *The Phenomenology of Perception*. New York: Humanities Press, 1962.

Merleau-Ponty's analysis of language as lived in a total bodily expressivity is very much at the heart of the way in which 'theory-as-lived-and-spoken' becomes lived-conviction for both therapist and patient.

Rank, Otto. *Will Therapy and Truth and Reality*. New York: Alfred A. Knopf, 1968.

Rank's description of Freudian therapy as an ideological brainwashing that undermines the patient's autonomous will is a powerful critique of the dangers of an overspecialized view of man. His general view of conversion to a system as inimical to the positive life and human will and creativity have helped to shape the criticisms found in the present text.

Schutz, Alfred. *Collected Papers. The Problem of Social Reality*, vol. 1. The Hague: Martinus Nijhoff, 1962.

Profound essays on social reality following a Husserlian approach. Schutz's distinction between specialized and commonsense consciousness, in which specialized views are seen as arising from, and grounded in, the common social order, provides the background for the discussion of the failures of specialization in therapy in this chapter.

Van den Berg, J. H. *Different Existence.* Pittsburgh: Duquesne University Press, 1972.

This lucid introduction to an existential psychopathology touches briefly on the way in which the therapist becomes the patient's unconscious. Van den Berg's view is that the patient, out of his isolation and alienation, seeks to come together with the therapist into the common space between them.

van Kaam, A. *Art of Existential Counseling.* Wilkes Barre, Pa.: Dimension Press, 1966.

A lively practical introduction to the fundamental spirit of existential counseling, with considerable emphasis on the grounding attitudes of the counselor-therapist.

————. *Existential Foundations of Psychology.* Pittsburgh: Duquesne University Press, 1966.

The present text is a small step along the way first described by van Kaam in his articulation of a program for remaking all of psychology along the lines of existential-phenomenology.

Wolpe, J. *Psychotherapy by Reciprocal Inhibition.* Stanford, Calif.: Stanford University Press, 1958.

A concrete description of a desensitization and relaxation therapy, used as an example in the present chapter, whose goal is to allow the person to become gradually less fearful by imagining previously feared things in a progressively relaxed way.

# DATE DUE

| | | |
|---|---|---|
| MAR 0 2 1998 | | |
| APR 2 1 1999 | | |
| APR 1 3 1999 | | |
| NOV 2 2 1999 | | |
| OC 29 '99 | | |
| OCT 2 7 2000 | | |
| OC 27 00 | | |
| DEC 15 2001 | | |
| | | |
| | | |
| | | |
| | | |
| | | |
| | | |
| | | |
| | | |